WITHDRAWN
From Toronto Public Library

TIME, SPACE, AND TRANSITION IN ANASAZI PREHISTORY

by

MICHAEL S. BERRY

University of Utah Press
Salt Lake City

Library of Congress Cataloging in Publication Data

Berry, Michael S.
Time, space, and transition in Anasazi prehistory.

Bibliography: p.
Includes index.
1. Pueblo Indians—Antiquities. 2. Pueblo Indians—History. 3. Indians of North America—Southwest, New—Antiquities. 4. Indians of North America—Southwest, New—History. I. Title.
E99.P9B38 1982 979 82-11102
ISBN 0-87480-212-1

CONTENTS

FIGURES

TABLES

ACKNOWLEDGMENTS

Time, Space, and Transition in Anasazi Prehistory is a revision of a doctoral dissertation completed at the Department of Anthropology, University of Utah. I would like to thank the members of my committee for their constructive criticism and guidance. The committee was comprised of Dr. James F. O'Connell (Chair), Dr. Robert Anderson, Dr. Philip C. Hammond, and Dr. Dennis O'Rourke. Special appreciation is acknowledged for the theoretical insight provided by Dr. Anderson, the initial stimulus to pursue Southwestern studies by Dr. John C. Ives, and for Dr. Jesse D. Jennings's continuous support throughout my graduate career.

Claudia F. Berry and Michael D. Windham assisted in many aspects of the research and made significant contributions to the development of the model elaborated herein. Many of the ideas expressed were inspired initially by James Benedict's emphasis in various articles and monographs on the importance of migration as an adaptive strategy. Benedict, John C. Ives, Thor N. V. Karlstrom, William D. Lipe, and R. G. Matson read the original manuscript in its entirety and offered many useful suggestions. In addition, David A. Breternitz, David Dechambre, James Schoenwetter, and John J. Wood have read and commented on various portions of the paper. Wood has been especially helpful in reviewing the statistical applications.

A revised manuscript was reviewed by Jesse D. Jennings and Claudia F. Berry, both of whom provided recommendations that greatly improved its quality.

An earlier version of Chapter 3 was presented at an Advanced Seminar of the School of American Research entitled "The Origins of Plant Husbandry in North America." Participants included Richard I. Ford (Seminar Chairman), David L. Asch, Wesley C. Cowan, Walton C. Galinat, Charles B. Heiser, Francis B. King, Paul E. Minnis, Dee Ann Story, and Patty Jo Watson. Many thanks are due to these scholars and to Douglas W. Schwartz, Director of the School of American Research, for valuable criticism and suggested improvements.

Chronology is the primary focus of the present work and a great many individuals have contributed to the accumulation of chronometric data. Jeffery S. Dean provided me with a complete set of the Laboratory of Tree-Ring Research Quadrangle series. This greatly facilitated the analyses described in Chapters 4 and 5. David A. Breternitz, Evan DuBloois, John Fritz, Cynthia Irwin-Williams, Jesse D. Jennings, Harold Krueger, William D. Lipe, Austin Long, William S. Marmaduke, R. G. Matson, Tom Matthews, Donald Morris, Fred Plog, Alan Simmons, Robert Stuckenrath, Richard and Georgia Beth Thompson, Charles Tucek, James VanStone, John Ware, and Mark Wimberly volunteered a great deal of invaluable unpublished information and directed me to additional sources of published data. Without this cooperation and assistance, the research task could not have been accomplished.

Finally, I wish to thank Norma Mikkelsen, Peggy Lee, and the excellent editorial staff of the University of Utah Press for transforming the submitted manuscript into final published form in a timely and professional manner.

TIME, SPACE, AND TRANSITION IN ANASAZI PREHISTORY

1. INTRODUCTION

The Anasazi sequence of the American Southwest generally is held to be one of the most securely documented examples of prehistoric cultural evolution in the New World. The interpretive framework has undergone little or no significant alteration since the formulation of the Pecos Classification in 1927 (Kidder 1927). The Basketmaker-Pueblo continuum, ranging from a hypothetical Basketmaker I (now classified as late Archaic) through the historically documented Pueblo V populations, is conceived of as a series of smoothly intergraded stages of cultural development. The segregation of the sequence into stages is thought to be an arbitrary analytical procedure, imposed upon the data for purposes of communication and data presentation. The continuum typically is assumed to represent reality, whereas the stage constructs are treated as convenient fictions.

This picture—gradual evolution necessarily distorted by stage representations—has prevailed for so long and been so indelibly imprinted on generations of Southwestern students that few have thought to question it. The accepted synopsis may be tersely stated: Following the demise of the Big Game Hunters, the Southwest was populated by Archaic hunting and gathering groups; maize farming was introduced from Mesoamerica at around 2000 to 3000 B.C., an event that initiated a long, slow, gradual shift from primary dependence on wild resources to primary dependence on domesticated resources; by the time of Christ these Archaic groups made the transition to settled, Basketmaker II village life; dependence on domestic crops continued to increase and new cultural traits gradually replaced the old, forming a pattern of transformation much like a Brainerd-Robinson seriation graph (Brainerd 1951; Robinson 1951); population steadily increased until late in the thirteenth century, at which time the "Great Drought" initiated the demise of the classic Anasazi urban centers, thus producing the scattered population distribution recorded at the time of European contact.

In the following chapters this "textbook" version of Anasazi prehistory is shown to be empirically false and conceptually misleading. Specifically, I maintain that:

1. Maize was not introduced into the Greater Southwest until around 500 B.C. in the southern Basin and Range province of New Mexico and Arizona. Its earliest well-documented occurrence on the Colorado Plateau is 185 B.C. In both provinces the introduction of maize had profound and immediate effects.

2. The subsequent Basketmaker-Pueblo evolutionary sequence was comprised of a series of temporally discrete stages, separated one from another by abrupt transitional events. That is, the stages of the Pecos Classification are "real" spatiotemporal entities rather than mere classificatory conveniences.

3. The discontinuities in the sequence were initiated by periodic Plateau-wide droughts, equivalent in magnitude and effect to the famed thirteenth-century drought. In every case, these caused widespread abandonment of Plateau sites and consequent migration to (primarily) high-elevation refugia. Forced coexistence and coalescence of immigrant groups in these various

refugia produced the syntheses of material culture traits that were to become diagnostic of the ensuing stage(s).

4. The population dynamics of the Plateau cannot be comprehended fully without consideration of coeval events in the Hohokam and Mogollon sequences in the adjacent southern Basin and Range province. The available chronometric data strongly suggest demographic complementarity in that the peaks of construction activity in one province are matched by markedly diminished activity in the other. It thus appears that the pattern described above of periodic migration to high-elevation refuge areas *within* the Plateau was superimposed upon a still broader pattern of population fluxion *between* the Plateau and southern Basin and Range.

This represents a radical departure from the accepted perspective, and I have no delusions that it will be embraced immediately by Southwesternists. For one thing, the model calls for considerably more population movement than most prehistorians are prepared to acknowledge. For another, it is incompatible with the view that the Anasazi sequence comprised a smooth developmental continuum. Quite to the contrary, the sequence consisted of abrupt, episodic stage transitions alternated with relatively lengthy periods of stability and conservatism. This contrast in perspective is in many ways analogous to the one drawn in biological evolutionism between "phyletic gradualism" and "punctuated equilibria" (Eldredge and Gould 1972; Gould and Eldredge 1977). In both paleontology and archeology gradualism represents the traditional view; however, in neither case does the gradualist perspective appear to be *empirically* based. Rather, gradualism has functioned as an "inarticulated major premise" that has exerted a powerful influence on the interpretation of the paleontological and archeological records (Gould and Eldredge 1977:141). As Eldredge and Gould point out (following N. R. Hanson [1969]), "*a priori* theorems often determine the results of 'empirical' studies before the first shred of evidence is collected. This idea, that theory dictates what one sees cannot be stated too strongly" (Eldredge and Gould 1972:83). They argue that the theory of phyletic gradualism and its attendant empirical expectation of continuous, "insensibly graded" series of morphological transformations have masked the true character of paleontological data patterning. That is, following the tenets of gradualism, macroevolution occurs as a consequence of incremental shifts in gene frequencies in whole populations. Discontinuities and apparent saltation in the fossil record must, perforce, be attributed to episodes of erosion or nondeposition. However, according to Eldredge and Gould's model of punctuated equilibria, macroevolution is primarily a consequence of allopatric speciation in relatively small subpopulations. Further, speciation and subsequent replacement of the ancestral population might occur so rapidly that in terms of geological time, the transformation will be preserved as an instantaneous "event" rather than as a gradual process. In short, the discontinuous nature of the paleontological record is precisely what is retrodicted by Eldredge and Gould's account. No recourse to the incompleteness of the fossil record is required to make the model empirically acceptable. In this context, the data are an accurate reflection of the salient processes rather than a patchwork of fragmentary evidence that poorly approximates reality.

The origins of gradualism in archeological thinking in general, and in the Southwestern culture area in particular, are difficult to pinpoint. The frequent allusions of Southwestern archeologists to gradualist biological principles suggest that a significant amount of theory borrowing has taken place. Alternatively, the parallel conceptual patterning may stem from a common intellectual tradition:

> The general preference that so many of us hold for gradualism is a metaphysical stance embedded in the modern history of Western cultures: it is not a high-order empirical observation, induced from the objective study of nature. The famous statement attributed to Linnaeus—*natura non facit saltum* (nature does not make leaps) may reflect some biological knowledge, but it also represents the translation into biology of the order, harmony and continuity that European rulers hoped to maintain in a society already assaulted by calls for fundamental change (Gould and Eldredge 1977:145).

Whatever the source, the effect of the gradualist premise on our understanding of North

American prehistory has been profound. As in paleontology, the empirical expectation of gradualism is *in situ* continuity accompanied by the slow-paced accretion of new traits at the expense of a similarly slow-paced deletion of ancestral traits. Consistent with this belief is the propensity—especially in the Southwest—to excavate sites in arbitrary, horizontal levels rather than by natural stratigraphy. This procedure virtually guarantees that a "punctuated" sequence will appear as a gradual series of transitions due to the artificial mixture of discrete artifact complexes. Abrupt transitions and temporal discontinuities are obliterated by an excavation technique thought by many to be the only acceptable "scientific" approach. Here we have a situation in which the dominant theoretical stance is paired with a data recovery technique that renders the theory immune to empirical falsification. Since each site is interpreted as a continuous, smooth, developmental sequence, regional "syntheses"—which typically consist of summaries of site report conclusions—tend to be simple inductive extensions of that pattern to more inclusive geographic areas. These syntheses reaffirm the gradualist stance in a subtly circular fashion, and since they are almost always cited in prominent textbooks, they also shape the conduct of future research to a considerable extent.

The method employed here is designed to circumvent the gradualist bias, insofar as it is possible, by focusing on the "raw" data rather than the interpretive statements made *about* the data. Since the primary objective is a reassessment of Anasazi evolutionary *tempo*, great emphasis is placed on tree-ring and radiocarbon dated sites. This information is used to generate regional chronological patterns, and these form the basis for the punctuational, spatiotemporal model of Anasazi stage transitions briefly outlined above.

2. THE TREATMENT OF CHRONOMETRIC DATA

Chapters 3 and 4 deal almost exclusively with chronological analyses. The intent of this chapter is to outline certain conventions employed in the handling of tree-ring and radiocarbon dates. Only these two methods of absolute dating will be considered even though other techniques, e.g., archeomagnetism, obsidian hydration, alpha recoil, etc., have been employed in the Southwest. This is because the newer methods are still in the experimental stages and have not been used at enough sites to be of much value for regional syntheses.

In the sections that follow, familiarity with the fundamentals of tree-ring and radiocarbon dating will be assumed and only a few critical issues will be addressed.

Tree-Ring Dating

Tree-ring dating was first developed in the Southwest and has been most intensively applied to problems of Anasazi chronology. The techniques of dendrochronological analysis improved rapidly following the initial development of the method by A. E. Douglass in the 1920s (Douglass 1929), but current standards were not attained until the early 1960s. The immense number of samples analyzed prior to that time constituted a "mixed bag" of highly reliable, probably reliable, and quite unreliable dates. Beginning in 1963 the Laboratory of Tree-Ring Research, University of Arizona, initiated a comprehensive reevaluation of all tree-ring dated archeological specimens from the Southwest (Bannister, Hannah, and Robinson 1966). The intent was to impose a uniform set of analytic criteria to the extant sample of specimens and publish the results in order to provide archeologists with regional compendia of reliable dates. The results were published in sixteen volumes between 1966 and 1975 (Dean and Robinson 1978). The impact of this effort has yet to be fully appreciated since the only major cultural-chronological synthesis of tree-ring dated Southwestern sequences (Breternitz 1966) is based on the earlier, unrevised data. This is unfortunate because the work of Bannister and his associates has significantly altered the picture of Southwestern chronology. For instance, Shabik'eshchee Village (Roberts 1929), the original type site of the Basketmaker III stage, has long been thought to date in the A.D. 700s (Gladwin 1945; Bannister 1965). However, a reassessment of the original beams using modern techniques failed to confirm this placement. The total collection of specimens yielded only five noncutting dates ranging from A.D. 327 to 581 (Robinson, Harrill, and Warren 1974). The construction date of this important site is obviously open to question, and until such time as Shabik'eshchee Village can be resampled for tree-ring or radiocarbon materials, no conclusive temporal placement will be possible. This is only one of many similar cases that might be cited. The point to be made is that the dendrochronological data which form the basis of currently accepted temporal models of Anasazi prehistory are, in a large number of cases, known to be incorrect. Hence, only the revised dates published in the Quadrangle Series of the Laboratory of Tree-Ring Research will be used in the development of temporal models in the following chapters. The use of dates published subsequent to the Quadrangle Series and the use of some recently analyzed, unpublished dates constitute the only exceptions to this general rule; these were all determined by Laboratory of Tree-Ring Research personnel and were, therefore, subject to the same standards as the main body of data.

All dates published in the Quadrangle Series are accompanied by qualifying symbols that convey the analyst's assessment of reliability. These are depicted in Table 1 along with a brief explanation of their meaning. Dean offers the following guidelines for the interpretation of these qualifiers:

> The symbols B, G, L, c and r indicate cutting dates in order of decreasing confidence, unless a + or ++ is also present.
>
> The symbols L, G, and B may be used in any combination with each other or with the other symbols except v and vv. The r and c symbols are mutually exclusive, but may be used with L, G, B, + and ++. The v and vv are also mutually exclusive but may be used in combination with all the other symbols (Dean 1975:10).

The appropriate symbols will be used in the text to facilitate interpretation of the dates.

The standard caveats regarding the possible use of dead wood (i.e., the "driftwood effect"),

TABLE 1
Qualifying Symbols Used with the Outer Tree-Ring Date

Symbol	Explanation
B	Bark present.
G	Beetle galleries are present on the surface of the specimen.
L	Characteristic surface patination and smoothness, which develops on beams stripped of bark, is present.
c	Outermost ring is continuous around the full circumference of the specimen. This symbol is used only if a full section is present.
r	Less than a full section is present, but the outermost ring is continuous around the available circumference.
v	Subjective judgment that, although there is no direct evidence of the true outside on a specimen, the date is within a very few years of being a cutting date.
vv	There is no way of estimating how far the last ring is from the true outside.
+	One or more rings may be missing near the end of the ring series whose presence or absence cannot be determined because the specimen does not extend far enough to provide an adequate check.
++	A ring count is necessary due to the fact that beyond a certain point the specimen could not be dated.

Source: Dean 1975

aboriginal stockpiling of timbers, and uncertain associations are too well known to bear repeating here, though these sources of error will be discussed in reference to particular cases taken up in later sections. While most researchers are aware of these potential problems, many have neglected to consider them in the interpretation of particular sites.

Another hindrance to effective dating is an apparent tendency to take too few specimens during excavation. A single cutting date or a handful of "v" or "vv" dates from a site fail to provide conclusive evidence for temporal placement. As a cursory examination of the Quadrangle Series reveals, virtually every well-dated Southwestern site, i.e., those with upwards of fifty dates, has a few specimens with cutting dates that are clearly aberrant. There are simply too many ways for "old" beams to find their way into more recent structures to place much confidence in temporal placements based on one or two dates. Large samples are required to make sense of simple to moderately complex sites. And *very* large samples may be necessary to detect "driftwood" effect or stockpiling.

Some of the misinterpretations of particular sites can be remedied and some cannot. In most cases no remedy short of reexcavation is possible. But it would be a mistake to dwell too long on the shortcomings of the dendrochronological data base on a site specific level. We have thousands of tree-ring cutting dates to work within the Anasazi area alone, and this provides a unique opportunity to construct a very precise macroscopic depiction of prehistoric temporal patterns. The utility of this approach is explored in Chapter 4 by means of a simple ten-year increment bar chart of tree-ring dated sites on the Colorado Plateau. However, that application of macroscopic method will be preceded by a similar, if somewhat differently oriented, presentation of the available radiocarbon evidence.

Radiocarbon Dating

The values of all radiocarbon dates presented in the following chapters are based on the Libby half-life of 5568±30 years. Even though it has long been recognized that this estimate is in error, published radiocarbon dates continue to be calculated in terms of the Libby half-life in order to avoid confusion and insure comparability (Flint and Deevey 1961). The plus-or-minus figure represents one standard error (Ralph 1971; Thomas 1976). Conversion from B.P. to the A.D./B.C. time scale is accomplished simply by subtracting 1950 years. If the result is positive, it is a B.C. date. If negative, it is an A.D. date (zero dates are, by convention, recorded as A.D. 1). Presentation of dates in the text will follow a set format with the radiocarbon age B.P. and the associated standard error appearing first, followed by the A.D./B.C. conversion with the lab number shown in parentheses. For example, a date of 1750 radiocarbon years with a standard error of 50 years would appear as 1750±50 B.P.: A.D. 200 (RX-99). Of course, the same standard error applies to the converted date; it is eliminated from the notation merely to avoid redundancy.

Contemporaneity Tests

Judgments regarding the probable contemporaneity of two or more radiocarbon dates can be of critical importance to the interpretation of both intra- and inter-site relationships, and it is mandatory—at least insofar as comparability of results is concerned—that all researchers use the same means and criteria to arrive at these decisions. Spaulding (1958) and Long and Rippeteau (1974) have published useful articles on the subject. Both treatments present versions of the t-test and F-test designed to assess the statistical difference between two or more radiocarbon determinations when each date is presented as a mean and standard error. The t-test and F-test are actually equivalent procedures when only two dates are involved (Mendenhall and Reinmuth 1971), and the sole reason for employing the former in such cases is that the computation is much simpler. Following Long and Rippeteau (1974:211), the value of t is

$$t = \frac{D}{\sqrt{\sigma_1^2 + \sigma_2^2}}$$

where D = the absolute difference in the means of the two dates and σ_1^2 and σ_2^2 are the associated squared standard errors. The t-test as used here is equivalent to testing the null hypothesis of no significant difference between the populations from which the samples were drawn. The test is two-tailed with infinite degrees of freedom, and the .05 level will be used as the criterion for rejection. Since the text includes large numbers of such tests, individual results will be reported in abbreviated fashion in parentheses. For example, a case in which the null hypothesis is rejected because $t=2.5$ and the region for rejection at the .05 level with infinite degrees of freedom is any value greater than 1.96, will be indicated by "($t=2.5>1.96$)."

Again, following Long and Rippeteau (1974:210), the value of F is

$$F = \frac{\bar{s}^2/n}{\bar{\sigma}^2}$$

where

$$\bar{s}^2/n = \frac{\sum (C_i - C_{av})^2}{n(n-1)}$$

and

$$\bar{\sigma}^2 = \frac{1}{\frac{1}{\sigma_1^2} + \frac{1}{\sigma_2^2} + \cdots \frac{1}{\sigma_n^2}}$$

where C_i = the mean value of the ith radiocarbon date, C_{av} = the average of the means of all the radiocarbon dates, n = the number of dates, and σ_n^2 = the squared standard error of the nth date. The F value is to be interpreted using a standard F distribution table with (n-1) and infinite degrees of freedom. As with the t-test, the .05 level will be used as the criterion for rejection of the null hypothesis. For the same reasons discussed above, a shorthand, parenthetic notation of individual tests will be used throughout the text. For example, a case in which the null hypothesis for three dates is rejected because $F=5.0$, and the region for rejection at the .05 level with two and infinite degrees of freedom is any value greater than 3.00, will be presented as "($F=5.00>3.00$: $df=2,\infty$)."

Averaging

If two or more dates are not sufficiently different to reject the null hypothesis, averaging may be appropriate (depending on archeological context). Long and Rippeteau (1974) suggest the use of a simple weighted mean formula

$$C_{av} = \frac{(C_1 \times W_1) + (C_2 \times W_2) + \cdots (C_n \times W_n)}{W_1 + W_2 + \cdots W_n}$$

where C_i = the mean value of the ith date and W_i = the weighting coefficient. Long and Rippeteau provide a table of approximate values for W, but it is clear that the true value for each C_i is equal to the quotient: largest squared standard error in the data set divided by the squared standard error associated with C_i. In short, the assigned weights are inversely proportionate to variance. This relationship rather than Long and Rippeteau's approximations will be used throughout the text. As an example, averaging of the two dates 1520±150 B.P. and 1470±100 B.P. would be accomplished as follows:

$$C_{av} = \frac{(C_1 \times W_1) + (C_2 \times W_2)}{W_1 + W_2}$$

$$= \frac{(1520 \times 150^2/150^2) + (1470 \times 150^2/100^2)}{(150^2/150^2) + (150^2/100^2)}$$

$$= 1485.4$$

The effect is to move the mean in the direction of the date with the lowest associated standard error.

The composite standard error of the averaged date is calculated by the following (after Long and Rippeteau 1974):

$$\bar{\sigma} = \frac{1}{\sqrt{\frac{1}{\sigma_1^2} + \frac{1}{\sigma_2^2} + \cdots \frac{1}{\sigma_n^2}}}$$

$$= \frac{1}{\sqrt{\frac{1}{150^2} + \frac{1}{100^2}}}$$

$$= 83.2$$

The standard error is always reduced considerably through averaging. The rationale for this has to do with effective sample size. When two dates are not found to be significantly different, they may be considered as two samples from the same hypothetical population. In effect, the sample size for the population in question has been increased, thus reducing the range of the standard error. Averaging, when justified by prior application of t-tests or F-tests, can have a marked effect on the precision of dating.

Comparability of Tree-Ring and Radiocarbon Dates

As demonstrated in later chapters, temporal control for the period from A.D. 600 to 1450 is primarily dependent upon tree-ring dating while the period from 185 B.C. to A.D. 600 is almost wholly controlled by radiocarbon dates. This raises the question of comparability of the two dating techniques.

It is now accepted fact that the concentration of atmospheric C-14 has varied significantly through time (De Vries 1958; Stuiver and Suess 1966). But it is quite obvious—as indicated by the scope of debate at a recent Nobel symposium (Olsson 1970)—that there is no general agreement as to the degree of the effect on radiocarbon samples of any given age. Numerous conversion curves and formulas are available (Olsson 1970), most of which depend upon the empirical process of radiocarbon dating tree-ring specimens of known age. Tree-ring and radiocarbon analyses of the venerable bristlecone pine have extended the range of calibration to beyond 7000 years B.P. However, the efficacy of conversion is far from being universally accepted (Burleigh 1973; Watkins 1975). The study of the comparability of tree-ring and radiocarbon dates is an ongoing, active, and (at present) conjectural field of inquiry. North American archeologists have, it seems, been too heavily influenced by the arguments of Damon et al. (1974) that conversion is a mandatory procedure. While it is clear that there is a significant departure of radiocarbon age from the true (calendric) age for samples older than ca. 3000 B.P., conversion of younger dates is of doubtful utility. This is demonstrated in Table 2, which depicts the results of a simple simulation based on the conversion tables of Damon et al. (1974). The time period involved is from 500 B.C. to A.D. 700. This covers the portion of the Anasazi sequence in which the comparability of radiocarbon and tree-ring dated events is most critical to the present study. The simulation simply treated the column for radiocarbon years in Damon et al. (1974) *as if* it represented a series of dates with associated standard errors of 100 years. Each date was then corrected to its corresponding tree-ring date, and the sigma was adjusted to include the correction uncertainty. Then, in order to test the significance of the conversion process, a t-test was performed on each pair (uncorrected/corrected) of dates. The region for rejection at the .05 level with infinite degrees of freedom is any value greater than 1.96. As shown in the last column of Table 2, none of the calculated t-values approaches this figure, hence conversion of radiocarbon dates does not seem warranted. I am not suggesting that the complex problem of comparability has been solved through this simple exercise. But given the fairly large standard errors that typify the extant radiocarbon data base and the considerable uncertainty associated with correction, nothing is to be gained by converting the dates for the time period under consideration.

Conclusions

Consistent application of these conventions and statistical methods should insure an unbiased view of the chronometric evidence. Of course, any systematic bias in the evidence itself is beyond our control. It is for this reason that most of the conclusions reached in the following analyses are macroscopic in nature. That is, the number of technically reliable tree-ring and radiocarbon dates is insufficient to engender much confidence in the inductively generated temporal patterns unless dates are pooled from broad geographic regions. To be sure, many of the arguments offered in Chapters 3 and 4 are site specific and deal with problems of stratigraphy, cultural assemblages, and associations. However, most of the arguments in this category are written in a negative vein to refute the inferences and conclusions drawn by the original investigators. Any positive, synthetic statements will rely on macroscopic data patterning.

TABLE 2
Simulation of Tree-Ring Corrected Radiocarbon Dates

Radiocarbon Years B.P.	Uncorrected Calendric Date and Hypothetic 100-Year Sigma	Tree-Ring Corrected Date	Correction Sigma	Tree-Ring Corrected Date and Composite Sigma	t
1227	A.D. 723±100	A.D. 744	51	A.D. 744±112	.140
1251	699±100	721	51	721±112	.147
1275	675±100	697	51	697±112	.147
1300	650±100	673	51	673±112	.153
1324	626±100	649	22	649±102	.161
1348	602±100	624	22	624±102	.154
1373	577±100	600	22	600±102	.161
1397	553±100	575	22	575±102	.154
1421	529±100	551	22	551±102	.154
1445	505±100	526	22	526±102	.147
1470	480±100	501	22	501±102	.147
1494	456±100	476	22	476±102	.140
1518	432±100	451	22	451±102	.133
1543	407±100	426	22	425±102	.133
1567	383±100	401	27	401±104	.125
1591	359±100	376	27	376±104	.118
1615	335±100	350	27	350±104	.104
1640	310±100	324	27	324±104	.097
1664	286±100	299	27	299±104	.090
1688	262±100	273	27	273±104	.076
1713	237±100	247	27	247±104	.069
1737	213±100	221	27	221±104	.055
1761	189±100	194	27	194±104	.035
1785	165±100	168	27	168±104	.021
1810	140±100	141	36	141±106	.007
1834	116±100	115	36	115±106	.007
1858	92±100	88	36	88±106	.027
1883	67±100	61	36	61±106	.041
1907	43±100	34	36	34±106	.062
1931	19±100	7	36	7±106	.082
1956	6±100 B.C.	20 B.C.	36	20±106 B.C.	.096
1980	30±100	48	36	48±106	.124
2004	54±100	75	36	75±106	.144
2028	78±100	103	36	103±106	.172

TABLE 2 (continued)

Radiocarbon Years B.P.	Uncorrected Calendric Date and Hypothetic 100-Year Sigma	Tree-Ring Corrected Date	Correction Sigma	Tree-Ring Corrected Date and Composite Sigma	t
2053	103±100	131	96	131±137	.164
2077	127±100	159	96	159±137	.187
2101	151±100	187	96	187±137	.210
2126	176±100	215	96	215±137	.228
2150	200±100	243	96	243±137	.251
2174	224±100	271	96	271±137	.338
2198	248±100	300	96	300±137	.374
2223	273±100	328	96	328±137	.396
2247	297±100	357	96	357±137	.432
2271	321±100	386	96	386±137	.468
2296	346±100	415	105	415±145	.392
2320	370±100	444	105	444±145	.420
2344	394±100	473	105	473±145	.449
2369	419±100	502	105	502±145	.471

3. THE AGE OF MAIZE IN THE GREATER SOUTHWEST

A wide variety of criteria may be used to distinguish the aboriginal Southwest from contemporaneous adjacent culture areas of North America, but perhaps the single most important discriminating attribute is maize agriculture. This is also true in a diachronic sense since it is maize agriculture which most clearly sets off the Anasazi, Mogollon, Hohokam, and Fremont life ways from that of the preceding Archaic stage. Given the obvious significance of this domesticate, the timing of its introduction to various parts of the Southwest is of critical importance to the understanding of subsequent evolutionary trajectories. However, Southwesternists have not afforded sufficient priority to the problem and, as a consequence, the temporal provenience of early maize is known only within very broad, imprecise limits. The reason for this chronometric negligence is readily identifiable. Virtually all research undertaken for the purpose of explicating the transition from hunting and gathering to farming in the Southwest has been conducted within a gradualist frame of reference. This is as true for the more recent "systemic" paradigms as it was for the cultural-historical approaches in vogue in the 1950s. Plog's characterization of the "systems approach" is particularly appropriate here.

> The use of systemic concepts has directed our attention away from the search for the earliest corn cob, domesticated wheat, and city, quests which are inherently impossible to complete, and toward answerable questions about the gradual processes that lead to domesticates and states, for example, at diverse times and places (Plog 1975:213).

If significant transformations are conceived of as long, drawn out processes, there is little motivation to obtain precise chronometric data for particular innovations or introductions that occur during a period of transition. It is enough to know the order in which they became components of the cultural system under investigation so that the long term, cumulative effects can be assessed. This is precisely how the Archaic/Anasazi transformation traditionally has been analyzed and this is why the chronometric evidence for the introduction of maize is so limited.

The approach taken here is decidedly antigradualist in character and stresses the instantaneity of the changes that accompanied the introduction of maize to the Southwest. This will entail a fairly lengthy evaluation of the extant data. In addition to providing certain insights into the processes of Southwestern Formative origins, the concluding section of this chapter establishes a plausible beginning date for the Anasazi sequence of the Colorado Plateau.

The Evidence for Early Southwestern Maize

According to current orthodoxy, the time and place of the introduction of maize are fairly well-established archeological facts.

> The early corn in Bat Cave, on the St. Augustine Plains of west-central New Mexico, was associated with a stone assemblage that differs little from Chiricahua Cochise. Radiocarbon dates from corn bearing levels in the cave run as early as about 4000 B.C., but data on the association

> of the corn and the charcoal samples dated have not yet been published. The earliest Bat Cave corn is exceedingly primitive—it cannot be said with certainty that it is not a wild variety—but reliable evidence of domestication comes early in the sequence, and we can infer that it was well advanced by 2000–3000 B.C. (Willey and Phillips 1958:128).

> The earliest appearance of maize in the greater Southwest . . . has been determined in the order of 3000 B.C. by radiocarbon means. The places are Bat Cave (Mangelsdorf and Smith 1949), Tularosa and Cordova Caves (Martin et al. 1952) in New Mexico, all in altitudes over 6,000 feet; and at Point of Pines, Arizona (Arz. W:10:112), in a valley floor geological context of first, possibly second, millenium B.C. age (Martin and Schoenwetter 1960) . . . (Haury 1962:113).

> To the small scattered bands of the Desert Archaic food collectors, specifically to those of the Cochise group, there came a series of new and, eventually, revolutionary traits. First, and ultimately the most important, maize—appearing in southwestern New Mexico more than four thousand years ago (E. Reed 1964:177).

> The Chiricahua period was a crucial one in Southwestern development for during this time agriculture was introduced from Mexico. One of the first indications of corn in the Southwest in the form of pre-Chapalote pod appeared in Bat Cave, New Mexico about 2000 B.C. (Whalen 1971:91).

> The first evidence of corn in and around Arizona occurs during the Desert culture stage. Corn pollen was recovered from sediments at the Cienega Creek Site in southeastern Arizona (Martin and Schoenwetter 1960:33–34). This pollen was deposited at 2000 B.C. or earlier. Corn dating to 2000 or 3000 B.C. was found at Bat Cave in west central New Mexico (Martin and Plog 1973:277).

> In addition, the San Pedro peoples began harvesting primitive corn as early as 3000 B.C., with squash and beans available by at least 1000 B.C. (Thomas 1976:455).

> As previously noted, domesticated plants were being cultivated on a small scale in the Southwest by 2000 B.C., if not earlier, and the Late Archaic was also a time of gradual population growth and increasing cultural complexity (Lipe 1978:341).

These statements, while certainly not exhaustive, are an accurate reflection of the prevalent view that maize was first introduced between 4000 and 5000 years ago in the southern Basin and Range province of New Mexico and Arizona. Furthermore, these statements—arranged in chronological order as they are—demonstrate that this belief has remained essentially unchanged for at least two decades. As a matter of fact, it has persisted for a somewhat longer period of time than the list of quotations indicates since, excepting Jelinek (1965) and J. D. Jennings (1967), no one has seriously questioned the validity of the Bat Cave chronology or cultural sequence as first set forth in the late 1940s and early 1950s (Mangelsdorf and Smith 1949; Dick 1952, 1954; Libby 1955). Neither has anyone openly criticized the interpretations of Bat Cave's companion sites, i.e., the handful of sites and locales that purportedly have yielded maize remains nearly as old as the Bat Cave complex. These include Cienega Creek (sometimes referred to as the Point of Pines alluvial site) in east-central Arizona (Haury 1957; Martin and Schoenwetter 1960), LoDaisKa in north-central Colorado (Irwin and Irwin 1959; Irwin and Irwin 1961), and the Arroyo Cuervo region of northwestern New Mexico (Irwin-Williams and Tompkins 1968; Irwin-Williams 1973). I will argue that (1) the evidence for 4000- to 5000-year-old maize at each of these sites is, at best, inconclusive, and that (2) a careful reading of the data yields a much more conservative age estimate. The implications of these conclusions will be considered in the final section of this chapter.

Bat Cave

Bat Cave is located on the southern fringe of the Plains of San Augustin, approximately 10 miles southeast of Horse Springs, New Mexico. The large main chamber contained very little evidence of human occupation and the bulk of the cultural materials came from four much smaller tunnellike caves.

Though the site was excavated in 1948 and resampled in 1950 (Dick 1952, 1954), the descriptive monograph did not appear in print until 1965 (Dick 1965). In the interim, the site and the interpretations of its excavator became firmly fixed in the tradition of Southwestern archeology. J. D. Jennings's (1967) review of the monograph and, to a lesser extent, Jelinek's (1965) critical assessment of the status of Southwestern radiocarbon dating, cast doubt on the credibility of the Bat Cave data. However, it seems clear that few students were influenced by these criticisms. Indeed, Jennings himself apparently has reversed his position on the matter (J. D. Jennings

1974:291). This is unfortunate since the points raised in his review article pertaining to excavation techniques and the nature of the radiocarbon samples constitute adequate grounds for rejecting the Bat Cave data as essentially meaningless, at least insofar as the age of maize is concerned. It will be useful here to discuss and further elaborate the two major features of Jennings's critique and to draw attention to a few additional problems.

First, Jennings noted that the site was excavated in arbitrary horizontal levels. Given the complexity of the midden deposits shown in Dick's Figures 10 and 17 (Dick 1965:14, 20), it seems obvious that the imposition of arbitrary levels must have had the dual effect of (1) obliterating the actual association of contemporaneous materials by artificial segregation into different levels and (2) creating fictitious associations by lumping distinct strata within the same level. Hence, there is nothing at all certain about the supposed association of maize and the charcoal samples that yielded fourth millenium B.C. radiocarbon dates. But even if it could be argued that Dick's arbitrary excavation units closely approximated the actual stratigraphic situation, two additional sources of uncertainty deserve our attention. The radiocarbon samples were collected during the 1948 and 1950 excavation seasons (see Table 1). The 1948 specimens consisted of maize cobs, wood, or combinations of both. According to Dick, these were

> selected by Mangelsdorf and Smith from the botanical specimens they were studying at the time. This material was sent to Libby without being checked by me so I cannot vouch for its exact provenience in the cave deposits (Dick 1965:18).

So, even given the tenuous assumption that excavation in arbitrary levels is an appropriate procedure, there is no way to ascertain which of the 1948 samples came from what levels. The 1950 excavations were designed primarily to rectify this problem of provenience control. Six additional samples were obtained, each of which consisted of

> small pieces of charcoal, picked by hand throughout a twelve-inch level in a five-by-six block. It was necessary to use this method to obtain enough charcoal, and this might well account for some of the discrepancies in the dates (Dick 1965:18).

"Necessary" or not, the practice of taking composite radiocarbon samples is of questionable utility even when stratigraphic excavation techniques are employed, but the composite sampling of arbitrary levels is a completely unacceptable procedure that is likely to produce erroneous radiocarbon dates. A hypothetical example will make this clear. Suppose a site has two distinguishable strata, A and B. Stratum A constitutes the refuse of the first occupation which ceased 3000 years ago. The site then remained unoccupied until 1000 years ago, at which time the deposition of stratum B was initiated. Now, if this site were excavated in arbitrary levels and one of these levels happened to bracket the stratigraphic break between A and B (as it almost certainly would), a composite radiocarbon sample from the level in question would (if collected by the method Dick describes) give a date of (3000 years+1000 years)/2=2000 years B.P. Hence the level would be dated to 2000 B.P. even though the site was actually unoccupied at that time. Needless to say, this line of argument could easily be extended to encompass the association of maize with early dates at Bat Cave.

Since the postulated associations are not to be trusted, the only possible means of demonstrating the great antiquity of the Bat Cave maize would be to date it directly. But, as J. D. Jennings noted, "the earlier dates come from apparently associated charcoal, *not* from the corn specimens themselves" (1967:123). And this brings up an interesting point that may not be a matter of general knowledge since Dick failed to include adequately detailed information on the type of material dated in his table of radiocarbon dates (Dick 1965:17). As a later albeit infrequently cited article entitled "Bat Cave Revisited" (Mangelsdorf, Dick, and Camara-Hernandez 1967) clearly shows, only one date was run on a sample consisting solely of cobs, and one more date was run on a mixed sample of cobs and wood. These yielded dates of 1752±250 B.P.: A.D. 198 (C-165) and 2249±250 B.P.: 299 B.C. (C-164; C-171), respectively. This is a far cry from the 3000 to 4000 B.C. temporal provenience originally suggested by

Dick (1965:95). It is also considerably more recent than the "guess date" postulated by Mangelsdorf, Dick, and Camara-Hernandez (1967) on morphological grounds. I quote the argument at length since it is of fundamental importance, and I have not seen it referenced elsewhere.

> One of the most important questions to be answered is the date of the [maize] remains. The radiocarbon determinations (Libby, 1951; Arnold and Libby, 1950) of samples of charcoal and other materials from the several levels are set forth in Table [3]. The data from the two excavations are fairly consistent for the three uppermost levels but differ widely for the two lower levels. There is reason to believe that the date of 5605 for the charcoal in the 48–60″ level is not valid for the associated earliest maize.
>
> On the basis of the characteristics of the cobs, especially those which represent evidence of teosinte contamination, we have concluded that the maize from the 48–60″ level of Bat Cave is later than the maize of the Abejas phase in the Tehuacan caves and earlier than that of the Ajalpan phase. This would date it at between 2300 and 1500 B.C. A similar correlation with the remains of maize in Romero's Cave, Tamaulipas, Mexico, excavated by Dr. Richard S. MacNeish, . . . makes it contemporary with the Guerrero phase dated by radiocarbon at 1800–1400 B.C. These correlations suggest that the earliest Bat Cave maize is probably not earlier than ca. 2300 B.C. and may be several centuries later (Mangelsdorf, Dick, and Camara-Hernandez 1967:4–5).

Here we have an apparent recantation of Dick's earlier pronouncements, but note that the proffered temporal placement is based on morphological comparisons with the Mexican maize sequence (which itself is imprecisely dated) and ignores completely the Bat Cave radiocarbon data. Obviously, morphological dating is a pretty hazardous business, and, as shown in Table 3, none of the dates fall anywhere near 2300 B.C. (4250 B.P.). If we ignore the 3655 B.C. (5605 B.P.) date as the authors suggest, then the next oldest dates in the sequence fall around 850–900 B.C. (2800–2850 B.P.). Of course, there is no way of knowing whether or not these dates mean anything for reasons discussed earlier, i.e., composite sampling and excavation in arbitrary levels. Finally, all of the dates from Bat Cave were determined using the solid carbon method. It has since been recognized that this technique is unreliable due to the effects of airborne radioactive contamination (Crane 1956) and self-absorption (Ralph 1971).

In sum, there is no reason to place much confidence in the Bat Cave data. It was a poorly excavated site that can be interpreted nearly any way one pleases by juggling the data and picking and choosing from the list of questionable dates those that fit a given hypothesis. It would seem that the only prudent alternative is to tentatively accept the radiocarbon determinations on samples that contain maize and ignore the rest. This

TABLE 3
Bat Cave Radiocarbon Dates

1948 Excavations			1950 Excavations		
Material	Level	Date B.P.	Material	Level	Date B.P.
Cobs	0–12″	1752±250			
Wood	12–24″	1907±250	Charcoal	11–15″	1610±200
Wood	24–36″	2239±250	Charcoal	24–36″	2816±200
Cobs & wood	36–48″	2249±250	Charcoal	36–48″	2048±170
Wood	48–60″	2862±250	Charcoal	48–60″	5605±290
Extrapolation	60–66″	3000–3500	Charcoal	60–66″	5931±310

Source: Mangelsdorf, Dick, and Camara-Hernandez 1967

may seem overly conservative, but I think the approach is justifiable. The burden of proof for "ancient maize" falls on the shoulders of those making the claims. Clear-cut and well-documented evidence is not too much to ask for, nor is it that difficult to obtain. Unfortunately, the Bat Cave data are not of the required quality and, as will be seen in the arguments that follow, evidence from the other Southwestern sites boasting "ancient maize" is similarly inadequate.

Cienega Creek

The Cienega Creek Site, located in east-central Arizona, was excavated in 1955–56 by Emil Haury and reported the following year in *American Antiquity* (Haury 1957). It is frequently cited along with Bat Cave as yet another site that demonstrates the very early occurrence of maize in the Southwest (in this case, prior to 2000 B.C.). The basis for these claims is a paper entitled "Arizona's Oldest Cornfield" (Martin and Schoenwetter 1960) in which the authors report the recovery of possible maize pollen from Bed D-1 of the site which was at that time thought to date as early as 2200 B.C. (Haury 1957). However, there were major inconsistencies in the original radiocarbon dating that had not been resolved at the time of Martin and Schoenwetter's publication, and a subsequent series of radiocarbon determinations did little to clarify the situation. The relevant data are summarized in Table 4. Figure 1 is a schematic profile of the site as published in Haury's 1957 article. At the time the article appeared, only the University of Arizona solid carbon series (Wise and Shutler 1958) and the University of Michigan gas dates (Crane and Griffin 1958a) were available. These are listed in stratigraphic order in the second and fourth columns of Table 4. As shown, there is a glaring discrepency between the Arizona and Michigan determinations on samples recovered from Bed D-1. The Michigan dates are contemporaneous ($F=.196<3.00$: $df=2,\infty$) with a weighted average of 2493±132 B.P.: 543 B.C. The three Arizona dates are also statistically contemporaneous ($F=1.99<3.00$: $df=2,\infty$) but their weighted average is 4238±91 B.P.: 2288 B.C., indicating an age for Bed D-1 roughly 1700 years older than the Michigan series. Haury, of course, had no way of knowing that the solid carbon method was soon to be discarded in favor of the gas counting technique by all major labs and chose to accept the older Arizo-

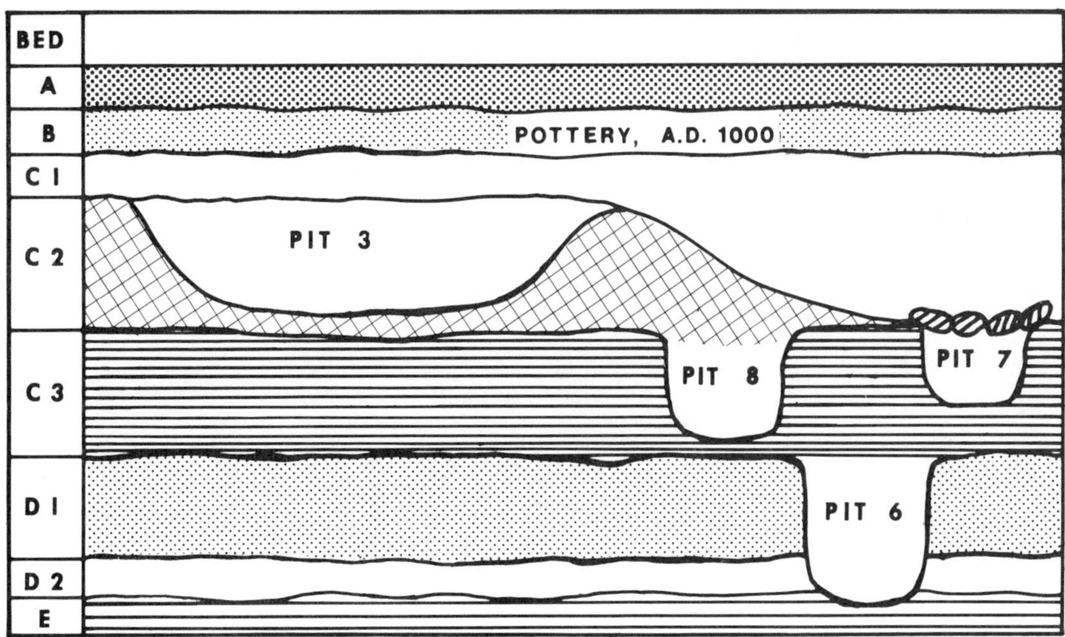

Figure 1. Schematic profile of the Cienega Creek Site (after Haury 1957).

TABLE 4
Radiocarbon Dates from the Cienega Creek Site

Provenience	Arizona Solid Carbon Series (Wise and Shutler 1958)	Arizona Gas Series (Damon and Long 1962)	Michigan Gas Series (Crane and Griffin 1958)
Pit 3, originating from the surface of C-2	2515±300 B.P. (A-28) carbonaceous material	1900±160 B.P. (A-28)*	1140±300 B.P. (M-462) fragmented solid charcoal
Pit 3, originating from the surface of C-2		2100±150 B.P. (A-20, A-23) charcoal (composite sample)	
Pit 7, originating from the surface of C-2	2150±200 B.P. (A-48) charcoal		
Pit 8, originating from the surface of C-3	3250±200 B.P. (A-50) 3025±200 B.P. (A-52) two runs on same sample of wet, charred wood	2720±150 B.P. (A-50 bis)*	
Within C-3	2610±200 B.P. (A-49) 2080±200 B.P. (A-53) 3380±200 B.P. (A-51) three runs on same sample of wet, rotten wood	3190±160 B.P. (A-51 bis)*	
Within C-3, above Cremation 36	3280±200 B.P. (A-26) carbonaceous material	2490±170 B.P. (A-26 bis)* 2900±150 B.P. (A-26B) organic material (rootlets removed before analysis)	
Pit 6, originating from the surface of D-1	3070±150 B.P. (A-27) charred, waterlogged pine branch	3190±150 B.P. (A-27 bis)*	
Within D-1	3980±160 B.P. (A-21, A-22) fragmented charcoal (composite sample) 4310±160 B.P. (A-19) fragmented charcoal 4400±150 B.P. (A-29) fragmented charcoal	2440±160 B.P. (A-25B) wood 2700±160 B.P. (A-25 bis)* 2430±150 B.P. (A-29 bis)* 2200±140 B.P. (L-432B) charcoal	2400±200 B.P. (M-540) fragmented charcoal (composite sample) 2530±250 B.P. (M-541) fragmented charcoal 2600±140 B.P. (M-461) fragmented charcoal

*indicates recombustion

na solid carbon series because the artifact complex of D-1 apparently was related to "the Chiricahua stage, though admittedly the identification had to be made on only a few traits (Haury 1957:24)." Since the Chiricahua complex had been elsewhere dated (also by the solid carbon method) between 2000 and 2500 B.C., the Arizona series was a reasonable choice. In their attempt to assign a date to the earliest maize pollen bearing stratum (Bed D-1), Martin and Schoenwetter (1960) mention the 1700-year discrepancy between the two sets of dates and accept the earliest on the basis of Haury's argument.

In 1959 the University of Arizona laboratory converted to the carbon dioxide gas-proportional counting method (Damon and Long 1962). During 1960 a number of repeat analyses were conducted on samples previously utilized in solid carbon determinations. Those from the Cienega Creek Site are shown in column three of Table 4. Dates marked with an asterisk are recombustions of the solid carbon used in the original dating. The others represent new runs on duplicate samples of charcoal, wood, and carbonaceous material. Also included in Table 4 is a La Jolla laboratory date (L-432B) originally run as a cross-check on M-540 (reported in Damon and Long [1962]).

The interpretation of this evidence is fairly clear cut for Bed D-1. The recombustion of sample A-29 yielded a date of 2430±150 B.P., which is compatible with the Michigan dates and invalidates the earlier solid carbon determination of 4400±150 B.P. Samples A-25B and A-25 bis, as well as L-432B, are also in agreement with the Michigan series. In fact, the seven gas dates for D-1 from the Michigan, La Jolla, and Arizona laboratories are statistically contemporaneous ($F=.84<2.1$: $df=6,\infty$). Such strong concordance allows for the unequivocal rejection of all three of the D-1 Arizona solid carbon dates. The weighted mean of the seven gas dates is 2442±66 B.P.: 492 B.C.

A somewhat different situation obtains for Bed C-3 in that the recombustion and same-sample analyses agree quite closely with the solid carbon determinations (excepting A-26 bis, which Damon and Long [1962] argue was probably contaminated by modern rootlets). The weighted average of the three contemporaneous ($F=1.1<3.0$: $df=2,\infty$) C-3 gas dates is 3104±92 B.P.: 1154 B.C.

As Jelinek (1965) has already noted, these results are anomalous since they indicate that Bed C-3 was deposited roughly 600 years earlier than the underlying Bed D-1. Damon and Long tentatively suggested that the D-1 dates were in error as a result of silica and limonite replacement.

> Although it is difficult to imagine contamination causing fortuitous agreement of all the D-1 layer dates, it is even more difficult to reconcile young ages with the cultural assemblage in D-1 and the older dates above it (Damon and Long 1962:243).

This line of argument is unconvincing for two reasons. First, the suggestion of fortuitous agreement as a consequence of replacement stretches credibility since the sample materials involved (unburned wood and wood charcoal) have considerably different contamination potentials. Second, the identification of the D-1 cultural assemblage as "Chiricahua" is, as mentioned earlier, tenuous at best since few diagnostic artifacts were recovered. Hence, a 500 B.C. temporal placement for the D-1 deposits is not necessarily contradicted by the associated items of material culture. If we accept the D-1 dating, we are left with the problem of explaining why the C-3 determinations are older than expected. Two solutions come immediately to mind, the most obvious of which is the ever-present possibility of some mixup in provenience assignments during the transfer of samples from field to laboratory to museum storage, etc. The only suggestion that this sort of error might have occurred is the discrepancy in published C-3 sample descriptions wherein Haury describes A-27 as "fragmented solid charcoal" (Haury 1957:22) and the radiocarbon analysts describe it as a "charred, waterlogged pine branch" (Wise and Shutler 1958:73). Apparently the specimen bearing the A-27 provenience label in the laboratory was not the same specimen described in the field. It seems unlikely, however, that provenience errors can be held to account for the inversion problem as a whole since no less than seven mistakes would have to have occurred in order to produce results of the type indicated.

Alternatively, the dating inversion might be

attributable to the origin(s) of the sample materials and the depositional processes by which they entered the site record. Apparent reversals in the stratigraphic ordering of well dated ceramic types are commonplace in the Southwestern alluvial settings. Hack (1942), for example, describes an inversion of Anasazi Pueblo III and Pueblo IV ceramics within the Naha formation of the Jeddito Wash alluvial sequence.

> The (a) member of the Naha formation was deposited, then cut by an arroyo, and the (b) member deposited, all between Pueblo III time and 1700 A.D. That the unconformity actually exists is proved by the assemblage of pottery fragments found in the two members. Member (a) (the oldest) yielded only 1 piece of Pueblo III pottery and 24 pieces of Pueblo IV pottery. Member (b) (the younger) on the other hand yielded 30 pieces of Pueblo III pottery and 6 pieces of Pueblo IV pottery. In other words the younger of the fills yields the highest proportion of the older pottery. . . . Both members must be dated by the youngest potsherds in them, so they are both Pueblo IV or later. The situation may be explained by assuming that during the deposition of the (b) member a portion of a Pueblo III ruin was being actively eroded by the wash (Hack 1942:53).

An analogous process could account for the anomalous dating of Cienega Creek. Referring again to Table 4, three of the four contemporaneous radiocarbon determinations from within Bed C-3, as well as the older than expected (i.e., older than D-1) date from intrusive Pit 8, were derived through recombustion of solid carbon originally prepared by Wise and Shutler from *waterlogged timbers*. The possibility exists that all of these were transported to the site by the same floods responsible for the laminated C-3 deposits. The similarity in ages of the specimens easily could have been the product of natural agency, e.g., alluvial burial or a forest fire, several centuries prior to redeposition at the Cienega Creek locale. In fact, death by forest fire would account for the charring reported for three of the four specimens (Wise and Shutler 1958). This is admittedly speculative, but no more so than the assumption that the age of the timbers equates with the age of Bed C-3 and the associated artifacts. If the wood *was* culturally introduced, why wasn't it subsequently burnt to exhaustion in campfires? In contrast, the radiocarbon samples from Bed D-1 are (with one exception) all fragmented charcoal associated with a great abundance of hearthstones. This leaves little doubt that the D-1 sample material was deposited *in situ* as a result of human activity. If this interpretation of the chronometric evidence is correct, the basal occupation of the Cienega Creek Site occurred at approximately 500 B.C.

As for the association of maize pollen with the earliest deposits, only 48 of the 51,170 grains analyzed from the preceramic levels were identified as *Zea*. These may in fact indicate that maize was being grown during D-1 and C-3 times. However, contamination from the overlying Mogollon occupation cannot be ruled out. This seems all the more likely in view of the numerous deep aboriginal pits, some of which originated in the Mogollon levels and were intrusive into Beds D-1 and C-3 (see Figure 1). Schoenwetter (personal communication, 1981) has suggested that the vertical distribution of corn pollen argues against contamination since the relative percentage drops between the Mogollon and San Pedro levels, then increases in the Chiricahua(?) level. However, this objection finds little statistical support. For one thing, the pollen sample comes from a single vertical column in this extensive and complex site. There is absolutely no way of knowing whether or not the relative pollen frequencies are representative of the site as a whole. Second, the percentages of corn pollen are so miniscule (Mogollon level = .081%, San Pedro level = .044%, Chiricahua(?) level = .13%) that the differences are not demonstrably significant. The case for association would be much stronger if cobs, kernels, stalks, or husks had been recovered from the early deposits. But none were found even though such normally perishable items as basketry, plant parts, and wild seeds were preserved in the bog-like C-3 deposits (Haury 1957).

In sum, despite the use of stratigraphic excavation techniques and the concern shown by Haury and others (Damon and Long 1962) for the accuracy of the absolute dating methods, there are major anomalies in the Cienega Creek record that cannot be resolved without additional excavation. The assertion that maize was being grown at the site as early as 2000 B.C. may now be discounted as wholly unsupportable. If we accept Damon and Long's argument and reject the D-1 dates, then the earliest dated occupation level is Bed C-3 with a mean determination of approximately 1150 B.C. If we accept the alternative interpretation offered above and reject the C-3 dates, then the most probable beginning date for occupation of the site is around 500 B.C. The presence of maize cannot firmly be demonstrated in either case due to the possibility of contamination.

The LoDaisKa Site

The LoDaisKa Site is located in the foothills of the Rocky Mountains roughly 15 miles west of Denver, Colorado. It was excavated in the late 1950s by Henry and Cynthia Irwin (Irwin and Irwin 1959, 1961). According to the authors, the site was occupied by four distinct, perhaps temporally overlapping, prehistoric cultures: Desert Archaic (Complex D), McKean (Complex C), Plains Woodland (Complex B), and Fremont (Complex A). (C. Nelson [1967] and Breternitz [1970] have disputed this latter assignment, noting that the ceramics are probably Shoshonean rather than Fremont. In the following argument, I have substituted "Shoshonean" for Irwin and Irwin's "Fremont" in order to acknowledge this generally accepted revision.) Again, according to the authors, maize was first utilized at the site by approximately 2000 B.C. As was the case with Martin and Schoenwetter's (1960) interpretation of the Cienega Creek Site, Irwin and Irwin accepted the Bat Cave evidence as valid and pointed to the Bat Cave maize complex as the probable progenitor of the early LoDaisKa maize.

> Since corn was present at Bat Cave (Dick, 1952) a site with certain Chiricahua Cochise affinities, it is not unreasonable to assume corn diffused to LoDaisKa from New Mexico or Arizona (Irwin and Irwin 1959:143).

> Maize cobs of Chapalote type and what is probably maize pollen occur earliest at LoDaisKa from 78 to 82 inches below baseline.... This level falls between 1140 and 2800 B.C., roughly 4000 years ago. This maize is morphologically very similar to maize of about the same age from Bat Cave in New Mexico (Irwin and Irwin 1961:115).

There are a number of reasons for questioning Irwin and Irwin's interpretations. First and foremost, the site was excavated in arbitrary horizontal levels, hence (for the same reasons discussed in connection with Bat Cave) the presumed association of maize with any particular radiocarbon date or, for that matter, with any particular cultural complex, is far from certain. In this case it would appear that the excavators had no choice but to employ arbitrary excavation units since the bulk of the deposits consisted of homogeneous, undifferentiated colluvium derived through chemical and mechanical weathering of the sandstone outcrop that forms the overhang and extends upslope above the site (Rodden 1959). The base of the site is well above the level of the local late Holocene alluvium, hence the culture-bearing deposits were never subject to the kind of rapid, intermittent inundation that typically produces clearly discernible stratification and simplifies the excavation process. As a consequence of the slow accretion of fill material and the resultant potential for mixing of artifacts from adjacent time horizons, interpretation of the cultural sequence is subject to certain ambiguities which Irwin and Irwin were unable to resolve.

> From the available material it is not possible to determine whether groups of divergent affiliation ever inhabited the area synchronously. The considerable overlapping of culture units seems to point in this direction; but, as indicated above, this phenomenon may be partially due to the telescoping of stratigraphy. This plus certain traditional continuums provide possible evidence of the influence of these groups on each other (Irwin and Irwin 1959:147).

Nowhere in the monograph do the authors make an unequivocal analytic decision as to how much of the typological overlap should be attributed to depositional factors and how much to cultural contemporaneity. This being the case, how much confidence attaches to either their proposed cultural reconstructions or the purportedly early temporal placement of maize at the site?

Some idea of the onerous nature of the interpretive task that faced Irwin and Irwin is conveyed in Table 5, which summarizes the distributional data from LoDaisKa. For convenience of presentation, the various tables scattered through their monograph have been juxtaposed. The projectile point data were taken from Irwin and Irwin's Table I (1959:37). Their types A through L are lumped together under the heading of "dart points," while types aa through xx

TABLE 5
Distribution of Artifact Types, Cultural Complexes, and Radiocarbon Dates at the LoDaisKa Site

Arbitrary Levels	Dart Points	Arrow Points	Ceramics	Maize	Radiocarbon Dates (years before present)	Desert Archaic	McKean	Plains Woodland	Fremont [Shoshonean]
0–12″									X
12–24″	3		4	1 kernel					X
24–36″	1	7	7					X	X
36–48″	16	50	32		970±150 B.P. (M-1003) 1260±150 B.P. (M-1002)			X	X
48–60″	34	36	21	1 cob	1150±150 B.P. (M-1005)	X	X	X	
60–72″	32	7	2		3400±150 B.P. (M-1004) 1150±150 B.P. (M-1008)	X	X		
72–84″	23			1 cob & frag-ments	3150±200 B.P. (M-1006)	X	X		
84–96″	12					X			
96–108″	4				4840±250 B.P. (M-1009)	X			

Source: Irwin and Irwin 1959: 37, 57

make up the "arrow point" category. The ceramic distribution originally appeared in Irwin and Irwin's Table II (1959:57), and the maize data were taken from Galinat's "Plant Remains from the LoDaisKa Site" published in the same volume (Galinat 1959). The radiocarbon dates were not available at the time the monograph was published but were the subject of a later article in *American Antiquity* (Irwin and Irwin 1961). In preparing Table 5, I have taken the liberty of collapsing the four-inch arbitrary levels to twelve-inch units in the interests of clarity and space. This produced no substantial alteration in the data patterns.

In retrospect, Irwin and Irwin's equivocation regarding the "overlap problem" should have been put to rest by the results of the radiocarbon analyses. As shown in Table 5, the region of greatest overlap of cultural complexes and artifact categories is also characterized by an inversion and intermixture of radiocarbon dates. This strongly suggests that the apparent contemporaneity of cultural complexes was artificially produced through (1) severe mixing due to "trampling" of deposits and aboriginal reuse of tools, (2) the imposition of arbitrary, horizontal excavation units on sloping deposits, or (3) some combination of these two factors. Whatever the case may be, virtually every instance of overlapping artifact types and complexes evidenced at the LoDaisKa Site is demonstrably anomalous in light of what is now known about the prehistory of the region. For instance, a face value reading of Table 5 indicates that the McKean complex lasted from some time prior to 1450 B.C. (3400 B.P.) to some time after A.D. 800 (1150 B.P.) and was partially contemporaneous with the Plains Woodland occupation. However, the twenty-four radiocarbon dates listed by Reeves (1973) for the McKean and closely related Oxbow complex of the central and northern Great Plains all fall between 3250 and 1200 B.C. There is no evidence that the McKean complex survived beyond 1200 B.C., nor is there any evidence that Woodland populations entered the Great Plains prior to A.D. 1 (Symms 1977). In fact, Woodland ceramics in the vicinity of the LoDaisKa Site do not appear to date any earlier than A.D. 200 and may date as late as A.D. 500 (D. Breternitz personal communication, 1969), so it is highly unlikely that the two complexes actually overlapped in time. Quite to the contrary, they were most likely separated by 1500 years or more. The absolute values of the radiocarbon dates from the site are consistent with this interpretation though their relative positions within the deposits are out of sequence.

As another example, there is general agreement that the bow and arrow was not introduced to the Great Plains until the inception of the Avonlea complex during the second or third centuries A.D. (Kehoe 1966, 1973; Reeves 1973; Symms 1977; Wood 1967). However, Table 5 suggests that arrow points occur as early as 1450 B.C. (3400 B.P.) in association with the Desert Archaic and McKean complexes. Again, a face value reading of the distributional data produces at least a 1500-year anachronism.

It is interesting in this regard that Irwin and Irwin saw fit to reject the early occurrence of arrow points as intrusive (Irwin and Irwin 1959:140), and I presume that they similarly rejected the ceramics from the same levels since no claim was made for the occurrence of pottery at 1450 B.C. Why, then, should a single corn cob and a few cob fragments recovered from a Desert Archaic "level" be accepted as a valid association? I strongly suspect that all of the maize remains from LoDaisKa, along with the ceramics and arrow points, are attributable to the Woodland and/or Shoshonean occupations. This is a testable proposition since the Chapalote specimen in question could still be submitted for radiocarbon analysis. If the above arguments are valid, it should yield a date well into the Christian era.

Whether or not such a test is ever conducted, I think it is clear that the evidence for "ancient maize" at LoDaisKa leaves much to be desired. It is certainly not the kind of data that will support higher level constructs regarding the introduction and diffusion of maize farming.

The Arroyo Cuervo Region

From 1964 through 1970 Eastern New Mexico University conducted an extensive program of survey and excavation in northwestern New Mexico under the direction of Cynthia Irwin-Williams (Irwin-Williams and Tompkins 1968; Irwin-Williams 1967, 1973). This research inspired

Irwin-Williams's definition of, first, the Picosa culture and, a few years later, the Oshara Tradition. The Picosa culture

> is defined as a continuum of similar closely related preceramic cultures existing in the southwestern United States during the last three millenia before Christ. It is seen as representing the elementary period of the development of the Southwest as a discrete culture area and is believed to be the result of a cultural synthesis of uniform developments originating as early as 8000 B.C. (Irwin-Williams 1967:441).

The Oshara Tradition was formulated for the "northern Southwest" and was based solely on data from the Arroyo Cuervo region. It purportedly represents

> an unbroken sequence of preceramic cultural development beginning in the sixth millenium before Christ and culminating in the early phases of the local Anasazi-Pueblo culture (Irwin-Williams 1973:2).

Both constructs are rather extreme statements of the gradualist school of evolutionary thought, presupposing as they do the slow-paced accretion of increments of culture change and implying biological and ethnic continuity within fairly restricted geographical domains for millenial periods. The gradualist perspective is quite compatible with the notion that maize farming was introduced to the Archaic hunter-gatherers of the Arroyo Cuervo region prior to 2000 B.C., but that it had no significant effect until the Basketmaker II–III period during the first few centuries A.D. More properly, gradualism demands that the problem be framed in this manner. Consequently Irwin-Williams's Picosa and Oshara constructs rely more on theoretical assumptions than they do on any archeological data. With respect to the current topic of investigation, what data allow the inference that maize has a 4000-year history of use in the Southwest? The evidence marshalled by Irwin-Williams is less than convincing.

> The one subsistence feature which sets the Southwest Picosa area off from all contemporary western Archaic cultures is the early presence and growing importance of horticulture. Probably introduced through the medium of the Cochise culture, its occurrence by about 2000 B.C. is documented in Arizona, New Mexico, and Colorado (Cienega Creek, Arizona [Haury 1957]; Bat Cave, New Mexico [Dick 1965]; Armijo Shelter, New Mexico [Irwin-Williams unpublished 1967 article]; LoDaisKa Shelter, Colorado [Irwin and Irwin 1959]) (Irwin-Williams 1967:443).

The list of citations would be impressive if not for the fact that three of the four sites named have been reviewed above and the evidence was found wanting. The fourth, Armijo Shelter, was excavated by Irwin-Williams as part of the Arroyo Cuervo, Anasazi Origins Project. However, the preliminary descriptive report cited above was for some reason never published and the relevant data cannot be evaluated. In fact, of the seven major excavations carried out in conjunction with the Anasazi Origins Project, only one site, En Medio Shelter (Irwin-Williams and Tompkins 1968), has been described in print. In that brief publication we learn that the evidence for the very early occurrence of maize consists solely of maize pollen recovered from alluvial and aeolian deposits dating from 1500 B.C. to 10 B.C. (laboratory numbers, material dated, and standard errors not given). Schoenwetter (personal communication, 1981) informs me that the 1500 B.C. date was on charcoal from a hearth, the "top" fill of which contained maize pollen. Maize pollen was also present in a sediment sample from the level of origin of the hearth and in seven of the samples between 7 cm and 82 cm above the hearth. It is Schoenwetter's view that this constitutes strong evidence for the 1500 B.C. occurrence of maize. I would argue, on the other hand, that these data leave much to be desired. For one thing, the dating of the hearth is based on a single uncorroborated radiocarbon determination. For another, the current evidence does not sufficiently establish the contemporaneity of pollen deposition and hearth ignition. In principle, the sediments containing the maize pollen could have been deposited subsequent to the hearth "event" following an interval of time ranging from a few minutes to several centuries in duration. Obviously, many more radiocarbon samples would be necessary to resolve these difficulties. Finally, as suggested for the Cienega Creek situation, the "early" occurrence of maize pollen may well be attributable to contamination from the overlying Basketmaker-Pueblo levels, which contained both maize pollen and macrofossils.

Schoenwetter (personal communication, 1981) also notes the presence of maize pollen in Archaic contexts at a number of other sites in the Arroyo Cuervo region. Since there are no published descriptions of these sites, any assessment of these proposed associations would be inappropriate at this time.

As I have maintained in previous sections, Bat Cave and its companion sites comprise a very weak body of evidence for early maize; hence, appeal to these data does nothing to enhance the probability of the early use of maize in the Arroyo Cuervo. Irwin-Williams's evidence must stand or fall on its own merits, but these merits cannot be evaluated until the results of this important project are published. As it now stands, little can be said about the age of maize in the Arroyo Cuervo region or Irwin-Williams's gradualist formulation of Anasazi origins.

Other Sites

In addition to the traditionally cited loci of ancient maize discussed above, there are a number of other sites that occasionally surface in the literature for which similar claims of great antiquity are made. Minnis (n.d.) has discussed these and, in general, summarily dismissed the supporting evidence as trivial or inconclusive. The relevant sites are the Chaco Canyon alluvial sequence (S. A. Hall 1977), the County Road Site (Plog 1974), Double Adobe (Paul Schultz Martin 1963), Fresnal Shelter (Human Systems Research, Inc. 1973), O'Haco Rockshelter (Bruier 1977), and Sand Dune Cave (Lindsay et al. 1968). I agree with Minnis's assessment since, in each case, the data are scant and far less convincing than the evidence for early maize at the sites I have criticized in detail. The dating of the County Road Site will be discussed in a different context in Chapter 4. Otherwise, the above listed sites require no further comment.

Recently, Simmons (1981) has reported the association of maize pollen and radiocarbon dates in the 1700 to 2000 B.C. range from two sites in northwestern New Mexico. LA17337 is a dune site containing a number of hearths. Three radiocarbon dates were obtained on charcoal from one of the hearths that contained maize pollen. Two of these are in close agreement and indicate an occupation date of 1700 B.C. However, the third date of A.D. 1700 suggests that the hearth may have been reused during the historic period or, more likely, that considerable post-depositional mixture has taken place as a consequence of dune activity. The situation is somewhat less equivocal at LA18103 where two charcoal samples dated at 2000 B.C. and 1700 B.C. were recovered from a subsurface pit that also yielded maize pollen. The problem with these two cases (as well as several others discussed earlier) is that pollen data do not provide evidence sufficient to demonstrate the presence of maize at specific proveniences within a site due to the likelihood of contamination. A considerable amount of contamination probably occurs as stratigraphic profiles are cut and subterranean features are exposed during the process of excavation. Complex depositional anomalies and aboriginal earth moving activities are also contributory factors. Then too, contamination during laboratory analysis cannot be discounted. Thus, while Simmons's evidence is interesting, confirmatory data in the form of macrofossils from stratigraphically controlled, well-dated contexts will be required before the very early occurrence of maize in northwestern New Mexico can be accepted.

Finally, it bears mention that Haury (1976; see also Gladwin et al. 1937) dates the beginning of the agricultural Pioneer Hohokam at 300 B.C. This temporal placement has been soundly criticized by Bullard (1962) and, more recently, by Berry and Marmaduke (1980), Haynes and Long (1976), Plog (1980), and Wilcox (1979). The consensus appears to favor a beginning date in the A.D. 300 to 500 range.

THE AGE OF MAIZE: A CONSERVATIVE ESTIMATE

Direct dating of maize specimens provides the most secure form of evidence though even that approach is subject to an uncertain degree of error due to isotopic fractionation in maize that produces anomalously high C-14/C-12 ratios and, hence, radiocarbon dates that are too recent. The amount of C-14 enrichment has been estimated indirectly through mass spectrometric analysis of C-13/C-12 ratios by Bender (1968) and Lowden (1969). Bender's work with both prehistoric and modern specimens suggests that a correction factor of 210 years is appropriate (Bender 1968:471). Lowden's analysis of modern maize suggests a correction factor of 234 years (Lowden 1969:392). Following Haynes and Long (1976), 250 years will be used herein as a rough approximation of the correction for fractionation.

Table 6 is a compilation of the earliest directly dated maize samples in the Southwest. The 250-year correction factor has been added to all but three of the dates. The three in question (C-585; C-612; C-164/171) consisted of mixed samples of maize and other organic materials. There is no way of knowing what percentage of these samples was maize and I have simply assumed a 50/50 split and added 125 years to the uncorrected radiocarbon dates. All of the dates are from the southern Basin and Range province except those from Cowboy Cave and Clyde's Cavern, both of which are located in southeastern Utah.

Obviously, these dates do not support the notion that maize was introduced to the Southwest

TABLE 6
Early Radiocarbon Dated Maize Samples

Site	Provenience	Uncorrected Radiocarbon Date (B.P.) and Lab Number		Corrected Radiocarbon Date (B.P.)	Reference
Jemez Cave	Square IX; Levels 7 to 9	2440±125	(M-466)	2690±125	Crane and Griffin 1958b
Tularosa Cave	Square 2R2; Level 10	1810±200	(M-716)	2060±200	Crane and Griffin 1960
	Square 2R2; Level 10	2145±160	(C-585)[a]	2270±160[b]	Libby 1955
	Square 2R2; Level 13	2300±200	(C-612)[a]	2425±200[b]	"
	Square 2R2; Level 14	2223±200	(C-584)[a]	2473±200	"
Bat Cave	0 to 1 ft. level	1752±250	(C-165)[a]	2002±250	"
	3 to 4 ft. level	2249±250	(C-164, 171)[a]	2374±250[b]	"
Cowboy Cave	Unit IVc	1865±70	(SI-2422)	2115±70[c]	R. Stuckenrath personal communication, 1978
Clyde's Cavern	Level 2	1490±100	(RL-175)	1740±100	Winter and Wylie 1974

[a]Solid carbon determination

[b]Mixed sample of maize and other organic material (see text)

[c]SI-2422 was originally corrected to 2075±70 B.P. on the assumption of 12 per mil δC-13 for fractionation (R. Stuckenrath personal communciation, 1978), and is probably closer to the true date than the value used here. I have increased the correction factor to 250 years for the sake of consistency.

prior to 2000 B.C. The earliest date is 740 B.C. (2690 B.P.) on maize from Jemez Cave described by Volney Jones as "of generalized Bat Cave character" (Crane and Griffin 1958b; Ford 1975). His description is of more than passing interest in light of the arguments offered earlier, since the date overlaps the earliest directly dated maize from Bat Cave within one standard error.

Admittedly, this is a very small sample upon which to base any far-reaching conclusions. But if maize *is* earlier than Table 6 suggests, it is surprising that none of the really ancient maize has been submitted for radiocarbon analysis in the quarter century that the method has been available. This is especially true considering the great amount of interdisciplinary attention that this particular topic has attracted.

Another secure means of dating maize is by association with clusters of radiocarbon dates recovered from discrete architectural proveniences in open sites containing only one or two cultural components. In such contexts, the chances for significant mixture are negligible and—*so long as there exists a tight clustering of radiocarbon dates*—aberrant determinations, such as might be caused by the aboriginal use of dead trees, can readily be identified and rejected. The three earliest sites, described briefly below, that meet these rather stringent requirements are Ariz D:7:152 (Gumerman and Euler 1976; J. A. Ware personal communication, 1977), NA14,646 (W. Marmaduke personal communication, 1978), and the Hay Hollow Site (Paul Sidney Martin 1967; Martin and Plog 1973; Bohrer 1972; Fritz 1974). The relevant radiocarbon evidence is presented in Chapter 4.

Ariz D:7:152

Ariz D:7:152 is located on Black Mesa northeast of Redlake, Arizona. It was excavated in 1974 in conjunction with the Black Mesa Project under the general supervision of George Gumerman (Gumerman and Euler 1976) of Southern Illinois University. The site is a single component pithouse village with abundant remains of maize cobs and kernels (J. A. Ware personal communication, 1977). The radiocarbon samples selected were either carbonized twigs and small branches from pithouse hearths or the outer ten rings of pithouse support posts or other structural timbers. The nine radiocarbon determinations are statistically contemporaneous ($F=.70<1.94$: $df=8,\infty$) and have a weighted mean of 2136 ± 27 B.P.: 186 B.C.

NA14,646

Site NA14,646 was excavated in 1977 by the Museum of Northern Arizona. It is located in Hardscrabble Wash near St. Johns, Arizona. Pithouse 1 was the earliest structure at the site. Maize macrofossils were recovered from the roof fall. Four radiocarbon dates were run on support posts and roofing material. These are statistically contemporaneous ($F=1.22<2.60$: $df=3,\infty$) with a weighted mean of 2135 ± 31 B.P.: 185 B.C.

Hay Hollow

The Hay Hollow Site is an agricultural pithouse village located in the Hay Hollow Valley near Snowflake, Arizona. It was excavated by John Fritz in conjunction with an extensive program of survey and excavation under the general direction of Paul Sidney Martin (Martin and Plog 1973). Maize pollen and macrofossils were recovered from the floors of several of the dated pithouses (Bohrer 1966, 1972). The 23 radiocarbon dates for the site range from 470 B.C. to A.D. 305 (J. M. Fritz personal communication, 1976), and published estimates of its maximum age range from 200 to 400 B.C. (Paul Sidney Martin 1967, 1972; Martin and Plog 1973). However, the earliest dates are on samples from external pits rather than pithouses and are well outside the range of the architectural dates. This seems to be a fairly clear-cut case of "driftwood" effect. If we consider only the seven dates from the three earliest pithouses at the site, a completely different picture emerges. The weighted averages are 1998 ± 60 B.P.: 48 B.C. ($F=.28<3.00$: $df=2,\infty$) for House 17, 1953 ± 61 B.P.: 3 B.C. ($t=.20<1.96$) for House 25, and 1972 ± 55 B.P.: 22 B.C. ($t=1.0<1.96$) for House 32. Published accounts notwithstanding, it would appear that the Hay Hollow Site was first occupied in the second half of the first century B.C.

Summary

Figure 2 is a graphic representation of the nine directly dated maize specimens and the three

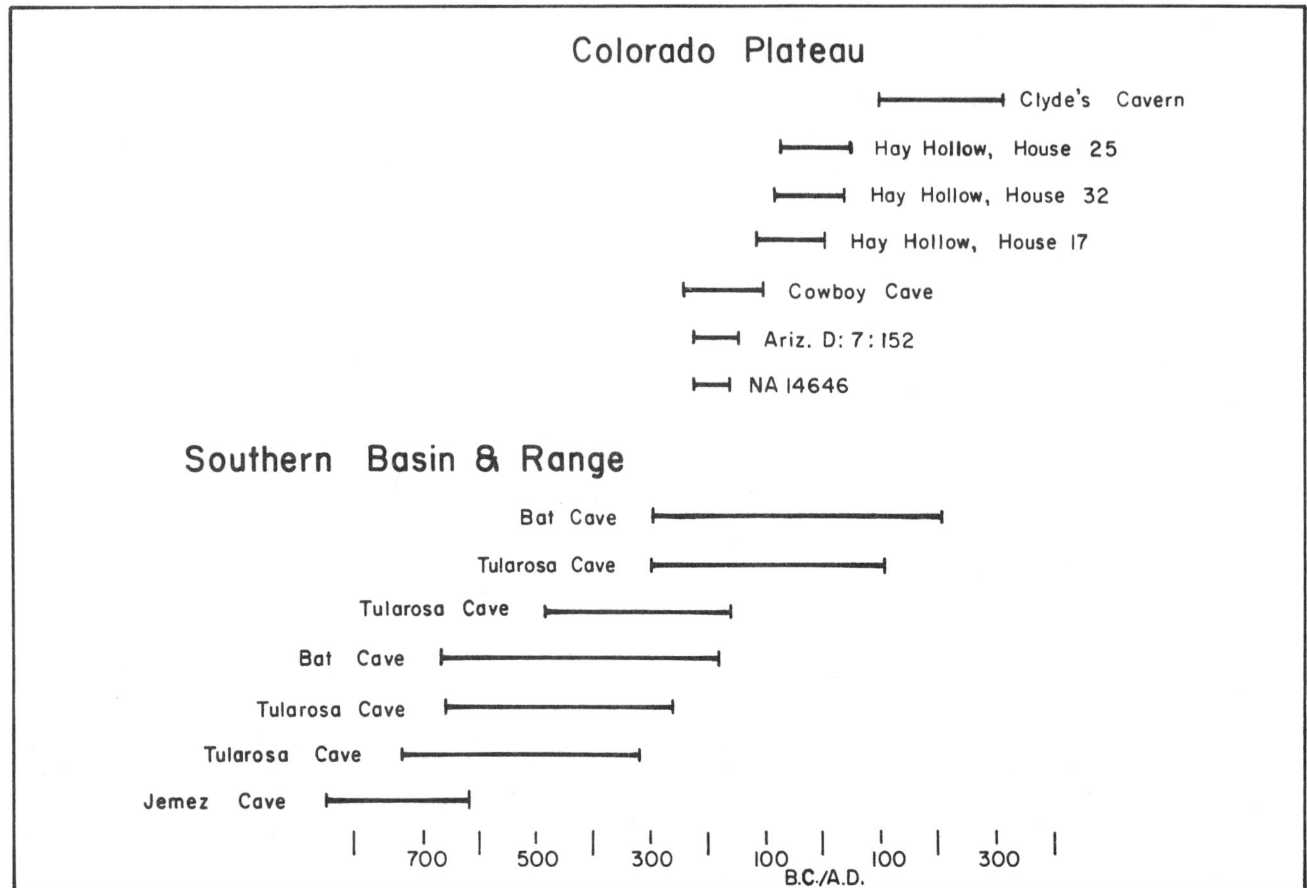

Figure 2. Direct maize dates and maize dated by reliable association.

adequately dated pithouse villages discussed above. Each date or weighted mean is depicted as a horizontal bar the length of which indicates the plus-and-minus one standard error range. The values shown for maize dates incorporate the corrections for fractionation (see Table 6). Dates for architectural features are the weighted means of contemporaneous radiocarbon determinations. I should point out that five of the nine maize dates were derived using the solid carbon method. This factor may, however, not be as debilitating as it seems since all of these were run by Libby at the University of Chicago laboratory (Libby 1955), and Libby's determinations are demonstrably more consistent with modern gas dates than any of the other pioneering solid carbon laboratories, e.g., Michigan (Crane 1956) or Arizona (Wise and Shutler 1958). The data shown in Table 6 suggest that a modest degree of confidence in the solid carbon dates may be warranted in the present case. The three solid carbon determinations for Tularosa Cave all overlap within one standard error, and C-585 from Level 10 is statistically contemporaneous with the Michigan gas date (M-716) from the same level ($t=.82<1.96$). A certain, if considerably weaker, degree of support can be mustered for the Chicago maize dates from Bat Cave (C-165 and C-164/171) since they are at least in the correct order suggested by their gross provenience levels.

Considering all the possible shortcomings and sources of error, the data of Figure 2 present a fairly coherent picture. The situation is clearest for the Colorado Plateau where both the earliest directly dated maize and the earliest maize-associated domestic architecture appear shortly after 200 B.C. The estimate for the southern Basin and Range depends on whether we are willing to accept the solid carbon maize dates on equal footing with the gas dates. If we do, the probable beginning date for maize, based on the clustering of the earliest dates from Tularosa, Bat, and Jemez caves, could then be placed at approximately 500 to 750 B.C. If we do not, then the very early date from Jemez Cave would have to be rejected as aberrant, leaving only the lone gas date from Tularosa Cave of 110±200 B.C. (M-716, corrected for fractionation) to serve as an estimate. This cannot be ruled out but it seems a bit too conservative given the current state of the data. For the time being, a "looser" estimate of 500 B.C., give or take 200 years, is probably appropriate.

Conclusions and Implications

There is no longer any reason to believe that maize made its initial appearance in the Southwest by 2000 B.C., much less 3500 B.C. The notion has its roots in the pioneering interdisciplinary efforts of the Bat Cave project, and it has been perpetuated through continual citation in standard textbooks and professional journals. Obviously the data are no better now than they were in 1948, and the time has come to put the myth of "ancient" maize to rest.

The realization that maize did not enter the Southwest until a few hundred years B.C. entails certain shifts in perspective with regard to traditional problems of both the diffusion of maize north of Mexico and its effects upon the recipient cultures. For one thing, we need no longer concern ourselves with the question of why it took so long for maize to appear in the midwestern and eastern United States after its initial occurrence in the Southwest. Struever and Vickery (1973) date the inception of maize in the Midwest riverine area at around 500 B.C. In a somewhat more critical assessment of essentially the same data, Yarnell (1976) concludes that maize was first introduced to the Midwest region by 200 B.C.±100. Regardless of which of the two estimates ultimately proves to be correct, it is, in light of the arguments offered earlier, quite conceivable that maize was introduced to the Southwest and Midwest at about the same time from a common Mexican source area.

A second issue of concern centers on the type(s) of models used to characterize the introduction of maize to the Southwest. It is generally held that maize farming was adopted by indigenous Archaic populations and, further, that the initial impact on these hunting and gathering groups was negligible. The process initiated by the addition of maize to the local resource base typically is envisioned as a slow shift from primary dependency on wild resources to primary dependency on domesticates. Acceptance of this view has been fostered by both the prevalence of gradualism as a theoretical orientation and the belief that maize had been present in the Southwest for thousands of years without producing any perceptible evolutionary consequences. The supposed great antiquity of maize has, I believe, been adequately refuted. The gradualist model and the related notion of negligible initial impact may, in like manner, be disposed of on empirical grounds. Figure 3 shows the relationship between the postulated introduction dates of maize (as indicated by the X's) and the relative intensity of cultural activity (as indicated by the radiocarbon bar charts) for the southern Colorado Plateau and the southern Basin and Range province. In both regions, there is a rapid, perhaps immediate, increase in the number of dated cultural events coincident with the probable inception of maize farming. The *meaning* of these increases is admittedly open to conjecture, but it no longer seems reasonable to speak of a gradual transition from hunting and gathering to agriculture in the Southwest. The transition was clearly abrupt and the impact immediate and profound.

The introduction of maize in the southern Basin and Range province appears to correspond with the emergence of the San Pedro stage of the Cochise culture. The San Pedro cultural assemblage is sufficiently distinct from the preceding Chiricahua stage to suggest an intrusion into the area by immigrating populations. The primary cause of this early agricultural dispersal may well have been the widespread "Fairbank Drought" which lasted from approximately 950 B.C. to 650

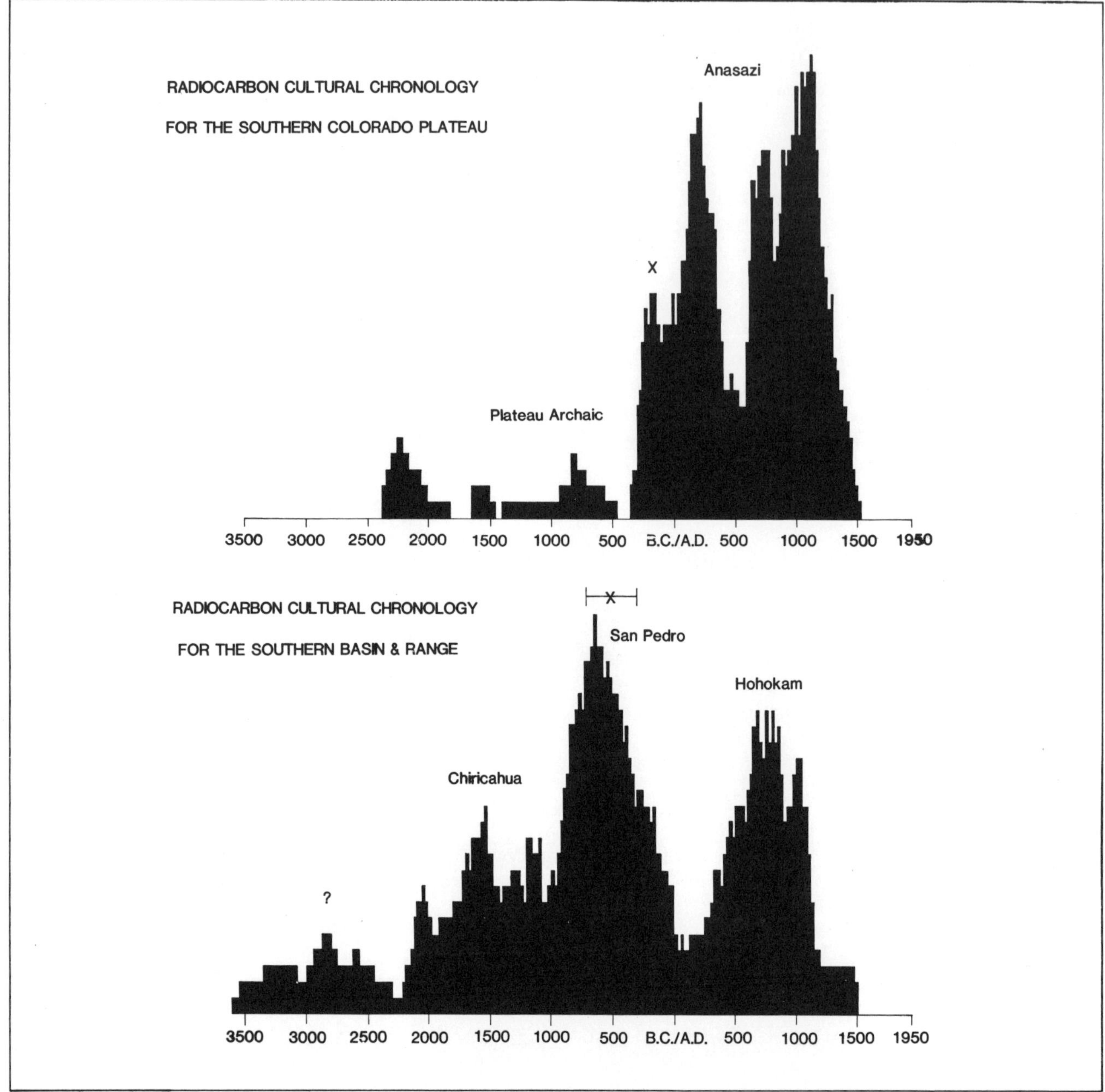

Figure 3. Bar charts of radiocarbon dated cultural remains from the southern Colorado Plateau and southern Basin and Range province. The X's indicate the probable introduction dates of maize in the two regions. The bar charts were constructed by first plotting all the radiocarbon dates on graph paper as plus-and-minus one sigma horizontal lines. Then, the number of lines crossing each 25-year increment was counted and plotted as the ordinate value for that increment of the bar chart. Not all of the available radiocarbon dates were used. Solid carbon determinations were eliminated as well as dates run on shell, bone, soil, and other questionable materials. In addition, dates clearly unrelated to cultural events and those that were demonstrably inconsistent with clusters of dates from the same site or stratum were excluded. No adjustments for variation in atmostpheric C-14 were made, but 250 years was added to each maize date to correct for fractionation. Southern Colorado Plateau dates are listed by site in the Appendix. The bar chart for the southern Basin and Range province was developed by Claudia F. Berry (Berry and Marmaduke 1980). Her list of dates has not been repeated here. The southern Colorado Plateau and southern Basin and Range bar charts were constructed from 151 and 133 radiocarbon dates, respectively.

B.C. (Haynes 1968). All of the sites that have yielded evidence of very early maize (750 B.C. to 500 B.C.) are located in the Mexican Highland Section of the southern Basin and Range at elevations between 6000 and 7000 feet (cf. Haury 1962). This is consistent with the notion of climatically induced population movement since these high-elevation sites would have served as excellent drought refugia for the small immigrant farming groups. Unfortunately, the source area(s) for this postulated migration cannot, at present, be identified.

Following the San Pedro peak, there was a rapid decline in cultural activity in the southern Basin and Range as indicated by the trough in the radiocarbon bar chart centered at A.D. 100 to 200. This corresponds precisely to the Basketmaker II peak for the Colorado Plateau. The complementary distribution of radiocarbon dates, combined with the fact that western San Juan dart points of the Basketmaker II period (Morris and Burgh 1954) are indistinguishable from San Pedro points, strongly suggests that Basketmaker II represents a migration from the southern Basin and Range to the Plateau. This interpretation gains further support from the extreme dissimilarity of late Plateau Archaic (San Jose/Pinto) and early Basketmaker II dart points (C. Berry personal communication, 1980).

Population movement from the mountainous region of the Basin and Range to the Plateau began at approximately 185 B.C. for reasons that are not entirely clear. One possibility is that the trend toward moister and cooler conditions following the Fairbank Drought may have drastically shortened the growing season in the high-elevation refugia while simultaneously increasing the potential for agricultural productivity on the Plateau. This of course assumes that the subsistence system centered on maize productivity. The fact that the early Basketmaker II sites are pithouse villages with abundant remains of maize macrofossils lends strong support to this premise, as does the absence of contemporaneous nonvillage sites.

If this reconstruction is essentially correct, there was no lineal, *in situ* relationship between Chiricahua and San Pedro or between the Plateau Archaic and Basketmaker II. In both cases the introduction of maize farming was accomplished through sociocultural intrusion rather than through diffusion of agriculture to indigenous hunter-gatherer populations. I suspect that this is true of the dispersal of maize agriculture in general throughout the Desert West. That is, there is no reason to expect that a successfully adapted hunting and gathering culture would voluntarily adopt a practice that imposes so many constraints on mobility and whose seasonal maintenance and harvest requirements conflict with the seasonality of so many productive wild resources, e.g., pine nuts, Indian ricegrass, amaranth, etc. The gradualist model alluded to earlier apparently was devised to accommodate this very problem. But the model errs in failing to acknowledge the all-or-nothing nature of maize agriculture. It is impossible to sustain a plant that is not self-propagating for any length of time without a total commitment to its planting, maintenance, and harvesting on a year-to-year basis. And that commitment minimally entails semisedentarism and a considerable reduction in wild resource exploitation during the growing season.

There is no evidence to indicate that a hunter-gatherer/agricultural transition ever occurred in the Southwest. Rather, everything seems to point to colonization by small groups of farmers as the primary mechanism responsible for the introduction of maize.

4. THE ANASAZI SEQUENCE FROM 185 B.C. TO A.D. 1450

With a plausible beginning date for the Anasazi cultural tradition established in Chapter 3, the available chronometric data for the sequence as a whole may now be summarized and critically analyzed. The chapter is divided into two parts: The first examines the earliest half of the sequence from the introduction of maize through the end of Basketmaker III; the second examines Pueblo I through Pueblo IV. The first part is far more detailed than the second because much of the evidence remains unpublished and is presented here for the first time. Then, too, the first half of the sequence encompasses the transition from radiocarbon dated events to tree-ring dated events mentioned in Chapter 2, and therefore requires careful and intensive analytic treatment. The intent of both parts is to provide an objective assessment of chronometric data patterning for the southern Colorado Plateau.

185 B.C. to A.D. 700

No in-depth analysis of early Anasazi architecture and chronology has been undertaken since the publication of the late William R. Bullard's (1962) excellent synthesis. A great deal of information has come to light in the past two decades, especially for the pre–A.D. 700 period. These data, and much of the evidence used by Bullard, are presented and reviewed below. The emphasis is on temporal controls; hence, many well-known, well-excavated, but undated sites are excluded from the analysis. Chronology building (as opposed to seriation) is best viewed as an empirical and inductive process, and it serves no purpose to include "guess-dated" or analogically dated sites or structures as constituents of an empirical generalization.

An attempt has been made to include every pithouse on the southern Colorado Plateau dated by tree-rings, radiocarbon, or both, to the pre–A.D. 700 era. (Site data published after the spring of 1980 are not included in the analysis). The reason for focusing on architectural proveniences has to do with the reliability of tree-ring and radiocarbon samples recovered from houses as compared to other contexts. Direct dating of building materials is much more likely to yield an accurate placement of cultural events than the dating of materials from firepits, external pits of unknown function, charcoal lenses, and other problematic features. This is due (at least inferentially) to the likely practice of using newly felled trees and freshly gathered thatching materials for construction purposes while using both contemporaneous logs and "dead" logs of *unknown* age for firewood. Additionally, recovered construction timbers are more likely to have their outer rings intact than logs consumed in a hearth fire.

The organization of data presentation is as follows: Sites containing the relevant structures are ordered from earliest to most recent. Discussion of each site or set of sites from a given area consists of (1) a brief statement of where, when, and by whom the work was conducted, (2) an assessment of the available chronometric evidence, and (3) a brief description of architectural features. By including all dated structures within the southern Colorado Plateau, a few sites normally considered to be in the Mogollon tradition will also be analyzed. This should cause no difficulty since the Anasazi-Mogollon distinction in the "border areas" is often hazy if not spurious.

Coal Mine Wash

Site Ariz D:7:152 is located adjacent to Coal Mine Wash on the northern part of Black Mesa in northeastern Arizona. It was excavated by John Ware in connection with the salvage program conducted by Southern Illinois University on Peabody Coal Company lease lands. The site is "an open, stratified pithouse village with numerous large 'bedrock' pithouses, surface hearths, and roasting ovens" (J. Ware personal communication, 1977). No architectural description is available at this time, and the site is included here only because of its early temporal provenience, precise dating controls, and the clear association of the dated structures with maize macrofossils (see Chapter 3).

CHRONOLOGY. The nine radiocarbon dates are shown below in Table 7. All samples were either small charred twigs or the outer ten rings of construction beams. These dates are statistically contemporaneous ($F=.70<1.94$: $df=8,\infty$), with a weighted mean of 2136±27 B.P.: 186 B.C. This evidence clearly overrides the single date of 600 B.C. reported by Gumerman and Euler (1976) for the site. That sample must have been a complete cross section of a large construction beam or a dead log that had been salvaged and used as firewood.

COMMENTS. This is one of the best-dated early agricultural sites in the Southwest. The dated features, as well as the site surface, were devoid of ceramics. It is unfortunate that no information is available on the architecture or associated lithic technology.

Hardscrabble Wash

Site NA14,646 is located along the course of Hardscrabble Wash roughly 20 miles north of St. Johns, Arizona. It was excavated in 1977 under the direction of James Bradford, Museum of Northern Arizona. The site had several compo-

TABLE 7
Radiocarbon Dates from AZ D:7:152

Provenience	Radiocarbon Age B.P.	Calendric Age A.D./B.C.	Lab Number
Feature 9	2210±80	260 B.C.	I-8402
Feature 6	2000±80	50 B.C.	I-8403
Feature 15	2180±80	230 B.C.	I-8404
Feature 24	2120±80	170 B.C.	I-8405
Feature 4	2205±80	255 B.C.	I-8406
Feature 18	2170±80	220 B.C.	I-8407
Feature 3	2150±80	200 B.C.	I-8408
Feature 16	2090±80	140 B.C.	I-8409
Feature 5	2100±80	150 B.C.	I-8410

nents, the earliest of which was represented by Pithouse 1. Pithouse 1 contained a few sherds of an unidentified plain ware in the fill above roof fall. These are thought to be intrusive from one of the later occupations since the floor of the structure was devoid of ceramics.

CHRONOLOGY. The four radiocarbon dates associated with Pithouse 1 are shown in Table 8 (W. S. Marmaduke personal communication, 1978). All samples were wood charcoal. These dates are statistically contemporaneous with respect to the precision of measurement ($F=1.22<2.60$: $df=3,\infty$) and have a weighted mean of 2135±31 B.P.: 185 B.C. This result is virtually identical to the weighted mean of radiocarbon dates from Ariz D:7:152 discussed above.

ARCHITECTURE. No description of NA14,646 has yet been published. The following summary of Pithouse 1 architecture has been taken from the field notes with the permission of William Marmaduke, project coordinator. (See Figure 4B for a plan map of the structure.)

Shape and size: Roughly circular in shape with a mean diameter of 4.5 m.

Depth: The fairly level floor surface ranged from 0.65 to 0.70 m below the level of origin.

Floor: Unplastered sterile sand.

Firepit: The firepit consisted of a shallow, ash-filled depression located slightly south of the center of the house. It was outlined by six large sandstone slabs placed horizontally on the floor surface. The maximum diameter of this semicircular enclosure was approximately 0.90 m. Depth of fill was 20 cm.

Other floor features: Floor features consisted of three postholes and one subfloor pit. Two of the postholes flanked the entryway at the southern edge of the structure. They averaged 0.25 m in diameter and contained the remains of charred post butts. The third posthole was located in the center of the pithouse. It was 0.1 m in diameter and also contained a charred post butt. The subfloor pit was located south of the firepit near the entryway. It was roughly diamond shaped and measured 0.48 m from east to west and 0.66 m from north to south. Maximum depth was 0.52 m. The fill consisted of charcoal-flecked, brownish gray sand.

Entryway/antechamber: The entryway was a short, southward extension of the house pit. It was 0.8 m long and contracted in width from 1.53 m at its intersection with the house wall to 0.9 m at its southern terminus. Like the main portion of the structure, the floor and walls consisted of unaltered sterile sand.

Superstructure: Combustion of roofing materials was fairly complete; hence, there is no certainty regarding roof construction. The single, centrally located post may have supported leaner poles whose butts were anchored at the base of the pithouse walls. This interpretation follows the traditional reconstruction of early Mogollon superstructures (Wheat 1955). However, a roof constructed of cribbed logs is an equally tenable possibility.

TABLE 8
Radiocarbon Dates from Pithouse 1, NA14,646

Provenience	Radiocarbon Age B.P.	Calendric Age A.D./B.C.	Lab Number
Roof fall, above floor	2180±60	230 B.C.	UGa2101
Roof fall	2145±60	195 B.C.	UGa2102
Roof fall	2185±65	235 B.C.	UGa2103
Roof fall, above hearth	2040±60	90 B.C.	UGa2104

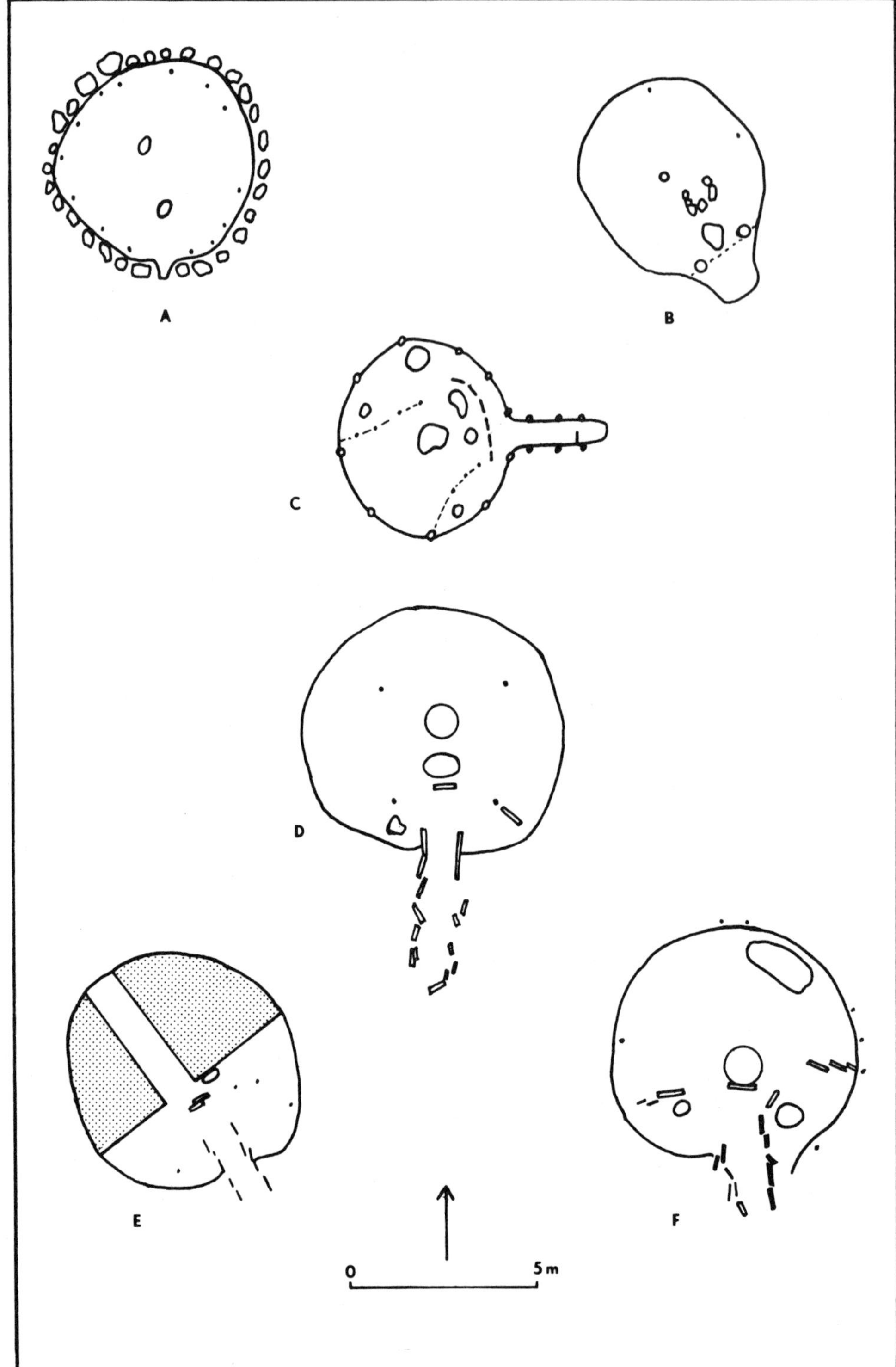

Figure 4. Early Colorado Plateau pithouses: A, House A, Tumbleweed Canyon (Martin et al. 1962); B, Pithouse 1, NA14,646 (W. S. Marmaduke personal communication, 1978); C, pithouse, County Road Site (P. R. Nelson 1964); D, pithouse, Veres Site (W. D. Lipe personal communication, 1978); E, pithouse, Lone Tree Dune (Sharrock, Day, and Dibble 1963); F, pithouse, Pittman Site (W. D. Lipe personal communication, 1978).

COMMENTS. Maize remains were recovered from the roof fall of this dwelling. The strong clustering of the radiocarbon determinations leaves little doubt that this was one of the earliest pithouses in the Southwest.

Comb Wash

Zero Plaza is located on the west side of Comb Wash approximately 40 miles east of Halls Crossing on the Colorado River. It was excavated in 1971 in conjunction with the Highway U-95 salvage project conducted by the University of Utah. Excavations were supervised by H. J. Hall (1973). The project as a whole was directed by Jesse D. Jennings. The site consisted of a single isolated pit structure.

CHRONOLOGY. A charcoal specimen recovered from the firepit yielded a date of 2050±120 B.P.: 100 B.C. (RL-240).

ARCHITECTURE. The following summary description is taken from H. J. Hall (1973).

Shape and size: Circular to oval in shape with a mean diameter of 4.6 m.

Depth: Maximum depth below level of origin is 0.9 m.

Floor: The floor was intentionally prepared and consisted of compacted pinkish sand over native earth.

Firepit: The firepit was centered along the north-south axis of the house but was only 1.5 m west of the east wall. It was roughly triangular in shape and contained eight sandstone slabs. Greatest transverse measurement was 0.6 m.

Other floor features: A deflector slab was set in the floor between the firepit and the east wall. It measured 30.5 cm in length, 25.4 cm in width, and was 7.6 cm thick. The only other floor feature was a circular pit located to the southwest of the firepit. It was 0.6 m in diameter and only 11.0 cm deep.

Entryway/antechamber: None.

Superstructure: Little evidence of a superstructure was found other than charcoal flecks in the fill. A single charred post butt was found on the western periphery of the structure.

COMMENTS. No ceramics were recovered from the structure.

The Hay Hollow Valley

Several early village sites have been excavated in the Hay Hollow Valley of northeastern Arizona by the Field Museum of Natural History, University of Chicago. These include the Connie, County Road, Petri, and Hay Hollow sites. None of these has been adequately described as yet, and the following account is based on information given me by the excavators and the few brief preliminary statements available in the published and unpublished literature.

CHRONOLOGY. The Hay Hollow Site has received more attention and detailed treatment than any of the others mentioned above. It consists of eight or nine pithouses and associated external pits. There is no doubt that it was a farming village as indicated by the abundance of maize macrofossils and pollen in association with pithouse floors (Bohrer 1966, 1972). But apparently considerable doubt exists as to the temporal placement of the site and the validity of the ceramic associations. For instance, Paul Sidney Martin, in the first published reference to the Hay Hollow Site, states that it was "occupied between 200 B.C. and A.D. 200 by a hunting-gathering folk who were in the process of adopting and adapting to corn agriculture" (Martin 1967:8). But later in the same article Martin makes a considerably different claim for the age of the associated ceramic complex. "Incidentally, this pottery may be among the earliest in the Southwest, because it was surely present at 400 B.C. or earlier" (Martin 1967:10). And in a more recent article: "The pottery is grayish-blackish, is friable, and not well-fired. It is among the earliest pottery of the area (about 300 B.C.)" (Martin 1972:3). Martin and Plog (1973) offer yet another interpretation of the temporal data.

> Radiocarbon dates from twenty-two discrete pieces of charcoal from house roof beams, from fire pits, and from other pits indicate the site was either intermittently occupied roughly between the dates of 300 B.C. and A.D. 300 or all occupied contemporaneously at some one period between those dates. The earliest house date [provenienced as Firepit 14 in Table 9] is 470 B.C.±115; the latest, A.D. 305±110. The older portion of the site (three houses and dozens of pits) yields a mean date of 30.7 B.C.±97.5. The younger portion (two to five houses and many associated pits) yields a mean date of A.D. 89.6±94.17 (Martin and Plog 1973:78).

Finally, John Fritz, who utilized the site data for his doctoral dissertation, estimates that "the site was occupied at one or more times between 200 B.C. and A.D. 300" (Fritz 1974:64).

While it is true that the dating accuracy attainable by the radiocarbon method is somewhat limited, e.g., as compared to tree-ring dating, there should not be this much disagreement over the interpretation of such a large number of determinations from a single open site. The 22 radiocarbon determinations are shown in Table 9 (J. Fritz personal communication, 1976) along with the provenience data and lab numbers. (The numbers used to designate features, e.g., "House 32," are functions of the provenience system employed by the investigator. They do not indicate the actual number of the various classes of named features found at the site.) Sample material has not been included since, with the exception of GX-0796 (human bone), all samples were wood charcoal. These data suggest a more elegant solution to the Hay Hollow dating problem. As shown, the radiocarbon samples were recovered from two classes of site features: houses and external firepits. As noted earlier, materials from structural house timbers are the most trustworthy since these are more likely to have been freshly felled trees. Dead, dry wood, on the other hand, was more likely to have been used in the external firepits, a practice that provides a potential source of significant error. I suspect (but obviously cannot prove) that the practice of burning dead wood accounts for the extremely early determinations on GX-0582 and GX-0807 from Firepit 14, which are two and a half to three centuries older than the earliest house date (GX-0540). Moreover, these 2 dates fail to overlap *any* of the remaining 20 charcoal dates at the one-sigma confidence interval, and there is no reason to believe that they correctly indicate the beginning of site occupancy. Worth noting is the fact that these dates are the only evidence for Martin's suggestion that pottery occurred at the site as early as 300 to 400 B.C. In addition, the earliest of the two (GX-0582) was erroneously assigned by Martin and Plog (1973) to a "house" provenience (see above quotation).

Nearly half the remaining dates are from structural timbers, and a brief consideration of these leads to a more conservative estimate of the age of the site. As shown in Table 9, the earliest dated structures are Houses 17, 25, and 32. The weighted averages of the dates from each house are in close agreement. They are 1998±60 B.P.: 48 B.C. (GX-0540, GX-0580, GX-0798[?]) for House 17 ($F=.28<3.00$: $df=2,\infty$), 1953±61 B.P.: 3 B.C. (GX-0792, GX-0727) for House 25 ($t=.20<1.96$), and 1972±55 B.P.: 22 B.C. (GX-0799, GX-0798[?]) for House 32 ($t=1.0<1.96$). Hence, the best estimate for the initial occupation of the site is the latter half of the first century B.C. The weighted average of the two dates from a later structure, House 13, is 1759±60 B.P.: A.D. 191 (GX-0539, GX-0579) ($t=.72<1.96$). As will be seen below, this date is consistent with the apparent onset of building activity at two other sites in Hay Hollow Valley.

The presence, temporal association, and typological status of the ceramics at the Hay Hollow Site are critical to an understanding of the origin(s) of the Southwestern pottery complex. Unfortunately, the available evidence does not allow any clear-cut statements regarding these important matters. The claim that pottery occurred as early as 300 to 400 B.C. can be dismissed on the strength of the arguments presented above. The possibility that the sherds were intrusive can also be dismissed on the basis of Fritz's statement that "it was only when sherds were found in unequivocal association with house floors, and other features that I and other excavators accepted Hay Hollow Site as being 'ceramic' " (Fritz 1974:376). This indicates that some care was taken to ascertain the correct provenience of ceramics and, presumably, other artifact classes as well. But the provenience data do not appear in Fritz's dissertation and they have not been published elsewhere. We are left to conclude that the ceramics were associated with (1) the early period of building activity around 50 B.C., (2) the later period of construction at ca. A.D. 200, (3) some intervening period, or (4) any combination of these three possibilities.

As for the type of pottery recovered from the Hay Hollow Site, the descriptive data are inadequate for comparative purposes. It has been described as "grayish-blackish, . . . friable, and not well-fired" (Paul Sidney Martin 1972:3), as noted earlier. But Martin and Plog say that "the pottery sherds are thin, brown in color, and may

TABLE 9
Radiocarbon Dates from the Hay Hollow Site

Provenience	Radiocarbon Age B.P.	Calendric Age A.D./B.C.	Lab Number
Firepit 14	2420±115 2350±95	470 B.C. 400	GX-0582 GX-0807
Firepit 1	2140±90	190	GX-0805
House 17	2095±105	145	GX-0540
Firepit 1	2040±90	90	GX-0800
House 32	2030±80	80	GX-0799
House 25	2030±80	80	GX-0792
Firepit 5	2020±110	70	GX-0808
House 17	1995±100	45	GX-0580
Firepit 1	1945±80	A.D. 5	GX-0801
House 32	1920±75	30	GX-0798(?)
Firepit 1	1920±85	30	GX-0802
House 17	1895±110	55	GX-0798(?)
Burial	1870±95	80	GX-0796
House 25	1845±95	105	GX-0727
Firepit 95	1820±80	130	GX-0809
House 13	1785±70	165	GX-0539
Firepit 95	1755±115	195	GX-0578
Firepit 3	1720±90	230	GX-0803
Firepit 2	1705±85	245	GX-0806
House 13	1685±120	265	GX-0579
?	1645±110	305	GX-0804

represent fragments of seed jars" (Martin and Plog 1973:78). Fritz's (1974) dissertation contains no artifact analysis and his few references to the Hay Hollow "plain ware" do little to clarify the situation. In short, no one but those directly involved in the project have any idea what the ceramics look like, and there is no indication that any in-depth analysis has been performed.

None of the many other early farming sites from the Hay Hollow Valley are as well dated as the Hay Hollow Site. The three for which some chronometric data are available include the Connie, Petri, and County Road sites. Dates from the Connie and Petri sites are, respectively, 1695±105 B.P.: A.D. 255 (GX-1656), and 1750±100 B.P.: A.D. 200 (GX-1659). These sites contained pithouses and "Hay Hollow type" pottery and were contemporaneous with House 13 at the Hay Hollow Site. The County Road Site is said to contain architecture nearly identical to examples from the Hay Hollow Site, but the temporal provenience is poorly controlled. This situation has not been helped by the numerous conflicting statements that have appeared in print since the excavation of the site. These may be summarized as follows:

1. Paul Sidney Martin (1967) originally gave a time span of 500 to 200 B.C. for "Country [sic] Road Village." No discussion of the supporting data was offered at that time.

2. Martin (1972) later estimated that the site was occupied from 1000 to 350 B.C. He gave two Geochron Laboratories numbers (GX-0274 and GX-0272) as the supporting data, but did not discuss the provenience or the material(s) of the samples.

3. Plog (1974) used the 1000 B.C. placement for the County Road Site in his overview of Hay Hollow Valley prehistory. He was apparently following Martin's lead, but he failed to cite the 1972 article or offer any discussion of the relevant data.

4. Fritz (1974) offered a different reading of the data. He stated that

> The estimated period of occupation falls between 70 and 5 B.C. . . . Three carbon-14 determinations have been performed on organic charcoal material from the site. The range of these dates, together with the presence of sherds of a plain ceramic ware similar to that recovered at the Hay Hollow Site . . . , indicates that this site might have been occupied at the same time or somewhat earlier than the Hay Hollow Site (Fritz 1974:374).

All in all, this is an incredible situation. There is quite a difference between 1000 B.C. and 5 B.C., and one would think that the investigators involved might be concerned over such a discrepency. Few Southwesternists would be surprised by the 1000 B.C. date for the maize associated with the site, though the arguments presented in the preceding chapter make this highly improbable. However, 1000 B.C. is an astonishingly early date for the occurrence of pottery in the Southwest and, if true, it would certainly warrant more discussion than, for instance, Plog's (1974) casual mention.

The three available dates are shown in Table 10 (H. Krueger personal communication, 1978). All materials were unidentified coarse fragments of charcoal. Obviously, these dates do little to support any of the various arguments for temporal placement of the site. The date of 1145 B.C. comes from an external pit rather than a structure and may indicate an earlier use of the site. There is certainly no justification for claiming that it relates to the maize and ceramics associated with House B. The two remaining dates come from a pit within House B, but they are not contemporaneous at the .05 level ($t=2.37>1.96$) and averaging is not justifiable. No accurate placement is possible given this scant data. The most recent of the two House B dates is probably the best estimate owing to the possibility of driftwood bias. This seems reasonable since a placement of 70 B.C. indicates contemporaneity with three of the four houses at the Hay Hollow Site. This is essentially the same interpretation proffered by Fritz (1974:374) and there is no compelling reason to think otherwise.

In sum, the dated structures in the Hay Hollow Valley fall into two temporal clusters. The first is represented at the Hay Hollow Site, and perhaps at the County Road Site, where construction activities date to the second half of the first century B.C. The second is represented at the Hay Hollow, Connie, and Petri sites beginning at around A.D. 200-250. It may be that pottery was associated with both sets of houses, but confirmation of

TABLE 10
Radiocarbon Dates from the County Road Site

Provenience	Radiocarbon Age B.P.	Calendric Age A.D./B.C.	Lab Number
House B, Pit A, floor	2020±95	70 B.C.	GX-0273
House B, Pit A, below 60 cm	2300±70	350 B.C.	GX-0272
Square #3, firepit, fill	3095±75	1145 B.C.	GX-0274

this possibility must await the publication of relevant data.

In pointing to the positive evidence for construction activities in two discrete periods separated by approximately two centuries, I am not denying the possibility that Hay Hollow Valley was occupied continuously during the interim. But neither am I assuming continuity to have been the case. As stated at the outset, the strategy employed in this chapter is to first provide a critical assessment of each site or locality and then to build a regional chronology through summation of the individual temporal placements. The method is inductive and empirical and must rely on the summation of chronometric facts rather than chronological assumptions.

ARCHITECTURE. The sources for the architectural summary that follows are P. R. Nelson (1964), Paul Sidney Martin (1967, 1972), and Martin and Plog (1973). All of these provide only brief, generalized descriptions of the structures; hence, it is impossible to determine the type and degree of change through time. Figure 4C is taken from Nelson's (1964) line drawing of a pit structure from the County Road Site. While obviously schematized, it is the only available plan for any of the early Hay Hollow Valley sites. (An overhead photograph in Martin's 1967 article on the Hay Hollow Site appears to be a picture of Pithouse B at the SU Site [Martin and Rinaldo 1940] in west-central New Mexico and, therefore, is not included in this descriptive summary.)

Shape and size: All structures were circular in shape and averaged 5.0 m in diameter.

Depth: Shallow and basin shaped in profile.

Floors: Use-packed, sterile earth.

Firepits: Circular to oval in plan view, shallow and basin shaped in profile.

Other floor features: Structure floors contained two or more large, deep pits from 0.5 to 1.0 m in diameter. These consisted of simple excavations into the sterile earth. None were plastered or slab lined.

Postholes set from 15 to 25 cm apart encircled the structure floors. At the County Road Site, alignments of three or four postholes occurred within the structures and posts may have supported partition walls.

At several of the houses a partition of upright sandstone slabs embedded in the floor stood between the entryway and the firepit (see Figure 4C). These are presumed to have served as deflectors.

Entryway/antechamber: Entryways consisted of parallel-sided trenches flanked by posthole alignments. The trenches emanated at right angles to the pithouse walls. None of the Hay Hollow Valley pithouses had antechambers.

Superstructures: According to Martin's reconstruction, the upright posts encircling the structures were fastened together by some means and then:

> The interstices between the upright poles were chinked with grass, brush and mud, very much like the chinking in

> early American log cabins. Great hunks of this chinking were actually found on house floors. The chinking *was* mud, leaving the imprint of grass, fingerprints, brush and twigs. . . . This kind of construction is called "wattle and daub," or by the Spanish term, *Jacal* (Paul Sidney Martin 1967:8).

The entry tunnels were probably roofed in a similar manner.

COMMENTS. The homogeneity suggested by the available information may be nothing more than an artifact of piecemeal description. As discussed earlier, I would be particularly interested in knowing if there were any significant architectural differences between the early and late components. Also of primary importance is the association of ceramics with particular structures. If ceramics are associated with the proposed early component of the Hay Hollow Site, this would mark the earliest known occurrence of pottery on the Colorado Plateau and, possibly, the Southwest as a whole. If the ceramics are associated with the later component at around A.D. 200, this would fit comfortably with the early occurrence of pottery at several other sites discussed later in this chapter. It is unfortunate that the relevant provenience data have never been published.

The Durango Area

The Durango Basketmaker II sites have played an important role in the development of Southwestern prehistory. Not only did they produce the oldest dendrochronological record (Haury 1938; Douglass 1943; Schulman 1949a, 1949b, 1951, 1952; Smiley 1951; Morris and Burgh 1954), but it was this area that yielded the first unequivocal evidence of houses in the "preceramic" Southwest.

CHRONOLOGY. While a great number of dates are available for these sites, the vast majority of the sample material was collected in the 1930s and early 1940s under less than ideal conditions and before the importance of exact provenience was fully appreciated. Dean (1975) has recently reanalyzed the Durango tree-ring material and thoroughly reviewed the extant information on the provenience and historic itineraries of the specimens. He tells a fascinating story of the careless storage practices, personality conflicts, and methodological debates that led to the splitting and resplitting of samples and consequent loss of provenience control as they were divided up among the various museums and tree-ring laboratories. To quote Dean:

> The condition of the Durango collections created several problems for the analysis of the material, not the least of which was the proper assignment of samples to the sites and the determination, if possible, of provenience within the sites. Provenience records for most of this material were inadequate to begin with. The exact context of seemingly inconsequential charcoal fragments was not of particular concern to pot hunters who were after artifacts and skeletons, and even the professional archaeologists of the day were not sufficiently aware of the necessity for good provenience control of tree-ring samples. Furthermore, the repeated division of the samples and the transmission of the material back and forth among various parties provided ample opportunity for specimens, tags, and labels to be lost or confused (Dean 1975:5).

Nonetheless, Dean managed to sort out the evidence in a careful and straightforward manner. The greatest confusion exists in the complexly stratified North and South Shelters. Dean interprets the data from North Shelter as follows:

> To summarize, the occupation of the North Shelter may have begun as early as the third century B.C. and continued until late in the third century A.D. A strong cluster of dates in the first century A.D. indicates a period of major utilization of the shelter that peaked around A.D. 50. It is unlikely that a date cluster such as this could be produced by the use of dead wood for construction or firewood, and these dates undoubtedly apply to actual use or construction events in the shelter. No recognizable house floors are associated with this episode. The floors themselves appear to have been built in the third century A.D., with those on Terraces II, III, and IV dated early in that century. Terrace I was apparently the last terrace occupied as indicated both by tree-ring dates in the 270's and the absence of cultural debris beneath Floors 1, 2, and 3 (Dean 1975:31).

The important point made by Dean is that *none of the structures can be placed any earlier than the first part of the third century A.D.* There was apparently an earlier occupation at 200-250 B.C. and another at around A.D. 50, but these groups were not responsible for any of the architectural phenomena in the North Shelter. There is no way of knowing the cultural affiliation of these earlier occupations since Morris and Burgh (1954) did not recognize "pre-Basketmaker" components and segregate the artifacts accordingly.

South Shelter shows a similar pattern; i.e., a

scattering of dates indicates that occupation may have started as early as the third century B.C., but dates on structural timbers place house construction between A.D. 217 and A.D. 337 (Dean 1975:31). Although Dean associates both the "B.C." and "A.D." tree-ring clusters with the Basketmaker II occupation, this is not demonstrably true, as suggested above. Moreover, it cannot even be demonstrated that occupation of the sites was continuous since, as Dean states:

> Both shelters are characterized by a gap in the sequence of dates between roughly A.D. 50 and A.D. 150. Whether this represents a hiatus in the use of the caves, a lull in wood-use activity, or a quirk of the archeological sampling is not known (Dean 1975:31).

More precisely, Dean's data show *only one* cutting date between A.D. 46 (GP-3847) and AD. 201 (GP-4164), i.e., between the terminal date for the "unknown" inhabitants of the shelters and the onset of the classic Basketmaker II occupation.

The dating of the open sites in the Durango area supports this interpretation in that none of the houses has yielded cutting dates earlier than the last half of the second century A.D. Dates of known provenience from Talus Village (Morris and Burgh 1954) range from A.D. 192 to A.D. 330 (Dean 1975:33), and Ignacio 12:46 may be securely placed between A.D. 356 and A.D. 372 (Dean 1975:61). The houses at both of these sites are identical to those excavated in the shelters, a fact wholly compatible with the chronological arguments offered above. Tree-ring dates from these two sites are given in Table 11.

The tree-ring data from the Durango sites would be important even if none of the proveniences were known insofar as the extension of the Southwestern dendrochronological record is concerned. However, the provenience of specimens becomes all important when attempting to date prehistoric cultural complexes. In this regard the Durango data are woefully lacking. As the situation now stands, the cutting dates falling between 200+ B.C. and A.D. 50 cannot be associated with any of the Basketmaker II houses. They may relate to an earlier occupation of the site or they might quite conceivably indicate the use of dead wood for fires. Dean is not necessarily correct in claiming that the use of dead wood cannot produce a tight clustering of apparent "cutting" dates. One natural event that comes to mind is the burial of local forests through alluviation or landslides. Karlstrom has documented numerous buried forests in the Black Mesa, Arizona, region (Karlstrom, Gumerman, and Euler 1974). The effect would be to make hundreds of trees—all with the same apparent "cutting" date—available for local aboriginal use. So it is possible that *all* of the "B.C." charcoal specimens from the Durango rockshelters were deposited (as firewood) by the occupants who built the houses at A.D. 200 and later. I do not intend this line of reasoning to be taken as proof; but it is an interesting possibility that, to my knowledge, has not yet been fully investigated. At any rate, the cutting dates from structures at North Shelter, South Shelter, Talus Village, and Ignacio 12:46 set the probable lower and upper temporal limits of building activity at A.D. 192 and A.D. 372, respectively.

ARCHITECTURE. The domestic architecture of the Durango area is amazingly uniform even in light of the relatively brief time interval adduced above. The descriptive data for the following summarization are taken from Morris and Burgh (1954) and Robert W. Biggs (personal communication, 1977). A total of 49 houses has been excavated: 35 at Talus Village, 9 in North Shelter, 4 in South Shelter, and 1 at Ignacio 12:46.

Shape and size: None of the floors was complete due to varying degrees of structural intrusion by later building activities. The houses appeared to be circular, oval, and subrectangular in shape. Greatest dimension varied from 2.5 to 9.0 m.

Depth: Shallow and basin shaped in profile.

Floors: Floors consisted of a graded surface (sometimes cut into sterile earth, sometimes into the fill of earlier structures) covered by a thin coat of clay plaster. Houses had cribbed log superstructures (see "Superstructures" below), and the floor plaster curved upward toward the periphery to meet the basal log course.

Firepits: Morris and Burgh (1954) use the term "heating pit" rather than firepit since none of the numerous floor pits showed evidence of *in situ* burning. Heating pits were shallow and basin shaped in profile. They averaged about 45 cm in diameter and 25 cm in depth and were lined with a thin coat of plaster. These pits contained sand,

TABLE 11
Tree-Ring Dates from Talus Village and Ignacio 12:46

Provenience	Date	Lab Number
Talus Village		
Area 1	176vv	IF-541
	193v	IF-634
	252vv	GP-3486
	276vv	GP-3452
	285vv	IF-612
	291vv	GP-3401
	296vv	GP-3461
	296vv	GP-3455
	298vv	GP-3293
	299vv	GP-3295
	300vv	GP-3454
	301vv	GP-3484
	305GB	GP-3392
	308vv	GP-3487-2
	314vv	GP-3395
	317vv	GP-3400
	317vv	GP-3399
	320++v	GP-3394
	320+v	GP-3397
	321vv	GP-3469
	324vv	IF-553
	324vv	IF-3445
	326+vv	GP-3485
	327vv	GP-3442
Area 2	85vv	IF-512-1
	192vv	GP-3357
	225vv	IF-512-2
Area 3	162vv	IF-504
	188r	GP-3347
	192rB	DUR-1
	214vv	GP-3344
	305vv	GP-3363
Ignacio 12:46		
Floor 1, log masonry wall beams	239vv	DUR-28
	262+vv	DUR-21
	289vv	DUR-6
	303vv	DUR-9
	332vv	DUR-23
	350vv	DUR-13
	354vv	DUR-12
	356vv	DUR-4
	356vv	DUR-16

TABLE 11 (continued)

Provenience	Date	Lab Number
Ignacio 12:46	356v	DUR-8
Floor 1, log masonry wall beams	356v	DUR-14
(continued)	360vv	DUR-17
	360rB	DUR-7
	372v	DUR-10
Floor 1, miscellaneous	281vv	DUR-24
	336++v	DUR-26
	356vv	DUR-19
	356B	DUR-25
	363vv	DUR-34

Source: Dean 1975

charcoal, ash, and large pieces of burned sandstone. Morris and Burgh (1954) suggest that the houses were warmed by heating the sandstone slabs in exterior firepits and then transporting the slabs to the interior pits. It was apparently common practice to dig new heating pits from time to time and fill in and plaster over the old ones.

Other floor features: Five types of storage cists were identified. All were circular in plan and up to 1.0 m in diameter. The first, and simplest, was an unplastered "jug-shaped" excavation. The second was very similar to the heating pits in design but considerably larger. These were basin shaped in profile and lined with a thin coat of plaster. The third and most frequently occurring type was a flat-bottomed cist with out-sloping sides. Sides were slab lined. The bottom was either slab lined or clay plastered. The fourth and fifth types were "beehive-shaped" mud domes. One variant was erected over a deep pit in the floor; the other was constructed directly on the plastered floor surface. The mud domes may have stood as much as a meter high.

A few of the small floor holes may have served as footing for vertical props, but these occur infrequently and never in a symmetrical pattern.

Entryway/antechamber: Morris and Burgh (1954) suggest that the houses may have been entered by means of a low crawl way, but there is no direct evidence of such a feature. None of the structures possessed identifiable antechambers. (See "Comments" below.)

Superstructures: Superstructures are cribbed-log, dome-shaped enclosures. Morris and Burgh (1954) describe them as follows:

> It is in reality a sort of masonry in which timbers were used in place of stones. The building of a wall of this character may be visualized as follows: Over the top of the previously prepared course a thick layer of mud was spread. Then pieces of wood, of whatever size and shape available, were laid on top of and pressed down into the fresh mud until they touched the solid substance of the course beneath. Their ends overlapping and joints broken wherever possible. This done, the interstices between sticks were tamped full of mud, and the joints of the exposed faces pointed with finger tips as a trowel. The thickness of the wall presumably would have varied in proportion to the size of the area being enclosed—the larger the room the more massive the shell. We believe the range in thickness to have been from about 18 to 25 cm. The fact that in cases where conditions were clear, the burned residue of walls lay upon the floors but did not extend appreciably beyond their margins, seems plainly to signify that the walls rose with an inward slant to what was considered a convenient head height (Morris and Burgh 1954:50).

The supporting bits of evidence for this reconstruction did not co-occur in any one house. It is a composite description built up from several of the most complete structures excavated. Nonetheless, it seems quite plausible, and no alternative reconstruction comes to mind that is as compatible with the available data.

COMMENTS. Due to structural intrusion or erosion, none of the excavations at early sites in the Durango area yielded complete structures. This raises the problem of missing data, especially in regard to the presence or absence of antechambers. As will be seen in the next section, certain houses from the Navajo Reservoir District match the Durango examples in every salient detail except that they possess rather large antechambers. It seems quite plausible that some of the Durango houses were originally antechambered and that these features were destroyed by subsequent construction or erosion. In fact, given the similarity in construction of antechambers and living floors in the Navajo Reservoir District, it is quite possible that some of the so-called houses in the Durango sites were actually antechambers whose associated living floors had been destroyed. I suspect this is the case for several of the essentially featureless floor areas depicted by Morris and Burgh (1954).

The Navajo Reservoir District

The early pithouse villages of the Navajo Reservoir District were excavated by representatives of the Laboratory of Anthropology, University of New Mexico, in the late 1950s as part of an extensive salvage archeology program (Eddy 1961; Dittert, Eddy, and Dickey 1963; Schoenwetter and Eddy 1964; Eddy 1966).

CHRONOLOGY. Two sequent phases were defined for the pre–A.D. 700 period: (1) the Los Pinos phase dated from A.D. 1 to 400, and (2) the Sambrito phase dated from A.D. 400 to 700. The A.D. 1–400 temporal placement of the Los Pinos phase sites (Eddy 1961) has been generally accepted among Southwestern specialists, and while the supporting radiocarbon data are less than ideal, there is no particular reason to doubt that the sites in question were constructed and occupied at some time during this 400-year period.

But there are serious problems with the ensuing Sambrito phase, which Eddy and his associates (cf. Dittert, Eddy, and Dickey 1963; Schoenwetter and Eddy 1964; Eddy 1966) assign to the period from A.D. 400 to 700. In the initial formulation of the local cultural sequence, Dittert, Hester, and Eddy (1961) proposed that the region was unoccupied during this 300-year period that separated the Los Pinos phase from the following Rosa phase. This interpretation has since been revised.

> As originally envisioned, a 300-year (A.D. 400–700) gap of non-occupation was thought to exist between the Los Pinos and Rosa phases; however, subsequent field excavations have turned up evidence indicating occupation during this period. These new data are referred to the Sambrito phase. . . . (Eddy 1966:13).

A careful review of the detailed reports available on this important salvage project leads me to believe that the original formulation was correct and that the gap-filling Sambrito phase is a fiction. I am, of course, not denying that the sites Eddy includes in the Sambrito phase exist, but I find no reason why these sites or site components should be separated in time from those included in the Los Pinos phase. In short, I submit that the two "phases" were contemporaneous and, further, that they are indistinguishable on either architectural or artifactual criteria. The evidence cited by Eddy in support of his Los Pinos–Sambrito sequential ordering includes a dubious ceramic distinction, stratigraphy, and radiocarbon dating. A critique of that evidence is long overdue.

To begin with, Los Pinos Brown and Sambrito Brown pottery types are said to be mutually exclusive diagnostics of these two phases. But the stated differences between these types do not seem adequately significant to serve as definitive indicators of phase assignment.

> The earliest brown paste types, Los Pinos Brown and Sambrito Brown, differ in vessel forms (of which few are known from the Los Pinos Phase), surface treatment (Los Pinos Brown is characterized by its pearly finish), and the tendency to use smaller and more uniform temper grains in Sambrito Brown. . . . (Eddy 1966:384).

Now, if Los Pinos phase vessel forms are poorly known, it is difficult to see how comparison of Los Pinos and Sambrito Brown vessel forms provides any useful typological criteria. Furthermore, the references to "pearly finish" and a tendency toward smaller and more uniform temper particles seem rather subjective. That such subtle, intergradational attributes could be applied by different analysts and consistently yield comparable results is inconceivable. Perhaps this is why Eddy's ceramic provenience table (Eddy 1966:558–66) has a column heading for "Los Pinos–Sambrito Brown" even though that transitional category is not discussed in the text. It is also remarkable that the ceramic provenience chart prepared by Dittert for Sambrito Village (Eddy 1966:568–71) makes no provision whatever for Los Pinos Brown. It is hard to believe that the type simply did not occur at this extensive, early village when Eddy claims its existence at all other early village sites in the project area. It seems more plausible to infer that Dittert did not find the Los Pinos–Sambrito Brown distinction useful—at least not at this site—and included all specimens under the latter heading.

The stratigraphic evidence for distinguishing the two phases is less than convincing. The examples of structural intrusion and superposition cited by Eddy come from a single site, Albino Village, which is purported to have been occupied during both the Los Pinos (A.D. 1–400) and Sambrito phases (A.D. 400–700) and briefly by "early Rosa Phase campers" (A.D. 600–750). However, Eddy's descriptions of the evidence (quoted verbatim) are not supported by the provenience data.

> Fill containing late Sambrito Phase pottery of Group 2c was found in both ring Structures 1 and 2. These relationships demonstrated the phase sequence Sambrito over late Los Pinos Phase (Eddy 1966:281).

According to Eddy's ceramic provenience chart, the above statement is not accurate. The chart shows that Structure 1 contained no Sambrito pottery whatever. Instead, Los Pinos Brown was recovered from "under ring" and both Los Pinos Brown and Rosa Gray occurred in the "upper fill." As for Structure 2, the provenience chart indicates that Sambrito Brown was the only type recovered from the floor, while the fill contained only Los Pinos Brown and Rosa Gray. These data imply the reverse of the situation described above by Eddy.

> Overlap of structures was found with ring Structure 1 overlying non-ring Structure 7. . . . The . . . series shows two superimposed late Los Pinos Phase structures each containing sherds of Los Pinos Brown (Eddy 1966:281).

Again, Eddy's statement is contradicted by the ceramic provenience chart, which shows that Structure 7 contained only Sambrito Brown in both "fill" and "floor" contexts while Structure 1, as noted above, contained only Los Pinos Brown and Rosa Gray. This, again, would indicate that the Sambrito phase preceded the Los Pinos phase rather than the other way around.

> Structure 2, which contains Group 1 pottery, overlaid Refuse Area 4, which also contained Ceramic Group 1. The ceramics agree with the stratigraphy (Eddy 1966:281).

Like the two previous quotations, this statement is not borne out by the provenience chart. While it is true that Refuse Area 4 contained only Ceramic Group 1 (Los Pinos Brown), the floor of Structure 2, (which presumably intruded the refuse area) yielded only Sambrito Brown, and the fill contained Los Pinos Brown. Hence, the ceramic sequence depicted in this stratified situation is Los Pinos Brown—Sambrito Brown—Los Pinos Brown.

These examples demonstrate that there is no consistent sequential relationship between the two pottery types. I think this adds considerable weight to the interpretation that only one pottery type and a single phase are represented in the early centuries of settled village life in Navajo Reservoir District prehistory.

Given the importance of the temporal placement of these sites to Southwestern prehistory, the radiocarbon evidence also leaves much to be desired. Only twelve samples have been run for the entire project, and Eddy has, for various reasons, seen fit to reject half of these (Eddy 1966:445). The first dates to be published were from two Los Pinos phase sites: 1640±90 B.P.: A.D. 310 (I-251) and 1420±80 B.P.: A.D. 530 (I-252) from Valentine Village; 1830±150 B.P.: A.D. 120 (M-1115B), 1740±150 B.P.: A.D. 210 (M-1115D), and 1690±150 B.P.: A.D. 260 (M-1115C) from Power Pole Site (Eddy 1961). These constitute a fairly tight clustering of dates with the exception of I-252, which appears to be considerably too recent. A possible explanation of this apparent anomaly is that all the other samples were from structural timbers, whereas I-252 was a composite sample from the fill of Structure 4, Valentine Village. As Eddy noted, "Very little wood was available in the ring structures, but a good sample consisting of large charcoal fragments had been collected by trenching the fill of ring Structure 4" (Eddy 1961:102). While Eddy did not question the date in the 1961 descriptive monograph, he opted to reject it in the 1966 synthesis of the Navajo Reservoir District data (Eddy 1966). I agree with this decision and think the Structure 4 date should be dropped from consideration since (1) it was a composite rather than a discrete sample; (2) the determination lies well outside the clustering of the other four Los Pinos phase dates, all of which overlap within one standard error; and (3) it was recovered from the fill rather than the floor of Structure 4 and probably was not contemporaneous with the Los Pinos occupation. Absolute dating of the Los Pinos phase is, therefore, based on four radiocarbon determinations, the means of which range from A.D. 120 to 310.

Six more dates have been run on materials derived from sites which Eddy includes in his Sambrito phase. Since Eddy rejected four of these, the temporal placement of the Sambrito phase between A.D. 400 and 700 rests on only two radiocarbon dates. I, too, would reject four of the six dates. But since my acceptance/rejection criteria are different from Eddy's, I disagree with him as to which of the dates actually relate to the materials in question. To facilitate discussion of the specific points of disagreement, I have listed the six dates, along with their provenience, in Table 12. Eddy's acceptance/rejection arguments are here quoted at length.

> Six samples of burned and rotted wood were collected from Sambrito Phase contexts. Only two of these matched the expected age range of the phase as shown graphically in Figure 46. Two of the remaining dates were too early (TBN and I-1342) falling within the Los Pinos Phase time range, although one of these, the Isotopes assay, would overlap the Sambrito age range by a two sigma confidence interval. This extension of sample I-1342 would match the early Sambrito Phase dating of Pit House 1 at LA 4169. Two other dates obtained from Sambrito Phase contexts vary widely from the expected results and are clearly erroneous. One of these, sample TBN-306-3 does not match the previous estimate within two standard deviations, being many centuries too early, while the other, sample I-1341, is considerably too late. In the case of the latter sample, there is a possibility that contamination

TABLE 12
Sambrito Phase Radiocarbon Dates

Site	Provenience	Radiocarbon Age B.P.	Calendric Age A.D./B.C.	Lab Number
Sambrito Village	External pit 21; lower fill	2191±264	241 B.C.	TBN-306-3
LA 3430	Structure 1; roof fall	1845±131	A.D. 105	TBN (?)
Oven Site	Pithouse 1; firebasin	1750±115	200	I-1342
Oven Site	External pit 13; fill	1480±120	470	I-1343
Uells Site	Refuse zone 10A	1390±170	560	I-1344
LA 3035	Pithouse; firebasin	935±130	1015	I-1341

Source: Eddy 1966:445

> from an overlying Piedra Phase structure may have introduced a log into a stratigraphically earlier Sambrito Phase pit house.
>
> The two reliable samples (I-1343) have ages of A.D. 470±120 and A.D. 560±170, respectively, and are consistent with the expected age range of the Sambrito Phase (Eddy 1966:448).

In short, Eddy throws out radiocarbon dates that do not match "the expected range" and accepts those that do. This approach negates much of the utility of radiocarbon dating as an *independent* evaluator of stratigraphically and seriationally derived cultural sequences. Only in the case of I-1341 does Eddy attempt to supply us with a plausible physical explanation of what might have gone wrong. One is compelled to agree with that interpretation since (1) the date of A.D. 1015 is more appropriate for the known range of the Piedra phase, the temporal limits of which have been established elsewhere by dendrochronology and ceramic cross dating, and (2) the structure at LA 3035 from which the sample was obtained was overlain by a later (possibly Piedra phase) surface structure, a situation which at least allows the possibility of intrusion.

This one point of agreement noted, the alternative interpretation offered here bears little resemblance to Eddy's. The two dates which most likely indicate the age of Eddy's "Sambrito" structures are TBN(?) and I-1342—A.D. 105 and A.D. 200, respectively. These two dates are on discrete samples from pithouses while the remaining three are on composite or otherwise questionable sample types from less than ideal proveniences. For instance, both of the dates accepted by Eddy were composite charcoal samples—a situation that can yield an "average" date due to the potential for mixing older and younger organic material. One of these (I-1343) "was obtained from the charcoal-flecked fill of Exterior Pit 13" (Eddy 1966) at the Oven Site. The pit contained only seventeen sherds of indigenous brown wares and "foreign" Mesa Verdean gray wares. The date of A.D. 470 might conceivably be associated with (1) the brown wares, (2) the gray wares, (3) both, if the wares were contemporaneous, or (4) neither, if the wares were separated in time but the composite radiocarbon sample produced an averaging effect. The point is that there is no way of determining which of these possibilities is correct. Hence, there is no reason to attach much significance to the date, and certainly no justification for treating it as *independent* evidence for a fifth-century placement of the Sambrito phase. The other date which Eddy found acceptable (I-1344) was on a composite sample "picked from Refuse Zone 10a" at the Uells Site (Schoenwetter and Eddy 1964). This midden layer contained Los Pinos Brown, Sambrito Brown, Rosa Brown, Rosa Gray, Twin Trees Plain, and Arboles Gray pottery types. Since these types span the entire period of Navajo Reservoir District settlement from A.D. 1 to A.D. 900, and considering the fact that these types do not co-occur in discrete proveniences (e.g., pithouse floors) at any other site described, it would appear that Refuse Zone 10a was a badly mixed deposit. The sixth-century date from this zone may be meaningless, and I see no way that it might be unequivocally related to "Sambrito" phase occupance.

In reappraising the evidence I conclude that the Los Pinos and Sambrito "phases" are actually two names for the same archeological entity. Since Los Pinos was the first of these designations to appear in the literature, I suggest that the term "Sambrito phase" be discarded and "Los Pinos phase" be retained to refer to the earliest period of village life in the Navajo Reservoir District. As for temporal placement, the six dates, which most probably relate to this occupation, are I-251, M-1115B, M-1115C, M-1115D, I-1342, and TBN(?). These dates are contemporaneous ($F = .41 < 2.21$: $df = 5,\infty$) with a weighted mean of 1730±51 B.P.: A.D. 220. It is quite conceivable that all the building activity associated with the Los Pinos phase (including the "Sambrito" remains) took place between A.D. 170 and 270.

ARCHITECTURE. The principal features of Los Pinos phase structures are summarized here, in brief, but with enough detail to give some indication of the range of variation. Consistent with the foregoing temporal reanalysis, structures placed in this category are those that (1) contained ceramics identified as Los Pinos and/or Sambrito Brown in floor contact, or (2) yielded no ceramics in floor contact but contained Los Pinos and/or Sambrito Brown in the postoccupation fill as the dominant type(s). Thirty-seven excavated structures in the Navajo Reservoir District meet these criteria: Structures 1 through 11 at Valentine Village; Structures 1 and 2 at the Power Pole Site (described in Eddy 1961); Pithouse 1 at LA 3035; Structures 1 and 2 at LA 3430; Pithouses 1, 2, 4, and 5 at the Oven Site; Pithouses 28, 30, 35, and 38 at Sambrito Village; Structures 1 through 10 at Albino Village; and Structures 1, 2, and 3 at the Tres Casas Site (all described in Eddy 1966).

In the initial Los Pinos phase monograph, Eddy (1961) made a major typological and temporal distinction between "ring" and "nonring" houses. The former were shallow pithouses surrounded by what Eddy interpreted as a broad layer of cobble paving. J. D. Jennings (1966) has suggested that since the cobbles always laid on top of local cultural debris layers, they probably represented fallen cobble-and-adobe walls rather than pavements. As indicated in the following quote, Eddy revised his interpretation in the 1966 monograph, albeit for different reasons than the point raised by Jennings.

> Distinctive rings of flat cobbles were found around many houses. Originally, these were thought to have been employed entirely as paved terraces or aprons. It is now known that some of the cobbles, particularly those found within the floor area and lying tilted in the house fill, were the remains of a low stacked masonry wall which leaned against the outside base of the wooden superstructure. Evidence for this consists of the tumbled cobbles in the house fill; cobbles found lying vertically stacked in series (Structure 2, Tres Casas Site); cobbles which overlay the fallen, horizontal log cribbing; and cobbles lying inside of wall braces (Structure 1, Albino Village). In opposition to this argument was the lack of cobble impressions on the construction clay which coated the wooden superstructure. It is assumed that this clay coat was allowed to harden before the cobbles were stacked in place. Except for Structure 2 at the Tres Casas Site, all of the structures with cobble-base walls also had surrounding terrace pavings, the walls serving as anchors to the wooden structure and the terrace as a walking platform. These walls were the oldest evidence of masonry known in the San Juan Basin, the use of cobbles in this fashion not appearing again in the reservoir until the early Piedra Phase, 450 years later, when free-standing masonry walls were erected at the Candelaria Site. . . . (Eddy 1966).

Unlike Jennings's argument, Eddy's reading of the data allows for some of the cobbles to be interpreted as paved terraces or aprons that served as "walking platforms." The main difficulty with calling any of these features pavements instead of fallen walls is that it leads to significant errors in stratigraphic interpretation. Obviously, if deliberately placed "pavements" of Structure X overlaid the fill of "nonring" Structure Y, there could be little doubt that the former was built after the latter had fallen into disuse. However, it is just as obvious that "walled" Structure X and "nonwalled" Structure Y could have been abandoned simultaneously, with the cobble wall disintegrating at some later date, producing the spurious impression of superposition. This was probably the case at both LA 3430 and Albino Village (discussed earlier) where Eddy utilized the overlap of cobbles with other structures as evidence of stratigraphic succession. While that interpretation was consistent with the "nonring" to "ring" house-type sequence originally proposed as a result of Eddy's work at Valentine Village (Eddy 1961), it no longer appears that this sequence is valid. The reappraisal of the temporal data presented herein suggests that all the structures in question were built during a fairly brief time interval and that the two types (ring and nonring) were contemporaneous. Hence, the interpretation of the cobble phenomena as walls rather than pavements is probably correct. Two examples of Los Pinos phase houses are shown in Figure 5.

Shape and size: All structures were circular to oval in shape with the exception of one subrectangular example at the Oven Site. Circular types ranged from 2.0 to 12.0 m in diameter with a mean of 8.0 m. Oval structures ranged from 7.0 to 15.0 m in length and 5.0 to 12.0 m in width with means of 9.6 and 7.1 m respectively.

Depth: Shallow and basin shaped in profile. Depth never exceeded 0.3 m and edge of floor area graded into original ground surface in most examples.

Floors: All but three of the structures had floors consisting of use-packed, sterile earth. The three exceptions were covered by thin clay plaster. These houses had cribbed log superstructures (see "Superstructures" below), and the floor plaster was continuous, with the clay covering the first log course.

Firepits: Circular to oval in plan view. Shallow

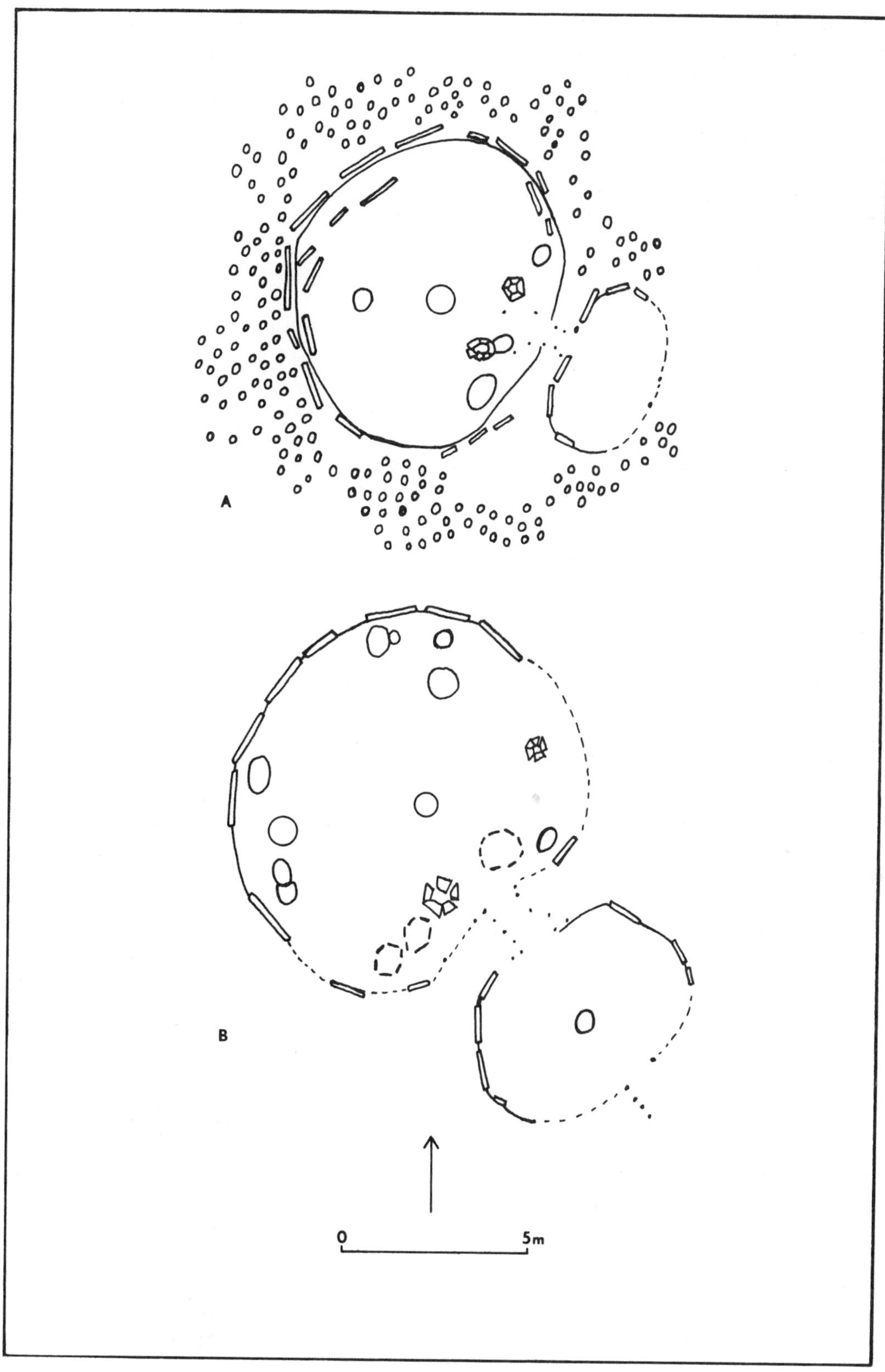

Figure 5. Los Pinos phase houses: A, ring structure, Cemetery Site; B, Structure 10, Valentine Village (Eddy 1966).

and basin shaped in profile. None of the examples had a prepared rim or slab or clay lining. Eddy (1966) notes several cases where the basin was discolored from firing. No information is available on size and depth.

Other floor features: The majority of structures for which adequate detail is provided contained fairly large (up to 1.0 m in diameter) circular pits. These were either straight sided or bell shaped in profile and were sometimes lined with upright slabs or clay plaster. Most of these were presumably storage pits, although a few with slightly discolored walls have been interpreted as "warming ovens" or "warming pits" (Eddy 1966:342).

At the Power Pole Site, Valentine Village, and Albino Village, floor pits of similar diameter were covered with coursed mud domes. These showed no evidence of firing and were probably used as storage structures.

Postholes associated with structure floors were of two types. The first consisted of parallel rows of three or four small (no metric data available) floor holes containing the charred butts of upright posts. These apparently served as footing for posts that supported the superstructures covering the connecting halls between main rooms and antechambers. The second type consisted of somewhat larger (no metric data available) holes containing charred or rotted timbers. These occurred in the floors of the main living chambers, placed in no apparent pattern such as might be expected if they served as superstructure supports. The only examples of intentionally patterned post placement are two structures that were ringed by postholes on the outside of the house depressions, hence, outside the floor area.

Entryway/antechambers: Of the 37 Los Pinos phase structures 9 had antechambers. Antechambers were quite similar in construction to the main living rooms, being shallow and basin shaped in profile and oval in plan view. Dimensions ranged from 2.0 to 8.0 m on the long axis and 1.0 to 5.0 m on the short axis with means of 5.7 m and 3.3 m, respectively.

Superstructures: Two types of construction techniques—used separately or in conjunction—account for nearly all the superstructural variability found in the Los Pinos phase. The first was a cribbed log, domed enclosure identical to that used in the Durango Basketmaker II houses (Morris and Burgh 1954). An example of this type is shown in Figure 5B. The second was a mud-and-cobble masonry technique. Figure 5A depicts a structure in which both techniques were used, i.e., a cribbed log dome with an encircling mud-and-cobble wall built to an unknown height. In all cases for which adequate data exist, the Los Pinos phase builders consistently employed the same construction techniques in both the antechamber and living room of any given structure.

Two Los Pinos phase houses, both at the Tres Casas Site, were roofed by means other than the two described above. Evenly spaced, vertical postholes around the perimeters of these structures served as the primary roof support members. Mud-and-cobble masonry was also employed, possibly to fill the interstices between the uprights.

COMMENTS. The overall impression of Los Pinos phase architecture is one of simplicity and homogeneity. There is a certain amount of variability, but this is best viewed as a consequence of the combination of a few basic elements and building techniques. All of this seems compatible with the relatively short time span allotted to the phase in the argument presented above. Ceramics were clearly associated with most, if not all, of the Los Pinos phase sites. An examination of the field notes and provenience records, along with a reanalysis of Los Pinos and Sambrito Brown ceramics, will be necessary in order to clarify the issues raised above.

Little Jug Site

The Little Jug Site (GC-663) was partially excavated by Richard and Georgia Beth Thompson (Thompson and Thompson 1974) of Southern Utah State College. Located on the north rim of the Grand Canyon in Grand Canyon National Monument, the site consists of at least five small pit dwellings and associated external storage pits.

CHRONOLOGY. The six radiocarbon dates currently available are given in Table 13 along with provenience data and lab numbers. All samples were discrete pieces of charcoal, but they were not necessarily from construction beams. These dates are statistically contemporaneous with respect to the precision of measurement ($F=.69<2.21$: $df=5,\infty$) and have a weighted mean of 1742±39 B.P.: A.D. 208.

The excavators were initially dismayed by the radiocarbon results since the samples were associated with ceramics which—according to the accepted framework (cf. Shutler 1961; Aikens 1966)—were not introduced into the area until after A.D. 500. However, the Thompsons ultimately were confident enough in their excavation procedures to assert the validity of the associations.

> These dates are surprisingly early even when considered by themselves but they become difficult to understand when it is recognized that all except the 230 A.D. date (from the edge of a feature not excavated) were from samples found in clear association with sherds. Much care was taken to trace any rodent holes in order to guard against the possibility that the sherds might be intrusive. In this precaution it is felt that the effort has been successful. To assert that all sherds were, in every case, introduced by rodents will require the postulation of a group of remarkable little animals that selectively intruded only plain ware sherds while completely ignoring the moderately numerous painted sherds found nearer the surface. Since painted sherds were found at these greater depths, even into sterile, in clearly defined rodent holes, we submit that no such creatures exist (Thompson and Thompson 1974:35).

All I can add to the Thompsons' "internal" argument is that the occurrence of plain ware ceramics at A.D. 200 is wholly consistent with the "external" comparative data from the Navajo Reservoir District, Hay Hollow Valley, and Forestdale Valley (see below). In fact, the patterning of the six dates from the Little Jug Site is virtually identical to that displayed by the dates from the Navajo Reservoir District which, as argued earlier, best represent the occupation span in that area.

ARCHITECTURE. At present, the brief description offered by Thompson and Thompson (1974) in their preliminary report is the only source of information on domestic architecture. Hence, the descriptive summary which follows will be necessarily cursory. No detailed plan maps are available for reproduction.

TABLE 13
Radiocarbon Dates from the Little Jug Site

Provenience	Radiocarbon Age B.P.	Calendric Age A.D./B.C.	Lab Number
Above a water deposited layer that overlies the F-73 pithouse floor	1850±90	A.D. 100	RL-339
F-73 pithouse floor	1810±100	A.D. 140	RL-338
Fill of the F-56 dwelling, 5 in above the floor	1750±100	A.D. 200	RL-337
Edge of partially excavated pithouse	1720±100	A.D. 230	RL-335
Pit F-79, under floor F-42	1690±100	A.D. 260	RL-336
Surface of floor F-78 in Pithouse F-225	1630±90	A.D. 320	RL-340

Shape and size: Circular to irregularly oval in shape with maximum dimensions varying from 3.0 to 3.4 m.

Depth: Houses were excavated to maximum depths ranging from 40 to 75 cm below level of origin.

Floors: Either use-packed sand or clay plaster. Pithouses F-73 and F-225 have, respectively, three and four superimposed floors indicating sequential reutilization of the initial pits.

Firepits: Circular in plan and basin shaped in profile. Diameters range from 38 to 60 cm, depths from 10 to 20 cm. The firepit in Pithouse F-82 was stone lined; the others were simple scooped-out depressions.

Other floor features: Pithouses F-56 and F-224 had shallow peripheral trenches encircling the floor areas. These may have served as footer trenches for cribbed log superstructures. Pithouses F-82 and F-225 had five and six postholes, respectively, placed symmetrically around the floor peripheries. The postholes varied from 10 to 12 cm in diameter.

Entryway/antechamber: No antechambers were present, and only two of the pithouses showed any evidence of entryways. Pithouse F-82 had a short trench projecting from its eastern edge, and one of the later occupation floors of Pithouse F-225 had what appeared to be a clay-lined entry ramp on the west side. It was 1.2 m wide and 0.75 m long.

Superstructures: The possible footer trenches in Pithouse F-56 and F-224 suggest cribbed log construction. The symmetrical posthole arrangements in Pithouses F-82 and F-225 suggest flat-roofed superstructures with leaner poles forming the side walls. The remaining six living floors excavated at the site show no evidence of superstructures.

COMMENTS. Pithouses at the Little Jug Site are marked by simplicity of design and small size. This is the westernmost site excavated to date exhibiting firm association of ceramics with second or third century A.D. dwellings.

Tumbleweed Canyon

The Tumbleweed Canyon Site is located northeast of Vernon, Arizona, on the west bank of the Little Colorado River. It was excavated in 1960 by the Field Museum of Natural History, University of Chicago, under the direction of Paul Sidney Martin. The site consists of three houses and associated storage pits on a narrow mesa top overlooking the river. Neither the houses nor the storage pits contained ceramics.

CHRONOLOGY. A single radiocarbon date of 1725±50 B.P.: A.D. 225 (GrN-2801) was obtained on a charred roof beam from one of the houses (Vogel and Waterbolk 1964). Neither the site report (Martin et al. 1962) nor the comment in *Radiocarbon* (Vogel and Waterbolk 1964) indicates from which of the three houses the sample was recovered. The age of the sample was incorrectly reported as 1685±50 in Martin et al. (1962:211).

ARCHITECTURE. Martin et al. (1962) is the sole source for the descriptive summary that follows. One of the houses is shown in Figure 4A.

Shape and size: Houses ranged from D-shaped to circular in plan. Greatest interior dimension ranged from 2.1 to 5.4 m.

Depth: Depth below surface very irregular, ranging from 20 to 65 cm.

Floors: Unmodified irregular surfaces with natural gravels protruding.

Firepits: Circular to roughly oval in plan and basin shaped in profile. Maximum dimension ranged from 30 to 80 cm, depth from 7 to 10 cm.

Other floor features: Houses B and D had no pits, postholes, or floor features of any kind. House A had both postholes and a possible heating pit. The pit was shallow and oval in shape with a length of 42 cm and a width of 27 cm. It contained "rocks" (no additional information given). The 18 postholes were spaced at irregular intervals around the edge of the house. They averaged 20 cm in diameter and 17 cm in depth.

Entryway/antechamber: No antechambers or obvious entryways were found.

Superstructures: Piles of basalt boulders encircled Houses A and D; these probably represent the remains of low masonry walls. Fallen roof beams in House A radiated out from the center of the structure to the periphery suggesting a central support post superstructure had been employed. However, no evidence of a central support post was found. It may be that the 18 peripheral postholes contained flexible saplings that were bent inward and lashed together over the center of the house. No burned, pole-impressed daub was recovered from the fill of any of the structures.

COMMENTS. The site was apparently without ceramics since, "diligent search . . . produced not a single sherd of pottery" (Martin et al. 1962:211). This being the case, it is unfortunate that more radiocarbon samples were not run.

Lone Tree Dune

The Lone Tree Dune Site was excavated in 1961 by Floyd Sharrock (Sharrock, Day, and Dibble 1963) in conjunction with the Glen Canyon salvage program under the general direction of Jesse D. Jennings, University of Utah. Located in the upper reaches of Castle Wash, a tributary of the San Juan River, northwest of Mexican Hat, Utah, the site consists of one house, an external slab-lined firepit, and an external storage cist.

CHRONOLOGY. A single radiocarbon date of 1700±80 B.P.: A.D. 250 (Y-1350) was obtained on a charred timber from the house.

ARCHITECTURE. Descriptive data are taken from Sharrock, Day, and Dibble (1963). A plan map of the excavated dwelling is shown in Figure 4E.

Shape and size: Roughly circular in shape with a mean diameter of 6.7 m.

Depth: Shallow and basin shaped in profile with an average depth of 0.46 m.

Floor: Unplastered sterile earth.

Firepit: A portion of a feature near the center of the house floor may have been a firepit. It was rectangular in plan and steep sided. Maximum width was 30 cm; depth 20 cm.

Other floor features: Six postholes were located in the southern portion of the floor surface. There was no apparent pattern to their distribution, although some symmetry might have emerged had a greater percentage of floor area been cleared.

Nine upright sandstone slabs were set in the floor flanking the entryway and extending ca. 1.5 m into the interior of the house. Two additional sandstone slabs set at right angles to this alignment probably served as a deflector.

Entryway/antechamber: The slab-lined entryway emanated from the southeastern portion of the structure. It was parallel sided with a total length of 2.2 m and an average width of 0.75 m.

Superstructure: Insufficient evidence remained to infer anything beyond the strong probability that some form of wattle-and-daub was employed to enclose the structure.

COMMENTS. Partial excavation of this early structure and the submission of only one radiocarbon sample undoubtedly reflect the limitations of time and funding inherent in most salvage projects. While this is understandable, it does not change the fact that vital information has been irretrievably lost.

Cedar Mesa

The Veres and Pittman sites (GG 69-1 and GG 69-18) are located in the Grand Gulch area roughly 15 miles west-northwest of Bluff, Utah. They were excavated in 1970 by William Lipe (Lipe and Matson 1971) during the initial phase of an extensive program of survey and excavation on Cedar Mesa. Neither the architectural descriptions nor the chronological data have been published. The information reported herein was acquired from the principal investigators, William Lipe and R. G. Matson.

CHRONOLOGY. Radiocarbon and tree-ring dates from the two sites are shown in Tables 14 and 15. Unfortunately, the tree-ring dates leave much to be desired, and the number of radiocarbon dates is less than ideal. Nonetheless, the construction dates of Pittman and Veres can be placed with a fair degree of confidence at shortly after A.D. 250 and A.D. 300, respectively. The earlier tree-ring dates can be safely discounted since the "vv" modifier indicates that an unknown number of rings were missing. Since there is no clustering, the most recent determinations are probably the best estimate of the true cutting dates. The radiocarbon dates are consistent with this interpretation. For example, the three dates and the additional rerun from the Pittman Site pithouse are statistically contemporaneous ($F=1.6<2.60$: $df=3,\infty$) and have a weighted average of 1695±49 B.P.: A.D. 255. This is in close agreement with the most recent tree-ring determination from external Feature 6 at the same site.

TABLE 14
Radiocarbon Dates from the Veres and Pittman Sites

Provenience	Radiocarbon Age B.P.	Calendric Age A.D./B.C.	Lab Number
Pittman Site, pithouse	1570±80	A.D. 380	GX-2141
Pittman, Site, slab hearth built in pithouse fill	1695±90 1759±176	A.D. 255 A.D. 191	GX-2142 GX-2142 Rerun
Pittman Site, external hearth	1870±100	A.D. 80	GX-2074
Veres Site, pithouse	1655±80	A.D. 295	GX-2072

ARCHITECTURE. Descriptive data are taken from line drawings provided by Lipe. These are reproduced to scale in Figure 4D and 4F.

Shape and size: Circular in shape with a mean diameter of 7.0 m.

Depth: Shallow and basin shaped in profile with an average depth of 0.4 m.

Floor: Unplastered sterile earth.

Firepit: The firepit in the Pittman Site pithouse was located in the approximate center of the floor. It was oval in shape, measuring 1.1 m east-west and 0.8 m north-south. An upright slab deflector was imbedded in the floor at the southern edge of the pit. The pithouse at the Veres Site had two firepits lying along the north-south axis of the dwelling in the approximate center of the floor area. The southernmost pit was similar in shape and dimensions to the one already described for the Pittman Site. The second firepit was circular in shape with an average diameter of 1.0 m.

Other floor features: Additional floor features include upright slabs, postholes, and assorted pits. Upright sandstone slabs were restricted to the southern portion of the house floors and were oriented east-west in line with the firepit deflector slabs. In both houses the rows of upright slabs that lined the entryways (see below) continued into the interiors of the structures.

Two distinct kinds of posthole patterns were apparent. The Pittman Site pithouse had seven postholes located at irregular intervals around the periphery of the floor surface. The Veres Site pithouse had a symmetrical four-post support system.

Both houses contained pits of unknown function varying from circular to oval in shape and ranging from 0.5 to 1.5 m in diameter.

Entryway/antechamber: Slab-lined entryways are located on the southern edges of the structures. Both were parallel sided and approximately 1.0 m wide. The Veres Site example was 4.0 m long while the Pittman Site pithouse entryway was only 2.0 m in length.

Superstructure: The peripheral postholes at the Pittman Site pithouse suggest a bent sapling superstructure. The symmetric configuration of the four postholes in the floor of the Veres Site pithouse resembles the four-post support system that was to become the "standard" form of later pithouses.

COMMENTS. These houses were nearly identical to the one already described for the Lone Tree Dune Site; neither contained ceramics.

TABLE 15
Tree-Ring Dates from the Veres and Pittman Sites

Provenience	Date	Provenience	Date
Pittman Site, Feature 6	106vv	Veres Site, pithouse	256vv
	173vv		278vv
	175vv		283vv
	191vv		288vv
	195vv		289vv
	215vv		309vv
	220vv		
	220vv		
	222vv		
	224vv		
	226vv		
	230+vv		
	241vv		
	253++vv		

TABLE 16
Initial Tree-Ring Dates from the Bluff Site

Provenience	Date	Lab Number
House 1	310±15	?
House 2	306±x	?
House 3	288±x	?
House 5	328 (bark date)	?
	320±5	?
House 6	287±x	?
	303±x	?
House 21	312±10	?

The Bluff Site

The Bluff Site is located in the Forestdale Valley about 10 miles southwest of the town of Show-low in east-central Arizona. It was excavated in 1941 by representatives of Arizona State Museum and the University of Arizona under the direction of Emil W. Haury. The site consisted of 24 structures scattered along the ridge that forms the southern boundary of the valley. Haury and Sayles (1947) assigned 15 of these to the Hilltop phase, with a temporal placement of A.D. 200–400. Three were assigned to the later Cottonwood phase (A.D. 400–600), one to the Corduroy phase (A.D. 800–900), and one to the historic Apachean occupation. (Four additional houses were tested but could not be assigned to any of the phases.)

CHRONOLOGY. Tree-ring dating of the site was initially performed by A. E. Douglass (1942, 1944). Douglass's determinations, as summarized in Haury and Sayles (1947), are listed below. The original system of qualifying symbols has been retained for reasons discussed earlier. All of these dates were on structural timbers from Hilltop phase houses and, taken as a group, indicated an early fourth-century placement. Haury and Sayles's broader estimate of the dates bracketing the phase was based on tenuous, but not altogether unacceptable, reasoning:

> For the Hilltop phase we have calculated a 200-year period from A.D. 200-400, allowing approximately a century before and after 300, where the tree-ring dates clustered. This seems reasonable, because the pottery presumably present at this time does not represent the first ceramic efforts. Some prior acquaintance with this art may be predicated, and the same attitude will apply with respect to architecture. The year 200 is thus stated as an arbitrary figure to acknowledge that something preceded the first dated remains, but we are fully aware that this date may be too liberal or too conservative. The phase ending date of 400 is based on the fact that at about that time the Basketmakers appear to have learned the art of pottery making. The total lack of Basketmaker pottery in Hilltop phase contexts, therefore, is some basis for the claim that there was no appreciable overlap between the Hilltop Phase and the Lino Phase of the Basketmaker, the initial period of pottery making among that group (Haury and Sayles 1947:87).

This early dating of the Bluff Site did not set well with H. S. Gladwin (1948) since it did not "fit" with his culture historical synthesis of Southwestern prehistory. Although Gladwin claimed that his reconstruction was based primarily on artifactual and architectural data, asserting that "the dating of ruins by means of tree-rings should be subordinate and supplementary to the archeological evidence" (Gladwin 1948:149), his criticism of Haury and Sayles cannot meaningfully be divorced from his ongoing methodological debate with Douglass. In reference to the Bluff dates, for instance, Gladwin argued that

> The importance of this dating can hardly be exaggerated since, if correct, it would mean that pottery was known in central Arizona many years before the Basket Makers acquired their knowledge of the art. It therefore poses the same problem which was raised at Snaketown and so deserves the most serious consideration. My reason for raising this question is that, at Gila Pueblo, we are unwilling to accept some of the dates which have been obtained by the Douglass method, particularly for those ruins which are peripheral to the Four Corners district, upon which the original Douglass chronology was based (Gladwin 1948:154).

Gladwin then applied his method to the three charcoal specimens figured in Douglass's (1942) article and concluded that they actually dated to the seventh and eighth centuries A.D. rather than the late third to early fourth centuries. Needless to say, this was exactly as Gladwin had predicted it should be since he included the Bluff Site in his "Stage of Polished Red," which was supposed to have begun in the early 700s.

Wendorf (1953) was forced to address this problem in attempting to use the Bluff Site evidence to cross-date the Flattop Site, a pithouse village in the Petrified Forest of north-eastern Arizona. While avoiding comment on the methodological differences involved in the Gladwin-Douglass controversy, Wendorf cited distributional, stratigraphic, and typological evidence which, while inconclusive, tended to support the early (Douglass) placement. A decade later Bullard (1962) arrived at a similar conclusion, albeit grudgingly, since it ran counter to one of his principal hypotheses. As he noted in summary,

> the review fails to find substantiation that any of the phases of the Hohokam or Mogollon cultures so far defined, with the questionable exception of the Hilltop phase, are demonstrably older than the Basketmaker III period of the Anasazi (Bullard 1962:93).

While the consensus has always seemed to favor the Douglass reading of the data, it was not until 1966 that the situation was finally resolved through reanalysis of the Bluff Site specimens (Bannister, Gell, and Hannah 1966). Unfortunately, many of the charcoal samples had been misplaced or lost in transit, but those available for rechecking were in close agreement with the results derived by Douglass a quarter of a century earlier. These data tend to confirm Douglass's dating of Houses 5 and 6 and, by implication, the early fourth-century dating of Houses 1, 2, 3, and 21.

TABLE 17
Reanalysis of Tree-Ring Dates from the Bluff Site

Provenience	Date	Lab Number
House 5	238vv	FST-289
	278vv	FST-231
	303rB	FST-230
	307vv	FST-332
	321vv	FST-261
	322vv	FST-260
House 6	298vv	FST-164

ARCHITECTURE. The 15 structures assigned to the Hilltop phase are Houses 1, 2, 3, 4, 4a, 5, 6, 7, 8, 9, 10, 12, 13, 15, and 21 (Haury and Sayles 1947). A total of 907 sherds was excavated from these houses, 95% of which were Alma Plain (either Bluff or Forestdale variety). Much has been said regarding the Hohokam and Anasazi ceramics found at the site (cf. Gladwin 1948; Wendorf 1953; Bullard 1962); but, to my knowledge, no one mentioned the fact that Haury and Sayles did not discriminate between "floor" and "fill" contexts. This being the case, the true association of these sherds with indigenous complexes or particular structures at the Bluff Site cannot be demonstrated. We can be sure that Alma Plain was made and utilized by the occupants of these houses, but all else is conjecture, and any cross-dating schemes that rely on the Bluff Site intrusives are highly suspect. The same problem affects the present study since presence, absence, or relative abundance of ceramic types in floor contact situations cannot be used to argue for or against the contemporaneity of undated and tree-ring dated houses. So, while we know that two of the houses (and probably the four others dated by Douglass) were built shortly after A.D. 300, there is no sure way of knowing when the other nine Hilltop phase houses were constructed. Nevertheless, I have included all 15 in the architectural summary that follows.

Shape and size: Eleven houses were circular in shape, three were oval, and one was rectangular with rounded corners. With one exception the circular houses were fairly uniform in size ranging from 4.0 to 6.1 m in diameter with a mean of 4.65 m. The one case that differed markedly from the norm was a circular structure 10.3 m in diameter which Haury and Sayles interpreted as a ceremonial structure. The oval structures ranged from 3.25 to 5.7 m in length and 2.6 to 4.0 m in width, with means of 4.6 and 3.7 m, respectively. The rectangular structure measured 2.5 by 2.7 m.

Depth: All of these structures are true pithouses. Depths ranged from 0.65 to 1.5 m, with a mean of 1.2 m. Houses were excavated into the sandstone bedrock.

Floors: Preserved sections of clay plaster in most houses suggest that the irregular bedrock floors were leveled by the application of a thick clay coating.

Firepits: The majority of structures lacked evidence of firepits. Two structures (Houses 5 and 9) had firepits consisting of circular depressions in the bedrock floors ringed with sandstone slabs.

Other floor features: Floor features of any kind were scarce in Hilltop phase houses; four examples were totally barren. House 8 contained two rock-rimmed storage pits 0.6 and 0.9 m in diameter. It also contained a clay storage bin built against the north wall. House 7 had a circular clay sill, 2.6 m in diameter, installed on the floor surface. The sill averaged .28 m high.

Only two of the houses had definite postholes (Houses 5 and 10). In both cases these formed a symmetrical four-post support pattern. House 5 also had an encircling trench cut into the bedrock. This feature is reminiscent of the footer trenches in the Durango houses.

Entryway/antechamber: Five of the houses had lateral entryways. All were ca. 1.0 m wide and 2.0 m long and were located on the east sides of the structures. The entryway of House 15 had two parallel floor grooves running along its edges.

Superstructures: The only evidence for roofing technique is the four-post support system inferred for both Houses 5 and 10. Postholes are absent from the other houses, and the fallen roof beams were apparently not well enough preserved to allow any reasonable interpretation.

COMMENTS. The houses do not vary significantly except in shape. Most are little more than holes in the ground with a few simple floor features. It should be noted that Gladwin (1948) gives the erroneous impression that four-post support is the predominant type of superstructure at the Bluff Site. As discussed above, only 2 of the 15 Hilltop phase structures were roofed in this manner.

Klethla Valley Sites

Sites in the Klethla Valley were excavated by the Museum of Northern Arizona in 1960 under the general supervision of Alan P. Olson and J. Richard Ambler (Ambler and Olson 1977). Two of the sites, NA8163 and NA8166, contained Basketmaker III structures.

CHRONOLOGY. Eight pithouses were excavated at NA8163, one of which yielded a cutting date of A.D. 555 (no lab number reported). The one excavated pithouse at NA8166 yielded a single cutting date of A.D. 703 (Bannister, Dean, and Robinson 1968).

ARCHITECTURE. Most of the pithouses were badly disturbed by road construction and erosion prior to excavation. Pithouses 1, 2, and 13 at site NA8163 (Figure 6) and Pithouse 1 at NA8166 are the only intact examples illustrated in the site report (Ambler and Olson 1977); hence, these are the only structures considered in the descriptive summary that follows.

Shape and size: The three houses at NA8163 were D-shaped with the flattened portion of the "D" located at the intersection with the antechamber. The house at NA8166 was oval in shape. Greatest transverse measurements ranged from 5.4 to 6.3 m, with a mean of 5.9 m.

Depth: Straight-sided pit walls ranged in depth below original surface from 0.4 to 1.2 m with a mean of 0.8 m.

Floors: Two structures had plastered clay floors. The other two had floors consisting of use-packed earth.

Firepits: Two of the firepits at NA8163 were circular in shape and the third was U-shaped. All

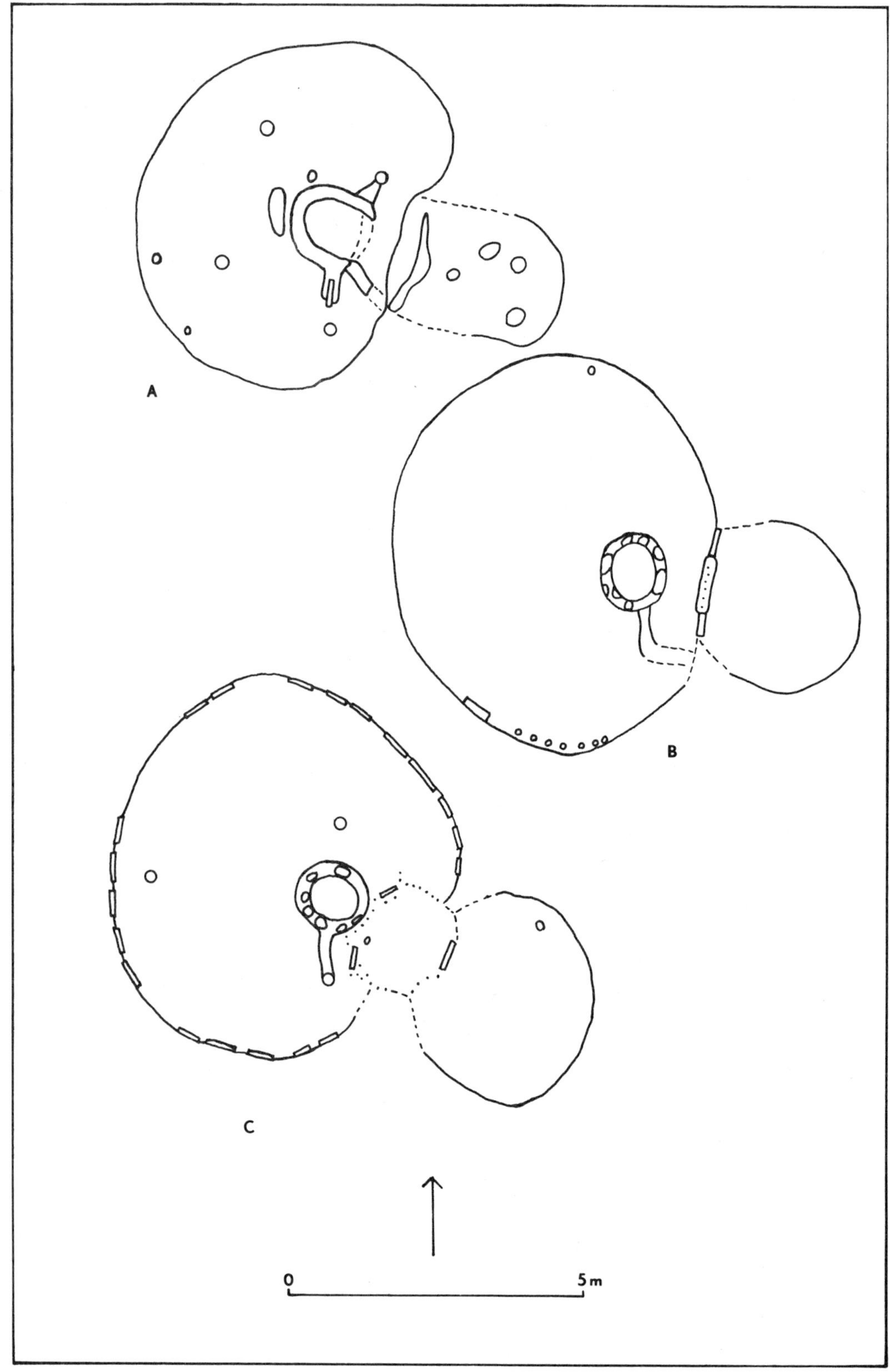

Figure 6. Klethla Valley pithouses, NA8163: A, Pithouse 13; B, Pithouse 2; C, Pithouse 1 (Ambler and Olson 1977).

three had rims formed of rocks plastered in adobe. The circular examples ranged from 0.9 to 1.2 m in diameter. The U-shaped firepit was 1.3 m long. The firepit at Pithouse 1, NA8166, was oval in plan and consisted of a simple basin-shaped depression scooped out of the floor. It measured 0.7 m north-south and 0.5 m east-west.

Other floor features: Floor features included upright slabs, partition walls, postholes, and floor cists.

The entire periphery of Pithouse 1, NA8163, was lined with upright sandstone slabs. Additional upright slabs were incorporated into partition walls in most of the other structures. However, the predominant building techniques involved in partition construction were jacal and unreinforced adobe. Partition walls separated the antechambers from the main floor areas. In at least two cases they were nothing more than short, low walls spanning the entryway formed at the intersection of the antechamber and pithouse. In the other, partition walls were angled inward so as to intersect the firepit.

Two types of posthole patterns were in evidence. Pithouse 2 at NA8163 and Pithouse 1 at NA8166 had small postholes along the pit peripheries. Only a few of these were preserved, but it seems likely that they once occurred around the entire circumference. The remaining pithouses had four major support posts forming a rectangular pattern inset from the pit walls. In some cases one or more of these support posts were incorporated in the partition walls.

Floor cists were few in number and fairly nondescript. They were unlined, irregular excavations with maximum transverse measurements of 20 to 50 cm.

Entryway/antechamber: All of the undisturbed pithouses had antechambers. These were circular to D-shaped in plan with the flat side of the D located at the intersection of the antechamber and the main structure. Greatest transverse measurements were quite uniform, ranging from 2.8 to 3.0 m, with a mean of 2.9 m. The antechambers had no floor features other than an occasional isolated posthole or a few shallow pits.

Benches: Pithouse 1 at NA8166—the most recent of the structures considered here—was the only structure with a bench. It encircled the entire floor area and varied from 30 to 53 cm in width and 48 to 61 cm in height. There was no evidence of adobe plaster.

Superstructures: Most of the structures probably were of the four-post support system type, i.e., a central rectangular framework supporting leaner poles, brush, and mud. The pithouses with peripheral posts may have had superstructures consisting of bent saplings similar to the wickiup style already described for the Hay Hollow Valley sites.

COMMENTS. The composition of the ceramic complex is difficult to describe in quantitative terms. The ceramic provenience tables make no distinction between "fill" and "floor" sherds. The only reference to floor contact ceramics was the occasional mention of whole vessels recovered during the course of excavation. These included Lino Gray, Lino Fugitive Red, and Obelisk Gray. The absence of Lino Black-on-gray whole vessels, combined with its virtual absence in the sherd tabulations (n=1), attests to the relatively early temporal provenience of NA8163 and seems consistent with the single cutting date of A.D. 555.

Prayer Rock District

The Prayer Rock District is located in extreme northeastern Arizona south of Carrizo Mountain and north of the Lukachukai Range. It is drained by numerous tributaries of Red Wash, which is in turn a tributary of the San Juan River to the north. The relevant sites were excavated by Earl H. Morris in 1930 while a member of the Bernheimer Expedition of the American Museum of Natural History and in 1931 as director of a Carnegie Institution expedition. The architectural descriptions and artifact analyses were not undertaken until Elizabeth A. Morris (1959) utilized these data as the basis for her doctoral dissertation.

The sites consist of groups of pithouses, cists, and surface masonry structures located in a series of rockshelters or alcoves. The quality of the available data is extremely variable. For instance, Elizabeth Morris was unable to find any field notes for Obelisk Cave, the earliest well-dated site in the region. Hence, the only description available for this important site is a brief summary statement provided by E. H. Morris (1936) in the

Tree-Ring Bulletin. On the other hand, the architectural descriptions and provenience data for Broken Flute Cave are quite detailed and useful. The remaining sites fall somewhere in-between.

CHRONOLOGY. The tree-ring dates for the region are given in Table 18. They are from Bannister, Dean, and Gell's (1966) reassessment of the specimens rather than E. A. Morris's (1959) account, since the former contains more dates and in some cases cutting dates that differ from the original analyses. Sites that are poorly described and have no cutting dates are excluded from Table 18.

The house in Obelisk Cave was the earliest structure in the district, with cutting dates ranging from A.D. 478 to 489. The early component at Broken Flute Cave, represented by Rooms 1, 2, (possibly) 3, and 8A, dates from A.D. 469 to 508. Evidence of subsequent building activity is lacking until the first half of the seventh century. At that time, there is a strong clustering of dates between A.D. 621 and 629 from Rooms 5, 6, 7, 8, 9, 11, and 12. This is followed by another strong cluster between A.D. 656 and 676 from structures at Caves 1 and 2. The area was apparently abandoned prior to A.D. 700 and remained unoccupied until the Pueblo II–III period.

ARCHITECTURE. The following descriptive account has been loosely abstracted from the section of E. A. Morris's dissertation entitled "Summary of Architectural Features" (1959:28–38). I have omitted discussion of the masonry structures since they are associated with the later Pueblo occupation.

Shape and size: Shape varied from rectangular with rounded corners to round. Greatest transverse dimensions varied from 2.25 to 8.5 m with most of the structures falling between 5.0 and 8.0 m.

Depth: Greatest depth was 1.5 m.

Floors: Typically consisted of a thin layer of adobe plaster over bedrock, native earth, or cultural fill. The one exception to this general rule was a floor consisting of clean sand. Floors were somewhat irregular and sloped inward toward the center.

Firepits: Circular or D-shaped in plan and basin shaped in profile. Diameters ranged from 0.5 to 1.0 m. Depths ranged from 10 to 50 cm. Firepits were slab lined with adobe plaster filling in the cracks between the slabs. Frequently a raised adobe collar encircled the rim. Only one of the structures had an ash pit located adjacent to the firepit.

Other floor features: Floor features consisted of partition walls, postholes, storage bins, cists, and deflectors.

Morris describes the various types of partitions in evidence as follows:

> In many pithouses one to four low mud partitions run from the hearth to the walls or to cists adjacent to the walls. These are located in the half of the house nearest the front of the cave. Usually these mud ridges have a log for a core, base, or cap. These logs are sometimes raised on a mud and stone base from 5 to 15 cm. high. In some instances, the height increases to as much as 40 cm. through the use of sandstone slabs set on end. In some houses one or two of the roof supports were included in the partition wall. The mud at the base of the radial partition ranges up to 27 cm. in total width. In one house the floor is 7 to 15 cm. higher in the area toward the edge than in the main part of the house (E. A. Morris 1959:31).

Storage bins were typically constructed of upright slabs and adobe plaster. These were usually incorporated into the partition walls. There were a few examples of jacal bins.

Floor cists were either deep irregularly shaped holes or shallow clay-lined basins. Both types are less than 1.0 m in diameter.

None of the houses contained upright sandstone slab deflectors. One structure had a possible deflector formed of upright planks placed in a floor slot.

All structures had four main support posts forming a rectangle slightly inset from the outer walls.

Entryway/antechamber: The houses were situated in the alcoves in such a way that antechambers and entryways—had they existed—would have been destroyed by erosion subsequent to abandonment. Morris adduces evidence for the occurrence of entry trenches in six structures; however, the data are less than conclusive.

Benches: Morris describes the benches as follows:

TABLE 18
Tree-Ring Dates from the Prayer Rock District

Provenience	Date	Lab Number
Obelisk Cave		
Burned room, east center	325v	GP-992
	438vv	GP-923
	480rL	MLK-280
General	446++rB	GP-932
	478GB	MLK-152
	479rB	GP-6673
	479rG	MLK-151
	480v	MLK-156
	480vv	GP-931
	484rGB	GP-930
	484v	MLK-150
	486B	MLK-153
	489rB	MLK-154
Broken Flute Cave		
Room 1	501rB	MLK-126
	508rLG	MLK-245
Room 2	468+r	MLK-244
	499cLBG	GP-920
Room 3	505v	MLK-226
Room 4	491rLBG	MLK-103
	628rB	MLK-99
Room 5	457+G	GP-887
	609vv	MLK-93
	628v	MLK-88
	629r	MLK-92
	629cB	MLK-142
Room 6	602vv	MLK-222-2
	606vv	MLK-77
	613vv	MLK-78
	622vv	MLK-76
	622rL	MLK-87
	622cL	MLK-134
	622cB	MLK-73
	623v	MLK-75
	623v	MLK-80
	623v	MLK-84
	623r	MLK-85
	623cL	MLK-127
	623cL	MLK-131

TABLE 18 (continued)

Provenience	Date	Lab Number
Room 6 (continued)	623rL 623cLB 627r	MLK-133 MLK-135 GP-885
Room 7	623cB 624rB 625cL 625rLB 625v 625r 625cL 626r	GP-6691 GP-879 GP-875 GP-876 GP-6690 MLK-140 MLK-137 MLK-51
Room 8	618vv 624v 624v 625v 625rB 627cL	MLK-64 MLK-65 GP-874 MLK-67 GP-872 MLK-66
Room 8A	469rL 469v 470rL 493v 494rG	GP-866 GP-868 GP-871 GP-870 GP-869
Room 9	515+v 611++LGB 613v 623rL 623rL 623rL 623c 624rL 624cLB 624rL 624rL 624rL 624L 624rLB	MLK-174 GP-848 GP-849 GP-853 MLK-175 MLK-173 MLK-170 MLK-164 MLK-165 MLK-167 MLK-169 MLK-171 MLK-176 GP-854
Room 11	491r 568++v 574vv 619+v 621rB 625cL 635++rG	MLK-144 MLK-147 GP-860 MLK-145 GP-859 GP-6686 GP-6683

TABLE 18 (continued)

Provenience	Date	Lab Number
Room 12	621B	GP-865
	623vv	MLK-55
	623rL	MLK-59
	623r	MLK-62
	623L	MLK-179
	623cL	MLK-178
Room 14	627v	GP-855
Room 17	489rL	GP-1426
	505r	GP-912
	605rL	MLK-266
Cave 1		
Pithouse 1	657vv	MLK-199
Pithouse 3	658r	MLK-24
Cave 2		
Room 1	626cL	MLK-12
	655vv	MLK-15
	657vv	MLK-14
	666c	MLK-18
	666c	GP-942
	667rB	GP-941
	667v	MLK-20
	667r	MLK-17
	667v	MLK-9
	668c	MLK-23-1
	668vv	MLK-5
	669rL	MLK-2
	669r	MLK-8
	669vv	MLK-19
	669vv	MLK-21
	669r	GP-939
	669vv	GP-940
	669r	GP-943
	669r	GP-945
	669cL	GP-948
	669cL	GP-950
	669c	GP-953
Room 2	667r	GP-954
	667vv	MLK-35
	668vv	GP-955
	669r	GP-958
	669vv	GP-959
	669r	MLK-30
	669r	GP-956

TABLE 18 (continued)

Provenience	Date	Lab Number
Room 2 (continued)	669r	GP-957
	669v	MLK-32
	676rB	MLK-29
	676c	MLK-42
Room 4	642v	MLK-191
	645vv	MLK-184
	654vv	MLK-195
	654vv	MLK-196
	655r	MLK-183
	656c	MLK-193
	657r	GP-964
	658++r	MLK-185
	658r	MLK-189
	658r	MLK-190
	658r	MLK-45
	660+r	MLK-186
	660+r	GP-966
	663++vv	GP-962
	665rL	GP-960
	668r	GP-967
	670cL	GP-961

Source: Bannister, Dean, and Gell 1966

> Most pithouses have an irregular sand bench along the remaining portions of the wall. These benches were poorly constructed over finished floors and vary considerably in height and breadth within a single room. The height varies from 10 to 60 cm., most of them being between 20 and 35 cm. The width varies between 25 cm. and 30 cm. In a few cases the benches are faced with sandstone slabs, neatly plastered in place. More often a thin mud mortar is used for surfacing. Some benches have a plastered rim along the outside edge, on others the slabs protrude, forming a small rim (E. A. Morris 1959:33).

Superstructures: Four-post support forming a central rectangular framework. Leaner poles formed the side walls which were covered with brush and adobe.

COMMENTS. The ceramic assemblage from Basketmaker III components in the Prayer Rock District may be divided into two groups. The earliest, dating from A.D. 470 to A.D. 508, consists of a single type, Obelisk Gray. The subsequent seventh-century assemblage includes Lino Gray, Lino Black-on-gray, Chapin Gray, Chapin Black-on-white, La Plata Black-on-white, fiber-tempered pottery, and an unidentified polished redware (Tallahogan Red?). There is a gap in the dating record of approximately one century between the two known "Basketmaker III" components, and it seems unlikely that occupation was continuous from the late 400s through the late 600s as E. A. Morris (1959) suggests.

Twin Lakes Site

The Twin Lakes Site (LA 2507) is located near Tohatchi, New Mexico, at the southern terminus of the Chuska Mountains. It is an extensive site containing both Basketmaker III and Pueblo I components. Only two of the structures have been adequately dated and described. The first was excavated in 1950 by William R. Bullard and Francis E. Cassidy (Bullard and Cassidy 1956a) in conjunction with a major archeological salvage project necessitated by construction of a pipeline for the El Paso Natural Gas Company's San Juan Project. Excavations were conducted under the

TABLE 19
Tree-Ring Dates from the Twin Lakes Site

Provenience	Date	Lab Number
Pithouse 1	584vv	RG-2504-4
	605rB	RG-2504-8
	606B	RG-2504-3
	610vv	RG-2504-12
	611+vv	RG-2504-11
Pithouse 5	283vv	RG-4308
	412vv	RG-4306
	586vv	RG-4307
	616vv	RG-4304
	619r	RG-4316
	622r	RG-4313
	622r	RG-4320
	622c	RG-4315
	622c	RG-4300
	623B	RG-4314

Source: Bannister, Robinson, and Warren 1970

general directorship of Fred Wendorf. The second structure was excavated and reported in 1962 by Chester Johnson in conjunction with a subsequent El Paso Natural Gas Company project.

CHRONOLOGY. The tree-ring dates for the two Basketmaker III houses are given in Table 19. Pithouse 1 apparently was constructed around A.D. 605 with additional repairs at 610 and later. Pithouse 5 was probably constructed in A.D. 622.

ARCHITECTURE. Information for the summary descriptions that follow has been taken from Bullard and Cassidy (1956a) and C. Johnson (1962) (see Figure 7B).

Shape and size: Both structures were rectangular in shape with rounded corners. Pithouse 1 measured roughly 4.0 m on a side. The dimensions of Pithouse 5 are unknown since C. Johnson (1962) failed to provide a scale in the plan map.

Depth: The floor of Pithouse 1 was approximately 1.0 m below the level of origin.

Floors: The floor of Pithouse 1 was use-packed native earth. Pithouse 5 had a prepared clay plaster floor.

Firepits: Firepits were circular in plan and basin shaped in profile with slightly elevated clay rims. The example in Pithouse 5 was also slab lined.

Other floor features: Additional floor features included postholes, partitions, storage bins, and deflector slabs. Floor cists were absent.

Both structures contained four main support posts, one or two of which were incorporated into the low clay ridges that radiated from the firepit and continued in a straight line toward opposite pit walls.

Pithouse 1 contained the only example of a storage bin. It consisted of two upright slabs set at right angles in one corner of the structure forming a rectangular enclosure.

Pithouse 1 had an upright slab deflector located midway between the entrance and the firepit. Pithouse 5 had a similar feature as well as a second deflector embedded in the antechamber floor near the outer end of the entryway.

Entryway/antechamber: Both structures had roughly circular antechambers connected to the main living area by short trench corridors. The antechamber of Pithouse 1 measured approximately 2.5 m in diameter. In both cases, floors and walls consisted of unplastered native earth.

Bench: Pithouse 5 contained a three-quarter bench. No dimensions are available.

Superstructure: Both structures were apparently roofed in the standard four-post manner. Preservation in Pithouse 5 was adequate to allow the following description of construction techniques:

> In Pit House 5, the fallen and burned roof material formed a level, about six inches thick, of burned plaster and logs. Log specimens were taken for tree-ring analysis. The roof was composed of logs and poles with sticks running at right angles and an over-all cover of grass capped with mud. The ceiling of the house was also plastered, as shown by dried mud containing log impressions without sticks or grass (C. Johnson 1962:160).

COMMENTS. Ceramic types associated with Pithouse 1 are limited to Chapin Gray and Chapin Black-on-white. Only Chapin Gray was found in floor contact. Floor-contact ceramic types recovered from the slightly later Pithouse 5 include Lino Gray, Lino Smudged, La Plata Black-on-

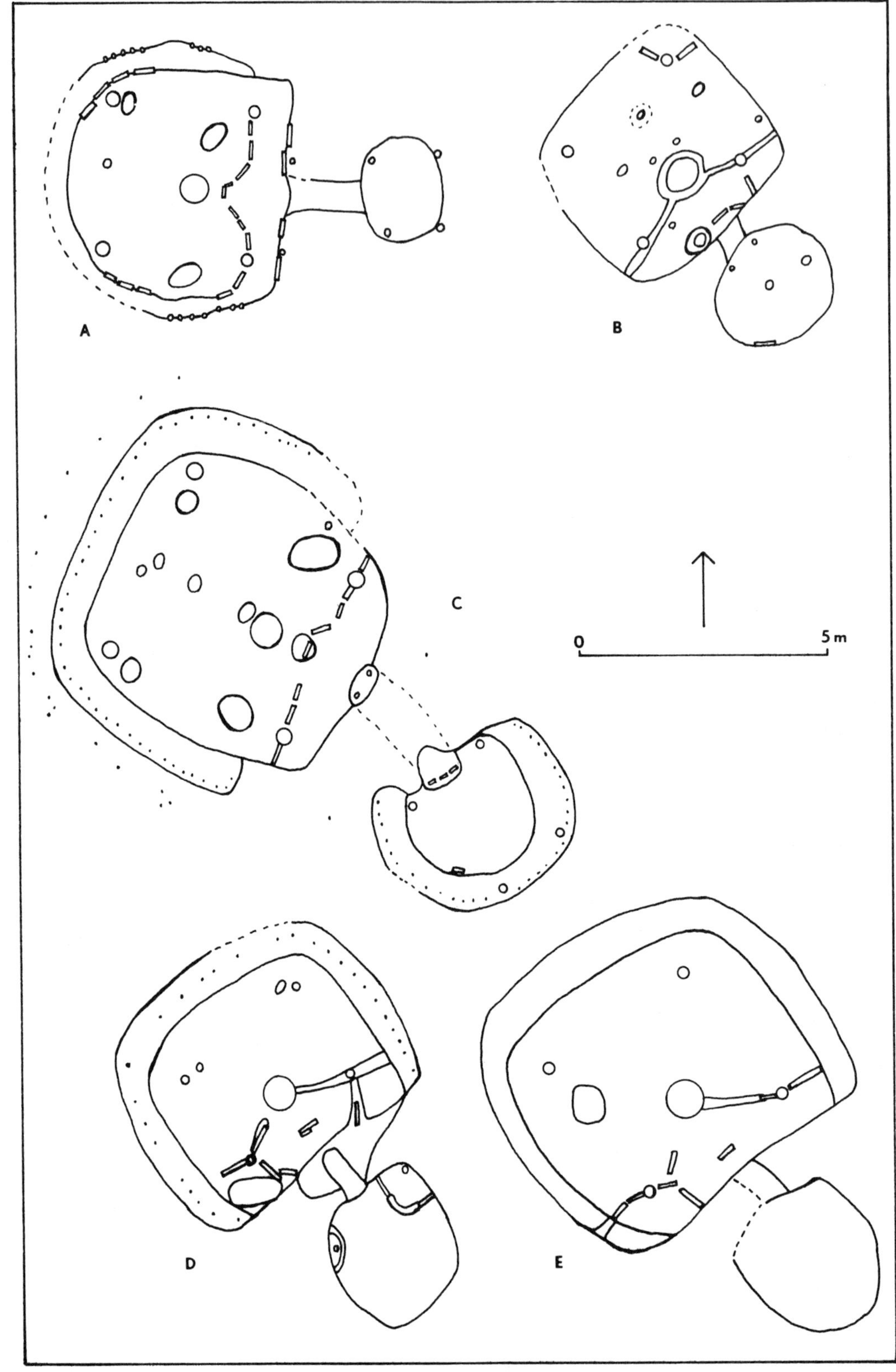

Figure 7. Basketmaker III pithouses from the southern Colorado Plateau: A, Structure 402, Cerro Colorado (Bullard 1962); B, Pithouse 1, LA 2507 (Twin Lakes Site) (Bullard and Cassidy 1956a; C. Johnson 1962); C, Structure 203, Cerro Colorado (Bullard 1962); D, Pithouse G, Site 1676, Mesa Verde; E, Pithouse A, Site 1644, Mesa Verde (Hayes and Lancaster 1975).

white, and Woodruff Smudged (Forestdale Variety).

The Cerro Colorado Site

The Cerro Colorado Site is located in west-central New Mexico approximately eight miles north of the town of Quemado. It was excavated in 1953 and 1954 by the Upper Gila Expedition of the Peabody Museum, Harvard University, under the general direction of J. O. Brew. William R. Bullard participated in the excavations and utilized the resulting data as the basis for his doctoral dissertation, which was published in 1962.

The Cerro Colorado Site is a moderately large Basketmaker III pithouse village that was subsequently reoccupied in late Pueblo I and Pueblo II times. Surface indications of occupation were clustered into four more or less discrete groups, and these areas were the most intensively investigated. Fifteen pithouses were excavated during the two field seasons.

CHRONOLOGY. Although vast quantities of charred timbers were salvaged for dendrochronology, the tree-ring chronology for the Quemado area was not sufficiently well developed until several years after the publication of the monograph. The determinations were finally published in 1970 by the Laboratory of Tree-Ring Research (Bannister, Hannah, and Robinson 1970). Dates from structures occupied prior to A.D. 700 are given in Table 20. These dates are consistent with the chronological interpretation of the site offered by Bullard (1962), and, as a matter of fact, the tight clustering of dates from well-controlled proveniences makes Cerro Colorado one of the best-dated sites in the Southwest. The earliest dated structure is Pithouse 3 with cutting dates at A.D. 604 and 626. This was followed by Pithouse 4 with a probable construction date of A.D. 630 to 637; Structure 208 with cutting dates ranging from A.D. 631 to 637 and repairs undertaken in the second half of the seventh century; Structure 203 from A.D. 654 to 671; Structure 104 from A.D. 650 to 668+; Structure 402 from A.D. 658 to 669; Structure 103 at A.D. 665; Structure 205 at A.D. 666; and Structure 101 at A.D. 695. Bannister, Hannah and Robinson (1970) suggest that the long span of cutting dates from Structure 405 (A.D. 642–687) is due to the aboriginal reuse of construction timbers. The probable building date is A.D. 670 with considerable refurbishing during the next two decades. The clustering of dates from the site as a whole indicates that the bulk of construction activities took place between A.D. 626 and 675. This was followed by a period of diminished activity and, finally, abandonment by the beginning of the eighth century.

ARCHITECTURE. The architectural summary that follows has been abstracted from Bullard's (1962) descriptive account (Figures 7A, C; 8A, D).

Shape and size: Virtually the whole gamut of house shapes occurred at the site including round, oval, D-shaped, and rectangular with rounded corners. Circular and oval examples varied from 5.0 to 7.1 m in diameter with a mean of 6.1 m. The two D-shaped houses (Structures 402 and 405) were 4.7 m along the greatest transverse measurement parallel to the flat side of the D and measured 5.1 and 4.1 m, respectively, along the axis at right angles to this side. The rectangular houses ranged from 3.2 to 7.3 m in length and from 2.9 to 5.3 m in width, with means of 6.0 and 5.0 m, respectively.

Depth: These were true pithouses ranging in depth from 0.6 to 2.0 m with a mean of 1.3 m.

Floors: The most common type of floor was unaltered native earth or bedrock. Two structures had clay plaster floors. Another two had a thin layer of "dirty" sand over native earth.

Firepits: Firepits were circular to oval in plan. Both clay-rimmed and unrimmed varieties were present. Diameters ranged from 35 to 60 cm; depths ranged from 10 to 20 cm. Two structures (Structures 103 and 203) had "ash pits" adjacent to the hearths.

Other floor features: Additional floor features included postholes, partitions, storage bins, floor cists, heating pits, and deflectors.

All structures had four main support posts forming a rectangular pattern. In several cases one or two of these were incorporated into partition walls or storage bins.

Partition walls generally were constructed perpendicular to the axis of symmetry, separating the house into two portions: (1) a large main

TABLE 20
Tree-Ring Dates from the Cerro Colorado Site

Provenience	Date	Lab Number
Pithouse 2	587vv	HAR-3407
	619vv	HAR-3292
	641v	HAR-3406
Pithouse 3	586v	HAR-3282
	604r	HAR-3226
	626rB	HAR-3301
Pithouse 4	583vv	HAR-W184
	621vv	HAR-W173
	626v	HAR-W182
	630r	HAR-W187
	631r	HAR-W185
	632vv	HAR-W180
	632vv	HAR-W181
	633v	HAR-W174
	633r	HAR-W176
	634vv	HAR-W177
	635vv	HAR-W186
	637r	HAR-W60
	637r	HAR-W63
	637r	HAR-W64
Structure 101	694vv	HAR-W26
	695r	HAR-W16
	695r	HAR-W22
	695r	HAR-W27
	695r	HAR-W160
Structure 103	580vv	HAR-W15
	660vv	HAR-W18
	665r	HAR-W129
	665rB	HAR-W11
Structure 104	598vv	HAR-W149
	602vv	HAR-W140
	611vv	HAR-W111
	623vv	HAR-W148
	639vv	HAR-W145
	641vv	HAR-W155
	648vv	HAR-W12
	650vv	HAR-W112
	650r	HAR-W105
	651r	HAR-W120
	652vv	HAR-W142
	652r	HAR-W109
	653r	HAR-W146

TABLE 20 (continued)

Provenience	Date	Lab Number
Structure 104 (continued)	653r 666r 667r 668vv	HAR-W14 HAR-W123 HAR-W143 HAR-W104
Structure 203	623vv 636vv 650v 651v 653v 653v 654r 658v 664r 665v 665r 667v 667r 667r 667r 667rB 671r 691vv	HAR-W241 HAR-W260 HAR-W259 HAR-W285 HAR-W277 HAR-W256 HAR-W281 HAR-W258 HAR-W257 HAR-W242 HAR-W283 HAR-W288 HAR-W248 HAR-W250 HAR-W280 HAR-W252 HAR-W278 HAR-W246
Structure 205	648v 651v 654v 666v 666r	HAR-W297 HAR-W296 HAR-W292 HAR-W294 HAR-W295
Structure 208	574vv 597++vv 631r 632v 633v 633r 633r 634r 637r 653v 653++v	HAR-W298-17 HAR-W298-1 HAR-W298-5 HAR-W298-14 HAR-W298-13 HAR-W298-16 HAR-W298-11 HAR-W298-4 HAR-W298-9 HAR-W299 HAR-W298-15
Structure 211	631+v	HAR-W300
Structure 213	699v	HAR-W301
Structure 402	601vv 602vv	HAR-W232 HAR-W222

TABLE 20 (continued)

Provenience	Date	Lab Number
Structure 402 (continued)	612vv	HAR-W216
	628vv	HAR-W225
	644r	HAR-W213
	648++vv	HAR-W218
	650vv	HAR-W210
	652r	HAR-W212
	654vv	HAR-W209
	655v	HAR-W202
	657vv	HAR-W237
	657vv	HAR-W234
	657+v	HAR-W220
	658r	HAR-235
	658B	HAR-228
	659r	HAR-W208
	661r	HAR-W221
	663vv	HAR-W227
	664vv	HAR-W215
	664r	HAR-W219
	665vv	HAR-W233
	669r	HAR-W203
Structure 405	638vv	HAR-W272
	641v	HAR-W303
	642r	HAR-W324
	646c	HAR-W316
	652vv	HAR-W307
	657r	HAR-W268
	657r	HAR-W310
	658vv	HAR-W306
	658r	HAR-W273
	658c	HAR-W264
	667r	HAR-W311
	670r	HAR-W276
	671r	HAR-W269
	675r	HAR-W321
	675r	HAR-W318
	675r	HAR-W308
	676v	HAR-W326
	676r	HAR-W314
	676c	HAR-W(A)1
	676c	HAR-W261
	685r	HAR-W323
	686r	HAR-W266
	686c	HAR-W(A)2
	686c	HAR-W262
	686c	HAR-W263
	686c	HAR-W275
	687r	HAR-W312

Source: Bannister, Hannah, and Robinson 1970

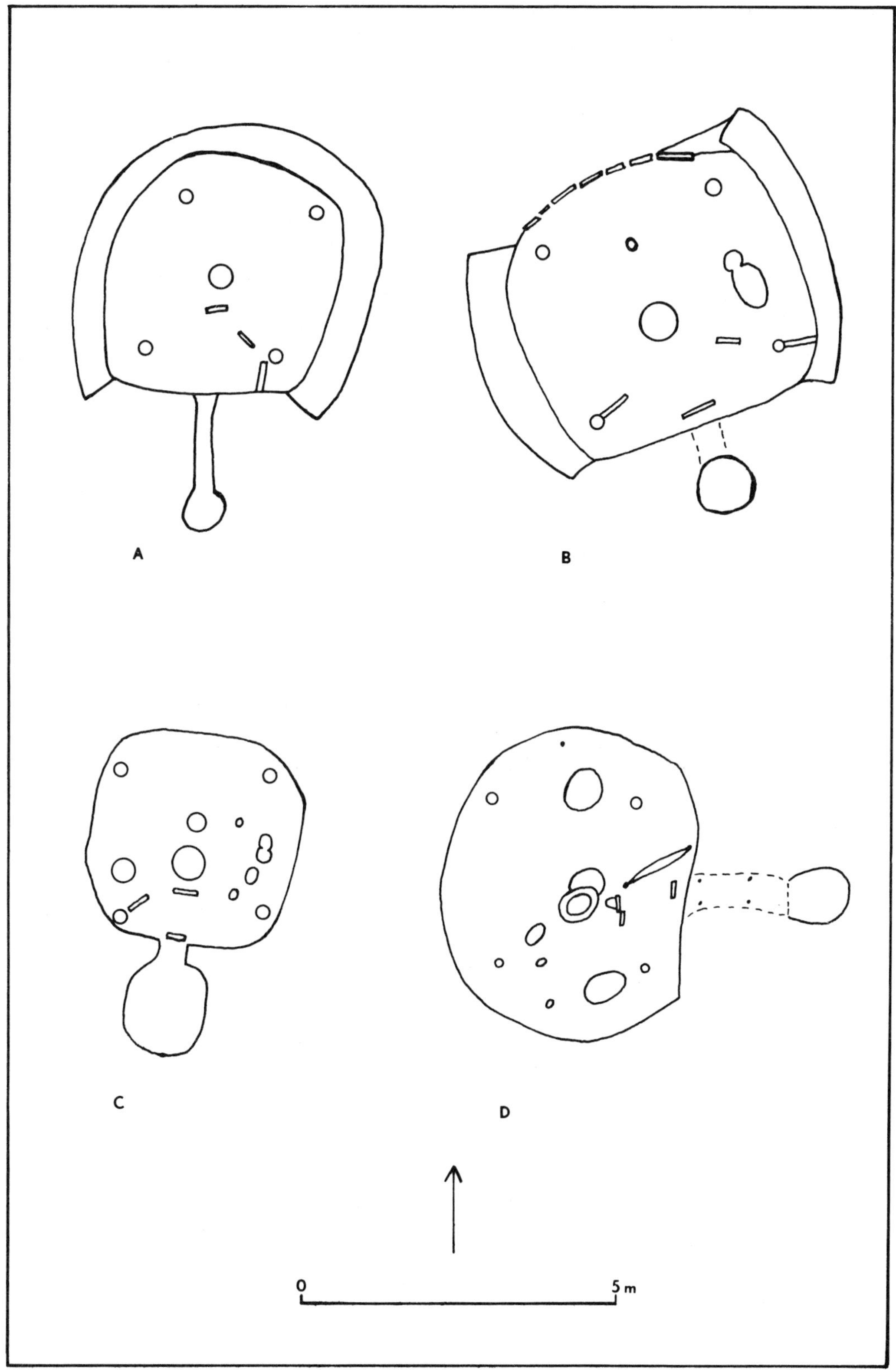

Figure 8. Basketmaker III pithouses from Mesa Verde and Cerro Colorado: A, Structure 405, Cerro Colorado (Bullard 1962); B, Second Pithouse, Twin Trees Site (Mesa Verde) (Lancaster and Watson 1954); C, Site 1060 (Mesa Verde) (Hayes and Lancaster 1962); D, Structure 103, Cerro Colorado (Bullard 1962).

living area and (2) a small compartment between the entryway, or ventilator tunnel, and the firepit. In only two cases (Structures 205 and 402) was the partition wall continuous (or nearly so) across the entire structure. Partitions were more frequently short free-standing walls or walls that abutted the pit edge at only one end. Construction methods included upright slabs set in a floor slot, upright slabs set in an adobe ridge, jacal, and unreinforced adobe.

Storage bins were of similar construction and were frequently attached to pit walls, partition walls, or main support posts.

Floor cists were basin-shaped, straight-sided, or bell-shaped excavations. They ranged from circular to oval in plan and were all less than a meter in diameter.

Six of the houses had one or more "heating pits" excavated into the main floor area. These were oval pits ranging from 0.75 to 1.0 m on the long axis and averaging 0.5 m on the short axis. The pits were filled with heat-cracked rocks.

Another six of these houses had deflector slabs set between the ventilator/entryway and the firepit. In two cases these slabs were incorporated in the lateral partition wall.

Entryway/antechamber: Three of the houses (Pithouses 2, 3, and 5) lacked both antechambers and vent shafts and had no discernible means of entry. These were presumably entered through the roof. The rest of the structures had either trenched entryways, trenched entryways connecting the main portion of the structure to an antechamber, or a ventilator shaft and tunnel.

The two well-preserved antechambers were D-shaped (Structure 205) or roughly oval (Structure 402) in shape. The D-shaped example was 4.0 m long and 3.1 m wide. The corresponding measurements for the oval example are 1.8 m and 1.5 m.

Entryways were, with one exception, unmodified trenches ranging in length from 1.5 to 2.6 m and in width from 0.6 to 1.0 m. The one exception falls within this size range but was lined with small support posts.

The vertical ventilator shafts were circular in plan and ranged from 0.7 to 1.1 m in diameter. The associated horizontal ventilator tunnels were from 0.3 to 0.6 m wide and 1.0 to 1.9 m long. These are not true "tunnels" but covered trenches. The only tunneled ventilator complex at the site occurred in Structure 201B, a late Pueblo II house.

Benches: Four of the houses had benches. The bench in Pithouse 2 was a fairly amorphous feature consisting of an unexcavated portion of the local bedrock. The three remaining examples were well-defined three-quarter benches. Two of these (Structures 203 and 402) had small postholes closely spaced along their peripheries. Benches varied in width from 0.5 to 1.2 m and in height from 0.65 to 0.75 m. The wall below the bench in Structure 402 was faced with upright slabs. The others were unmodified.

COMMENTS. Both Anasazi gray wares and Mogollon brown wares are associated with these structures. The former predominates, making up 90–95% of the ceramic complex. Anasazi types include Lino Gray, Lino Smudged, Lino Fugitive Red, and La Plata Black-on-white. Principal brown ware types are Alma Plain, Alma Smudged, and San Francisco Red.

Sites on Mesa Verde

The Mesa Verde in southwestern Colorado was apparently unoccupied until the onset of Basketmaker III settlement at the beginning of the seventh century A.D. (Hayes 1964). Nine excavated sites on Chapin Mesa and seven on Wetherill Mesa have been tree-ring dated between A.D. 600 and 700. Unfortunately, only eight of these have been adequately reported. The University of Colorado initiated an extensive program of excavation in 1970. This included the excavation of five well-dated seventh-century sites on Wetherill Mesa. Publication of these data will contribute significantly to knowledge of Basketmaker III architecture in the region.

The eight reported sites were excavated between 1932 and 1963 and include Mesa Verde Pithouses B and C (Lancaster and Watson 1943), Mesa Verde Pithouse No. 1 (Smiley 1949), Site 145 (O'Bryan 1950), the Twin Trees Site (Lancaster and Watson 1954), Site 1060 (Hayes and Lancaster 1962, 1968), and Sites 1644 and 1676 (Hayes and Lancaster 1975).

CHRONOLOGY. The tree-ring data for these sites are presented in Table 21.

TABLE 21
Tree-Ring Dates for Seventh-Century Mesa Verde Sites

Provenience	Date	Lab Number
Mesa Verde Pithouse B	526+vv	GP-5505
	538vv	GP-5494
	541vv	GP-5478
	543++vv	GP-5562
	566+vv	GP-5481
	570vv	GP-5495
	572+vv	GP-5508
	580+r	GP-5493
	583vv	GP-5491
	589vv	GP-5477
	595r	GP-5479
Mesa Verde Pithouse C	437++vv	GP-3601
	520vv	GP-5511
	531vv	GP-5517
	547vv	MV-233-1
	551vv	MV-235
	556vv	MV-180
	557vv	MV-233
	571vv	GP-3602
	574vv	MV-180-1
	582vv	GP-5513
	587vv	GP-5510
	587vv	GP-3608
	597vv	MV-236
	600r	MV-180-2
	608vv	GP-5515
	628vv	GP-3599
Site 1644		
Pithouse A	641vv	MV-1828
	648vv	MV-1833
	649vv	MV-1824
Pithouse B	622vv	MV-1868
	623vv	MV-1873
	626vv	MV-1880
	628vv	MV-1889
	630vv	MV-1871
	630vv	MV-1885
	630vv	MV-1897
	632vv	MV-1892
	635+vv	MV-1893
	636vv	MV-1882
	638vv	MV-1867
	643vv	MV-1886
	645vv	MV-1887

TABLE 21 (continued)

Provenience	Date	Lab Number
Pithouse B (continued)	645vv	MV-1891
	649vv	MV-1874
	649vv	MV-1884
	650vv	MV-1848
	650vv	MV-1888
	667vv	MV-1856
Site 1676		
Pithouse G	556vv	MV-2329
	567+vv	MV-2317
	581+vv	MV-2323
	581vv	MV-2326
	613vv	MV-2320
	631vv	MV-2319
Site 145		
Pithouse 1	521vv	GP-6884
	532	GP-6867
	537vv	GP-6873
	560vv	GP-6874
	562vv	GP-6880
	571++vv	GP-6876
	577++vv	GP-6869
	579vv	GP-6883
	580+vv	GP-6866
	582vv	GP-6865
	587vv	GP-6868
	595vv	GP-6877
	606r	GP-6870
	618r	GP-6871
	623vv	GP-6864
	630vv	GP-6879
Pithouse 2	355vv	GP-6895
	588+vv	GP-6921
	589vv	GP-6889
	590++vv	GP-6933
	598vv	GP-6936
	598vv	GP-6930
	618vv	GP-6887
	628vv	GP-6927
	631vv	GP-6896
	641++vv	GP-6942
	641vv	GP-6913
	642vv	GP-6925
	642vv	GP-6886
	653vv	GP-6897
	654vv	GP-6910

TABLE 21 (continued)

Provenience	Date	Lab Number
Pithouse 2 (continued)	655vv	GP-6920
	655vv	GP-6929
	657vv	GP-6898
	658vv	GP-6904
	659vv	GP-6916
	660vv	GP-6935
	660vv	GP-6885
	661vv	GP-6030
	662vv	GP-6902
	662r	GP-6909
	663vv	GP-6912
	663r	GP-6907
	663r	GP-6931
	663r	GP-6937
	663r	GP-6928
	663rB	GP-6888
	665r	GP-6894
Twin Trees Site		
First Pithouse	574vv	MV-486
	583vv	MV-487
	627vv	MV-489
	656vv	MV-488
	673vv	MV-491
	674vv	MV-4861
	674vv	MV-493
	674r	MV-490
Mesa Verde Pithouse No. 1	609+vv	GP-4944
	650vv	GP-4959
	657vv	MVPH-39-1
	673vv	MVPH-39-9
	679vv	MVPH-39-3
	683vv	MVPH-39-4
	687vv	MVPH-39-5
	688vv	GP-4957
	689vv	MV-437
	689vv	GP-4967
	691vv	GP-4981
	691vv	GP-4953
	692vv	MVPH-39-7
	692vv	GP-4972
	695vv	GP-4962
	696vv	GP-4978
	697vv	GP-4987
	697vv	GP-4984
	698vv	GP-4954
	700vv	GP-4963

TABLE 21 (continued)

Provenience	Date	Lab Number
Mesa Verde Pithouse No. 1 (continued)	700v	GP-4969
	700r	GP-4964
	700r	GP-4950
	700r	GP-4982
	700r	GP-4971
	700r	GP-4983
	700r	GP-4960
	700r	GP-4970
	700r	GP-4976
	700r	MV-440
	833vv	GP-4956
	858vv	MVPH-39-8
	859vv	GP-4947
	862r	GP-4946
	864vv	MVPH-39-10
	864vv	MVPH-39-6
Site 1060 Pithouse	544vv	MV-1008
	562+vv	MV-1002A
	575vv	MV-1002B
	579vv	MV-1007A,B
	586vv	MV-1009A,B
	587vv	MV-1002C
	608vv	MV-1006A,B

Source: Robinson and Harrill 1974; Hayes and Lancaster 1975

From Table 21 it may be inferred that Mesa Verde Pithouses B and C and Pithouse 1 at Site 145 were among the earliest houses built on Mesa Verde, with construction dates ranging from A.D. 600 to 630. Pithouse 2 at Site 145, First Pithouse at the Twin Trees Site, and Mesa Verde Pithouse No. 1 form a well-dated sequence from A.D. 662 through A.D. 700. The data for the remaining structures are inconclusive but suggest construction in the mid- to late seventh century.

ARCHITECTURE. Seventh-century pithouses on Mesa Verde are similar in form and show little significant change through time. Selected examples are depicted in Figures 7 and 8.

Shape and size: House shapes intergraded from rectangular with rounded corners to D-shaped. Sizes ranged from 3.9 m east-west by 4.2 m north-south for Pithouse 1 at Site 145 to 7.8 m east-west by 7.3 m north-south for Pithouse B at Site 1644. Means were 5.8 m east-west and 5.2 m north-south.

Depth: All of these structures were true pithouses with depths ranging from 0.7 to 1.7 m. Mean depth was 1.2 m.

Floors: Five of the houses had plastered clay floors. One had a layer of hard-packed sterile sand. The remaining four were unprepared beyond packing through use.

Firepits: Firepits were circular in plan and basin shaped in profile. Diameters ranged from 0.6 to 1.0 m. Five examples had raised adobe collars, four were unlined, and one was lined with upright slabs.

Other floor features: Additional features included postholes, partitions, storage bins, floor cists, wall cists, and deflectors.

With one exception, all structures had four main support posts forming a rectangular pattern. The two posts in the southern end of the structures were frequently incorporated in the partition walls. Pithouse 1 at Site 145 (O'Bryan 1950) had a single main support post located in the approximate center of the floor area.

Partition walls were generally constructed from east to west across the southern portion of the floor area. They were built of upright slabs, either set in the floor or in a low ridge of adobe. In no case did the partition form a continuous wall. Rather, it consisted of two separate partitions attached to opposite pit walls and in line with the firepit. This configuration left an open passage from the entryway to the main portion of the pithouse living area.

Storage bins were also constructed of upright slabs. Bins were normally incorporated in the partition and were either triangular or quadrilateral in plan. They were in all cases located adjacent to the pithouse walls.

Floor cists were basin-shaped, straight-sided, or bell-shaped excavations. All were roughly circular in plan and less than 1.0 m in diameter. The larger cists were apparently used as storage chambers. A special class of smaller cists interpreted as "sipapus" occurred in six of the houses. These are located immediately north of the firepit and are 15 to 20 cm in diameter and 20 to 30 cm deep.

Wall cists or storage niches occurred in only four houses: Mesa Verde Pithouses B and C (Lancaster and Watson 1943), and Pithouses 1 and 2 at Site 145 (O'Bryan 1950). These were small, irregularly shaped chambers dug into the pithouse walls above floor level.

Six of the houses had deflector slabs set in the floor between the entryway and the firepit.

Entryway/antechamber: All but one of the structures had an antechamber to the south of the main living room. These ranged from rectangular with rounded corners to oval in shape. Sizes ranged from 1.9 to 3.9 m long and from 1.0 to 2.9 m wide. Five of the antechambers had four main support posts, two had two support posts, and the remainder had none.

The antechambers were connected to the main structures by short passageways. At Site 1060 the passageway was lined with upright slabs. However, at the rest of the houses it was simply an unlined trench cut into sterile earth.

The one structure without an antechamber was Second Pithouse at the Twin Trees Site. It had a ventilator tunnel and shaft complex located at the south end of the structure. The shaft was circular in plan and approximately 1.0 m in diameter. It intersected the horizontal tunnel at right angles.

Bench: Seven of the structures had a three-quarter bench. Four of these contained closely spaced peripheral postholes. The pithouse at Site 1060 had a full bench, while Mesa Verde Pithouse B lacked a bench. Height above floor level varied from 20 to 70 cm. Width varied from 20 cm to 1.0 m.

Superstructure: A four-post rectangular framework with leaner posts for the side walls is the most reasonable reconstruction. The leaner poles were probably footed either at the intersection of the bench surface and the native earth pit walls or in postholes excavated into the bench surface. These were then covered with brush and adobe.

COMMENTS. This group is perhaps the most homogeneous class of houses considered in the present study. No pattern of change through time is apparent even though the examples were constructed over a 100-year period.

Jeddito 264

Jeddito 264 was excavated in the late 1930s by representatives of the Peabody Museum as one aspect of the extensive Awatovi Project, which was under the general directorship of J. O. Brew. Jeddito 264 was excavated by Richard B. Woodbury and written up many years later by Hiroshi Daifuku (1961), who used these data as the basis of his doctoral dissertation.

The site is located on Antelope Mesa near Keams Canyon, Arizona. It consists of 7 pithouses, 26 slab-lined storage chambers, 1 rectangular room, and 6 outdoor firepits. Only three of the pithouses are considered in this analysis. The remaining four, while similar in many ways, date well into the eighth century A.D. and represent a reoccupation at the site.

CHRONOLOGY. The maximum range of cutting dates from Pithouse B is A.D. 672 to 692 with a clustering and, hence, probable building date at A.D. 690. Cutting dates for Pithouse F range from A.D. 666 to 685 with a strong cluster at A.D. 684–685. No dates were ever run for the structurally similar Pithouse C. (See Table 22.)

TABLE 22
Tree-Ring Dates from
the Early Component of Jeddito 264

Provenience	Date	Lab Number
Pithouse B	672r	L-2281-6
	675r	L-2283
	690r	L-2275-1
	690r	L-2276
	690c	L-3378
	692r	L-2275-2
Pithouse F	661vv	L-2251
	666r	L-2250
	667c	L-2258
	670r	L-2257
	670r	L-2330
	671vv	L-2340
	672r	L-2253
	675v	L-2334
	675r	L-2259
	676r	L-2332
	684vv	L-2269
	684vv	L-2339
	684v	L-2328
	685vv	L-2329
	685v	L-2338
	685v	L-2335
	685r	L-2266
	685r	L-2333
	689v	L-2337

Source: Bannister, Robinson, and Warren, 1967

ARCHITECTURE. On the basis of ceramic associations, Pithouse C is considered roughly contemporaneous with the two dated structures; it will, therefore, be included in the architectural summary that follows (Figure 9). All information has been abstracted from Daifuku's site report (1961).

Shape and size: All three structures were circular with diameters ranging from 5.28 to 5.68 m (bench included).

Depth: All three structures are true pithouses with depths ranging from 0.8 to 1.0 m. Pithouse F was excavated into sandstone bedrock.

Floors: Floors consisted of unaltered bedrock, clay plaster over bedrock, or unaltered native earth.

Firepits: All three examples were circular with a raised adobe collar. Each had a second adobe-rimmed depression, or "ashpit," adjacent to the firepit on the east side. Firepits averaged 50 to 65 cm in diameter. The encircling adobe collars were 10 to 12 cm in width and 8 to 10 cm high.

Other floor features: All three structures had clay ridges radiating from the firepit to the floor edge. These divided the house floor into two sections—a western and a somewhat smaller eastern section. Pithouse C had a floor slot carved in the sandstone bedrock in the eastern section. This was located between the firepit and the entryway and presumably supported an upright deflector slab. No evidence of deflector slabs was found in the other two structures.

Two types of posthole patterns were in evidence. Pithouse F had twelve postholes evenly spaced around the outer edge of the floor area. Pithouse B probably had a similar configuration, but much of the floor area was obliterated by later construction and erosion. Pithouse C had four postholes symmetrically placed to form a rectangle. Two of these were adjacent to the adobe ridges radiating from the firepit in the eastern portion of the structure.

The structures were otherwise devoid of floor features except for haphazardly placed postholes that may have contained ancillary roof support posts.

Entryway/antechamber: Pithouses B and C had lateral entryways located on the east sides of the structures. Their floors were level and cut to the same depth as the main house floors. The Pithouse B entryway was 2.6 m long and 60 cm wide. The Pithouse C entryway was 3.0 m long and 65 cm wide. Pithouse F had no lateral entryway.

Bench: All three pithouses had an encircling bench. Height above floor level varied from 40 to 60 cm; width varied from 40 to 70 cm. The walls below the benches were plastered with adobe.

Superstructures: Pithouse C had four main

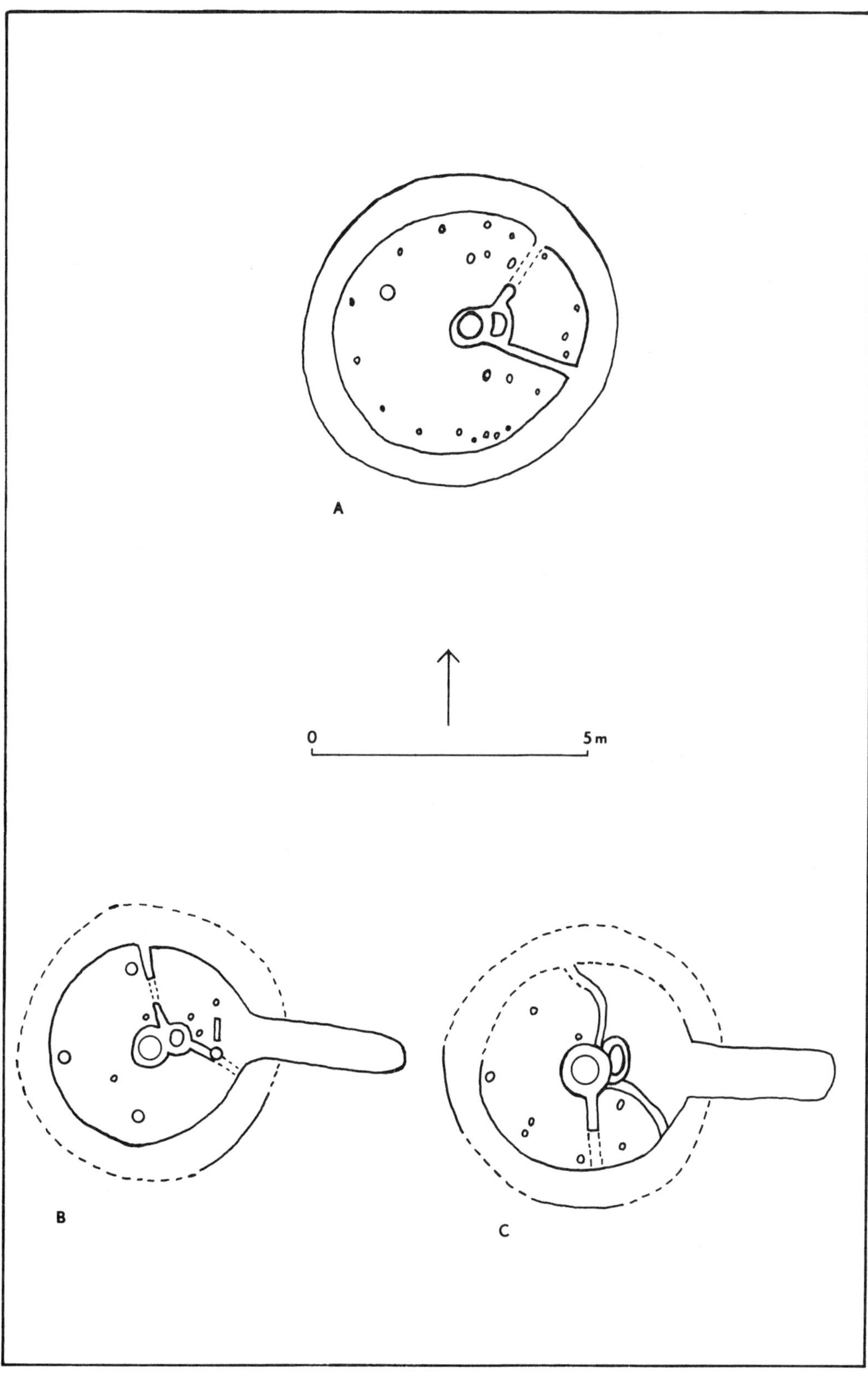

Figure 9. Pithouses from Jeddito 264: A, Pithouse F; B, Pithouse C; C, Pithouse B (Daifuku 1961).

support posts, which indicates a rectangular central framework with side walls composed of leaner poles whose butts were anchored in the bench. Daifuku (1961:21) suggests that Pithouses B and F had conical or truncated-conical superstructures.

COMMENTS. The ceramic complex for the three pithouses is classic Basketmaker III. Lino Gray predominates, making up more than 90% of the assemblages. Decorated types include Lino Fugitive Red, Lino Smudged, Tallahogan Red, and three sherds of Kana-a Black-on-white, which were apparently intrusive from the later occupation at the site. Also present were a few sherds of an unidentified brown ware.

Discussion

Figure 10 is a graphic summary of the chronological interpretations offered above. The dating ranges of individual structures, sites, or site clusters upon which Figure 10 is based are given in Table 23. The order of presentation in Table 23 corresponds to the left-to-right ordering of the symbols in Figure 10.

Wherever possible an attempt has been made to depict each structure individually rather than grouping all houses from a site or region under a single heading with a composite temporal range. While this ideal circumstance was realized in most instances, the empirical situation in a few cases necessitated averaging of several dates from different structures within a site or site cluster. For example, all of the structures from the Little Jug Site are assigned the same temporal placement based on the weighted mean of radiocarbon dates from six different architectural proveniences because the relationship between the

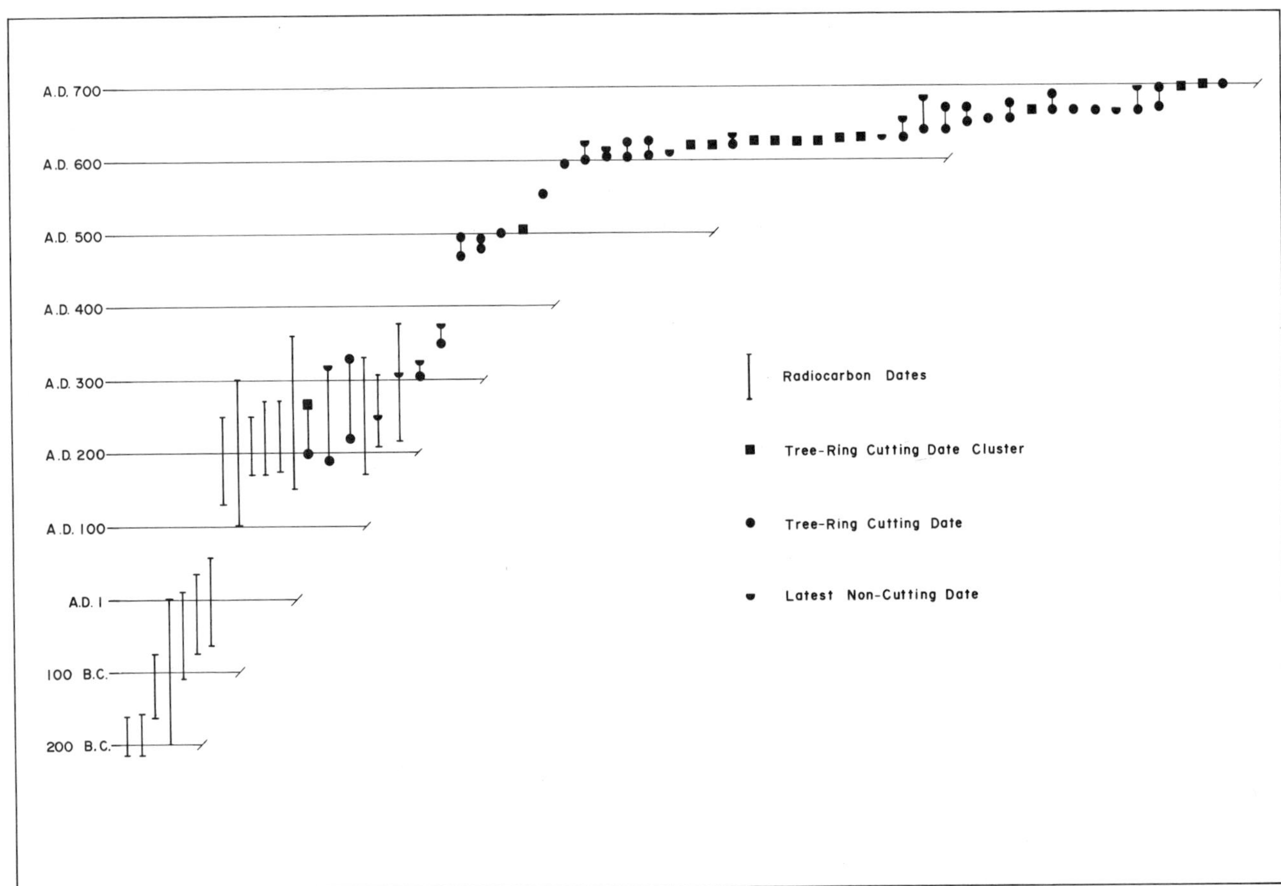

Figure 10. Graphic depiction of radiocarbon and tree-ring dated structures prior to A.D. 700.

TABLE 23
Summary of Dated Structures, Sites, and Regions Prior to A.D. 700

Provenience	Date	Dating Method
AZ D:7:152; pithouse	186±27 B.C.	C-14
NA14,646; pithouse	185±31	C-14
Zero Plaza; pithouse	100±120	C-14
County Road Site; Pithouse B	70±95	C-14
Hay Hollow Site; House 17	48±60	C-14
Hay Hollow Site; House 32	22±55	C-14
Hay Hollow Site; House 25	3±61	C-14
Hay Hollow Site; House 13	A.D. 191±60	C-14
Petri Site; pithouse	200±100	C-14
Little Jug Site	208±39	C-14
Navajo Reservoir District	220±51	C-14
Tumbleweed Canyon; pithouse	225±50	C-14
Connie Site; pithouse	255±105	C-14
Falls Creek Area; North Shelter	200 to 270	Tree-Ring
Talus Village	190 to 330	Tree-Ring
Falls Creek Area; South Shelter	217 to 337	Tree-Ring
Lone Tree Dune; pithouse	250±80	C-14
Pittman Site; pithouse	255±49	C-14 and Tree-Ring
Veres Site; pithouse	295±80	C-14 and Tree-Ring
Bluff Site; House 5	300 to 320	Tree-Ring
Ignacio 12:46; Floor 1	356 to 370	Tree-Ring
Broken Flute Cave; Room 8A	469 to 494	Tree-Ring
Obelisk Cave	478 to 489	Tree-Ring
Broken Flute Cave; Room 2	499	Tree-Ring
Broken Flute Cave; Room 1	501 to 508	Tree-Ring
NA8163; pithouse(?)	555	Tree-Ring
Mesa Verde; Pithouse B	595	Tree-Ring
Mesa Verde; Pithouse C	600 to 628	Tree-Ring
Twin Lakes Site; Pithouse 1	605 to 611	Tree-Ring
Cerro Colorado; Pithouse 3	604 to 626	Tree-Ring
Mesa Verde Site 145; Pithouse 1	606 to 630	Tree-Ring

TABLE 23 (continued)

Provenience	Date	Dating Method
Mesa Verde Site 1060; pithouse	608	Tree-Ring
Twin Lakes Site; Pithouse 5	619 to 623	Tree-Ring
Broken Flute Cave; Room 12	621 to 623	Tree-Ring
Broken Flute Cave; Room 6	622 to 627	Tree-Ring
Broken Flute Cave; Room 7	623 to 626	Tree-Ring
Broken Flute Cave; Room 9	623 to 624	Tree-Ring
Broken Flute Cave; Room 8	625 to 627	Tree-Ring
Broken Flute Cave; Room 11	621 to 635	Tree-Ring
Broken Flute Cave; Room 5	629	Tree-Ring
Cerro Colorado; Pithouse 4	630 to 637	Tree-Ring
Mesa Verde Site 1676; Pithouse G	631	Tree-Ring
Cerro Colorado; Structure 208	631 to 653	Tree-Ring
Cerro Colorado; Structure 405	646 to 687	Tree-Ring
Cerro Colorado; Structure 402	658 to 669	Tree-Ring
Cerro Colorado; Structure 104	650 to 668	Tree-Ring
Red Rock District; Cave 1, Pithouse 3	658	Tree-Ring
Red Rock District; Cave 2, Room 1	626 to 669	Tree-Ring
Red Rock District; Cave 2, Room 2	667 to 676	Tree-Ring
Red Rock District; Cave 2, Room 4	655 to 670	Tree-Ring
Mesa Verde Site 145; Pithouse 2	662 to 665	Tree-Ring
Jeddito Site 264; Pithouse F	666 to 689	Tree-Ring
Jeddito Site 264; Pithouse B	672 to 692	Tree-Ring
Cerro Colorado; Structure 103	665	Tree-Ring
Cerro Colorado; Structure 205	666	Tree-Ring
1664; Mesa Verde Site Pithouses A and B	667	Tree-Ring
Cerro Colorado; Structure 203	664 to 691	Tree-Ring
Mesa Verde; Twin Trees Site, First Pithouse	674	Tree-Ring
Cerro Colorado; Structure 101	695	Tree-Ring
Mesa Verde Pithouse No. 1	700	Tree-Ring
NA8166; Pithouse 1	703	Tree-Ring

published provenience data and the architectural/stratigraphic context was not entirely clear. In another case, the bracketing dates of the Los Pinos phase of the Navajo Reservoir District had to be based on the weighted mean of six dates from four sites. However, it must be stressed that this sort of approach was never undertaken unless the group(s) of dates in question were statistically contemporaneous. Hence, there is no chance that any fictitious dates—as might be produced by the averaging of widely disparate values—have been incorporated in the resultant temporal pattern.

As shown in Figure 10, the transition from radiocarbon to tree-ring dating is centered between A.D. 200 and 300. This occurs within a relatively tight cluster of dated phenomena attributable (primarily) to the classic Basketmaker II stage. The fact that the radiocarbon evidence closely approximates the range of tree-ring dated structures for this period tends to support the use of uncorrected radiocarbon dates as the simulation in Chapter 2 suggested.

It seems reasonable to assume that the three discrete temporal clusters depicted in Figure 10 represent something much more interesting than sampling error. The sample is more properly described as haphazard than random, but there is no compelling reason to suspect systematic error. If this can be accepted as a working assumption, then the evidence suggests that occupation occurred in three discrete periods, each separated in time by significant hiatuses. A brief, geographically limited construction event, which occurred midway between the second and third periods, constitutes the only exception to the general pattern.

PERIOD I: 185 B.C. TO A.D. 1. Sites in this period have been classified as either "late" Archaic or Basketmaker II by the original investigators. However, following the arguments offered in Chapter 3, Period I sites coincide with the introduction of maize farming to the Plateau and appear to be unrelated to earlier indigenous Archaic hunter-gatherer populations. Therefore, use of the term "Archaic" in reference to Period I sites would be misleading. It is tempting to refer to this grouping of sites as Basketmaker I—a stage whose existence was predicted by the original formulators of the Pecos Classification—but this would probably lead to confusion since Basketmaker I has, in common usage, come to be equated with late Archaic (J. D. Jennings 1974). As a compromise solution, Period I sites are classified as "early" Basketmaker II. This serves to delineate the cultural content of this temporal cluster from the nonagricultural Archaic, as well as partitioning it off from the succeeding Period II sites, which are termed "late" or "classic" Basketmaker II.

The period is represented by seven dated structures. Two of these, Ariz D:7:152 and NA14,646, are the earliest well-dated houses in the Southwest. Claims of earlier temporal proveniences for structures associated with Wheat's (1955) Mogollon I, the Vahki phase of the Hohokam sequence (Haury 1976), and the San Pedro stage of the Cochise culture are not well substantiated. For instance, Wheat's placement of the beginning of Mogollon I at 300 B.C. (Wheat 1955) is based solely on the radiocarbon dates for the earliest maize from Tularosa Cave. This maize is thought to be associated with Mogollon I ceramics, but since Tularosa Cave was excavated in arbitrary levels (Martin et al. 1952; Bullard 1962), and the radiocarbon dates were determined using the solid carbon method (see Chapter 3), little certainty attaches to this purported association. Actually, the earliest Mogollon *structure* is House 5 at the Bluff Site (Haury and Sayles 1947) with a fairly convincing cluster of dates at A.D. 300–320. Fitting, Anderson, and Klinger (1972; Fitting 1973) report that Mogollon pithouses in southwestern New Mexico may date somewhat earlier, but the radiocarbon evidence is equivocal (Yamasaki, Hamada, and Hamada 1977).

Similarly, Haury's (1976) estimate of 300 B.C. for the beginning of the Vahki phase is based on very scant and questionable data. Haury rejects Haynes and Long's (1976) conclusion (which was based entirely on the radiocarbon evidence) that Snaketown was first occupied no earlier than A.D. 1, preferring instead to accept the archeomagnetic dates from presumed Vahki phase contexts. However, as Haury notes, the archeomagnetic dates are subject to an alternative interpretation (Haury 1976:332) that would move the 300 B.C. estimate forward in time to approximately A.D.

400. This is consistent with the nine Snaketown radiocarbon dates from Vahki, "Early Pioneer," and "Transition" contexts, which range from A.D. 60 to 850 (a tenth date of 425 B.C. was rejected by Haynes and Long [1976] as clearly aberrant). It is also in general agreement with Plog's (1978), Wilcox's (1979), and C. Berry's (Berry and Marmaduke 1980) reassessments of the Snaketown chronology.

Finally, a number of pit features thought to be associated with the San Pedro stage have been interpreted as houses; however, the published descriptions of these features (Sayles and Antevs 1941; Eddy 1958) leave considerable doubt that they were actually used as pithouses. It seems more likely that they were storage structures of some type.

Besides being the earliest known Southwestern houses, AZ D:7:152 and NA14,646 provide the earliest evidence of maize farming on the Colorado Plateau (J. Ware personal communication, 1977; W. Marmaduke personal communication, 1978). Four of the five remaining structures in Period I—i.e., the County Road Site pithouse and Houses 17, 25, and 32 at the Hay Hollow Site—also yielded maize macrofossils (P. R. Nelson 1964; Paul Sidney Martin 1967, 1972; Martin and Plog 1973; Fritz 1974).

Both AZ D:7:152 and NA14,646 lacked ceramics. The uncertainties of ceramic associations at the County Road and Hay Hollow sites have been discussed earlier in this chapter. Suffice it to say that ceramic technology *may* be earlier than A.D. 1 in the Hay Hollow Valley. The problem is that pottery is certainly associated with the poorly dated County Road Site and uncertainly associated with the well-dated Hay Hollow Site. In the latter case, the ceramics *may* be associated with both the early (ca. 50 B.C.) and the most recent (ca. A.D. 200) components of the site. But since Fritz (1974) neither discusses the possibility of two components at the site nor provides provenience charts, the question remains open.

PERIOD II: A.D. 200 TO 370. Following the end of Period I, or early Basketmaker II, there is a break in the record of dated structures of approximately two centuries. Period II, or classic Basketmaker II, begins slightly before A.D. 200 and lasts until A.D. 370. Included are three structures from the Hay Hollow Valley (i.e., the late component from the Hay Hollow Site, the Petri Site, and the Connie Site), all Los Pinos phase sites from the Navajo Reservoir District, the four sites from the Durango area (i.e., North Shelter, South Shelter, Talus Village, and Ignacio 12:46), three structures from southeastern Utah (i.e., the pithouses at Lone Tree Dune, the Pittman Site, and the Veres Site), all of the structures at the Little Jug Site, a single house from the Tumbleweed Canyon Site, and House 5 at the Bluff Site. Of interest is the fact that some of these structures contain pottery while others do not. In particular, the four Durango sites, the three sites from southeastern Utah, and the Tumbleweed Canyon pithouse lacked ceramics, while the remaining sites and individual structures are positively associated with pottery technology. Even the most recent summaries of Southwestern prehistory employ absence of ceramics as one of the prime diagnostics of the Basketmaker II stage (Rohn 1977; Lipe 1978). However, since roughly half the known sites from Period II contain ceramics, it is no longer feasible to retain this criterion in the monothetic definition of Basketmaker II.

PERIOD III: A.D. 600 TO 700. Period III equates with Basketmaker III and begins at A.D. 600. The cutoff date of A.D. 700 was somewhat arbitrarily selected, but, as discussed in a subsequent section, it turns out that A.D. 700 marks the beginning of a significant decline in the occupational density of the southern Colorado Plateau and, hence, has a certain degree of empirical reality as a bracketing date for Basketmaker III. The period is represented by 35 dated structures, all of which are associated with plain gray utility vessels and black-on-gray decorated bowls. These sites blanket the Anasazi area, and architecture is surprisingly uniform over the entire region.

The end of classic Basketmaker II and the onset of Basketmaker III are separated in time by over two centuries. The few structures that date to this intervening period are not clearly assignable to either Basketmaker II or Basketmaker III and may represent intermediate forms as the temporal provenience suggests. The sites in question are Obelisk and Broken Flute caves (E. H. Morris 1936; E. A. Morris 1959), and NA8163 (Ambler and Olson 1977), all of which are located in northeastern Arizona. The ceramic assemblages from all three sites consist entirely of undecorated gray wares (Lino Gray and Obelisk Gray).

Discussion

The temporal patterning for the first half of the Anasazi sequence is shown schematically in Figure 11. The results are inconsistent with the currently accepted perspective of *in situ* Anasazi development. Matson and Lipe (1978) recognize a break in the sequence between Basketmaker II and III for the Cedar Mesa area of southeastern Utah, but this sort of interpretation is unusual and runs counter to the general trend. That is, most Southwesternists, even when faced with the same kinds of evidence as Matson and Lipe, assume continuous development from stage to stage within a given area regardless of what the chronometric data indicate. As a consequence, Plateau-wide syntheses based on the cumulation of the chronological interpretations found in site reports tend to incorporate chronological assumptions on an equal footing with chronometric facts. It should be evident that sound *empirical generalizations* cannot be built in this manner. The results of such an approach can be seriously misleading and frequently entail the delineation of "pseudoproblems." A good example is Glassow's (1972) proposed explanation of the transition from Basketmaker II to Basketmaker III as a response to "stress" resulting from a steady increase in population density.

> I argue that population density was increasing through the Early Basketmaker period [Basketmaker II] throughout the San Juan Basin, and that this disequilibrium between population input and output in Early Basketmaker cultural systems eventually caused enough stress on other components to induce a change to Late Basketmaker [Basketmaker III] systems (Glassow 1972:295).

What kind of evidence does Glassow offer in support of increasing population density?

> The available data do indicate that the numbers of sites increased markedly during Late Basketmaker times. This is apparent in the remarks of Morris and Burgh (1954:73) and Gladwin (1957:53) concerning Late Basketmaker sites in the Durango District, and it is also evident in Morris's work in the La Plata District and Herold's summaries of site distribution of Mesa Verde and adjacent regions (1961) (Glassow 1972:300).

Obviously Glassow has relied on the assumptions and interpretations of others rather than the data *per se* and has, as a consequence, set for himself the problem of explaining a series of events that probably never happened. What the data *do* indicate is that there was a strong temporal clustering of Basketmaker II sites separated from an even denser clustering of Basketmaker III sites by a 200-year period, during which the Plateau was very sparsely inhabited. Glassow's increasing population density model is hardly applicable to such a situation.

This is only one of many cases that might be cited. The point is that empirical generalizations must be based upon the inductive summation of data. They cannot be based on the summation of statements that others have made *about* the data. It is not enough to accept on faith the temporal placements proffered by the authors of particular site reports and then use this information to build regional chronologies. It is necessary to assess the chronometric and stratigraphic evidence in detail in order to separate assumption from fact. This has been the primary intent of the arguments and summarizations presented above, and the wholly unexpected nature of the data patterning revealed through the various analyses seems to bear out the utility of the approach.

A.D. 700 to A.D. 1450

The latter half of the Anasazi sequence from Pueblo I through Pueblo IV is—as might be expected—much more complex than the first half. Paradoxically, an analysis of temporal patterning comparable in rigor to that presented in the previous section is a much simpler undertaking. This is due to the very large number of tree-ring dated sites between A.D. 700 and A.D. 1450. As a consequence of large sample size, it is feasible and reasonable to proceed directly to the generation of macro-pattern, thus avoiding the tedious process of site-by-site argumentation. The data base, as mentioned earlier, is found in the highly valuable Quadrangle Series of the Laboratory of Tree-Ring Research (Bannister, Hannah, and Robinson 1966). The approach employed here is the construction of a bar chart of tree-ring dated sites for the Colorado Plateau relying almost wholly on the dates published in the relevant issues of the Quadrangle Series (in a few cases dates determined subsequent to the publication of that series have been incorporated). The chart (Figure 12C) is based entirely on cutting dates; i.e., dates with "v" and "vv" modifiers have been disregarded. For reasons discussed earlier, only dates on architectural features have been included and sites with only a single uncorroborated cutting date have been eliminated from consideration. Sites meeting these criteria are listed, by period, in Table 24.

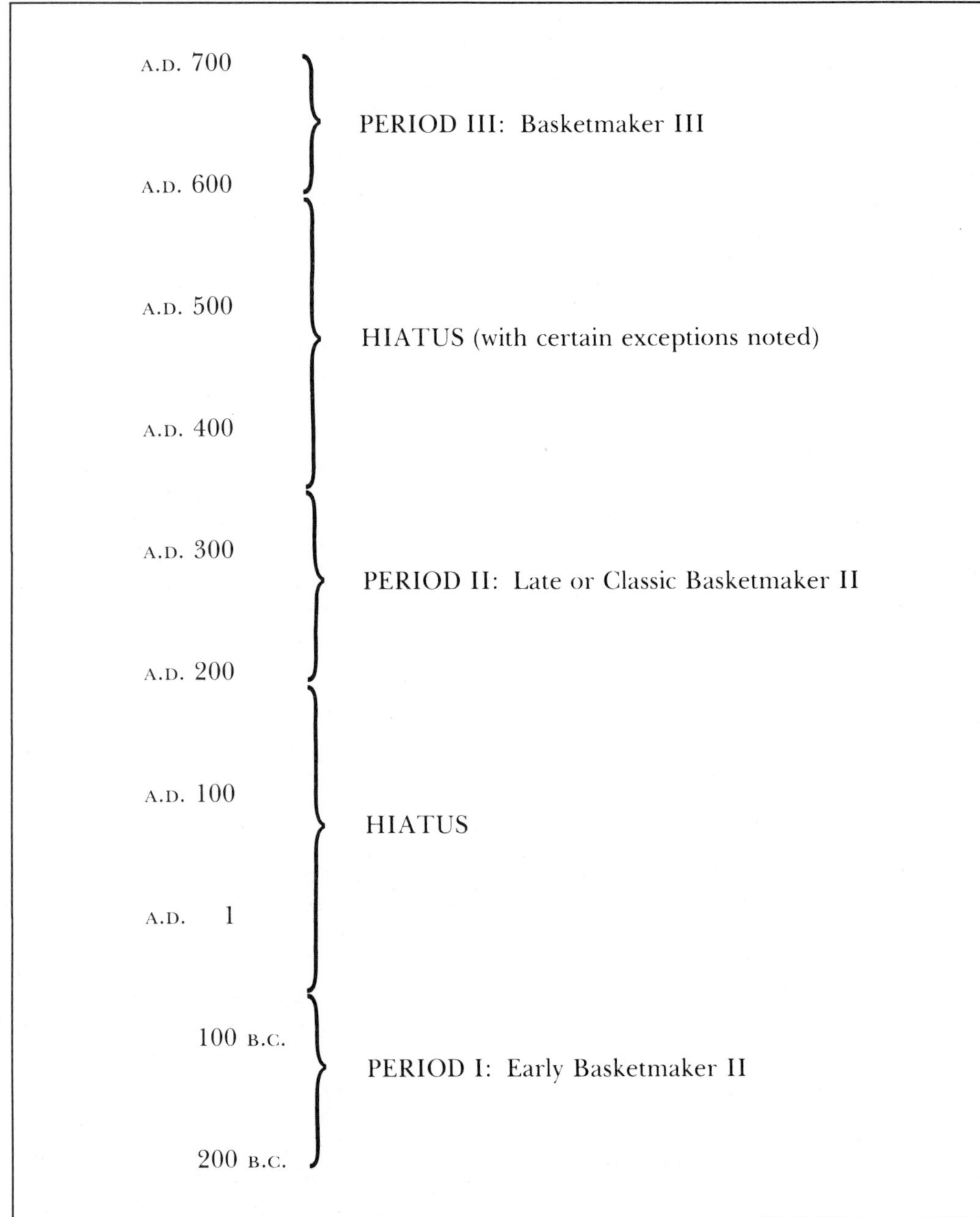

Figure 11. The early Anasazi sequence.

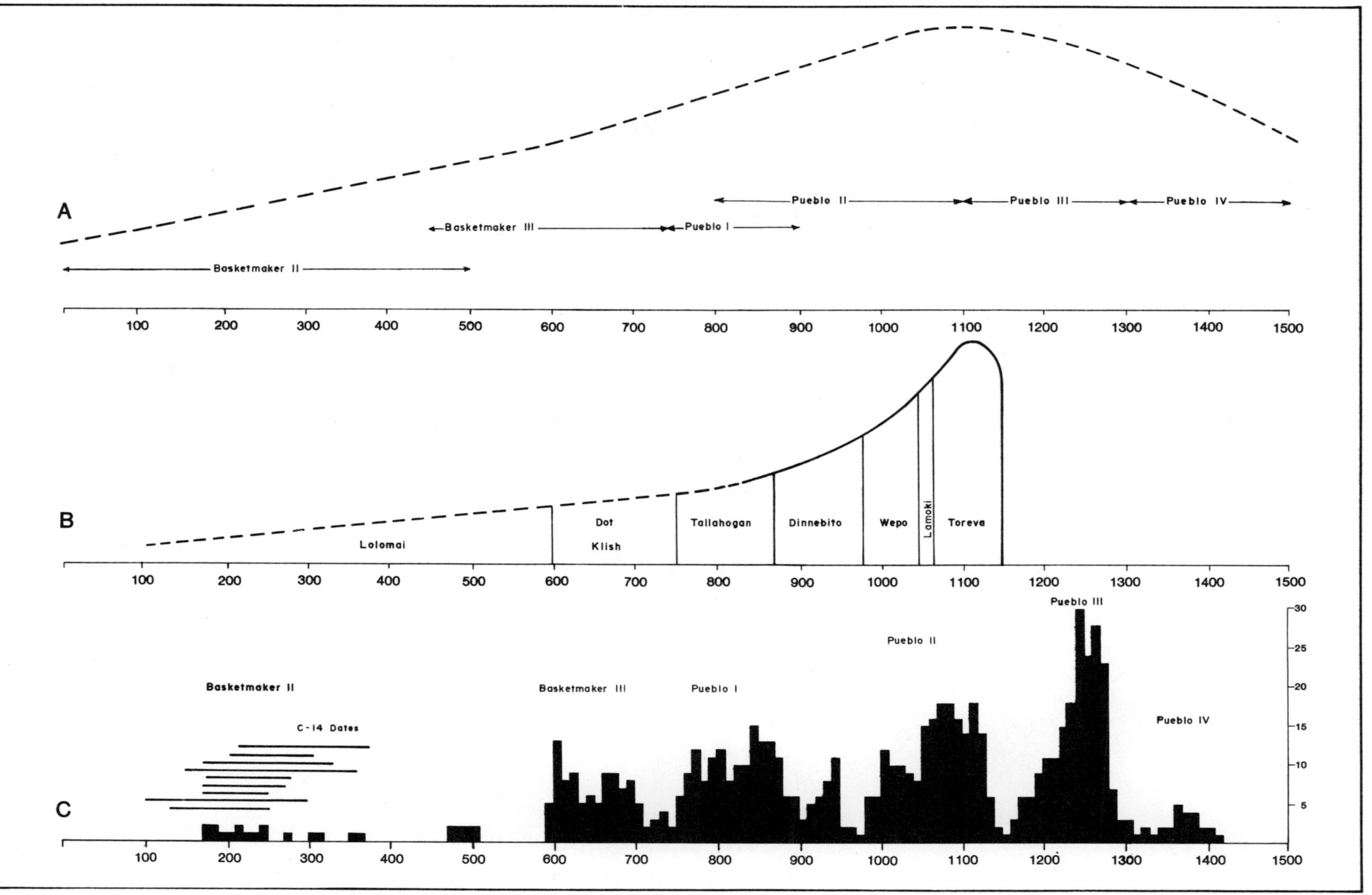

Figure 12. Currently accepted gradualist evolutionary curves of Anasazi prehistory compared to the actual chronometric evidence. A, J. D. Jennings's (1974: 38) curve depicting the rise and decline of Southwestern culture. Superimposed time spans of Pecos Classification stages are from Jennings (1974: 301); B, Gumerman and Euler's (1976) curve depicting population trends on Black Mesa, northeastern Arizona; C, ten-year increment bar chart depicting the number of contemporaneously occupied sites on the southern Colorado Plateau from A.D. 1 to 1450. Tree-ring data from the Laboratory of Tree-Ring Research Quadrangle Series. Radiocarbon dates for Basketmaker II sites based on evidence discussed in Chapter 4.

TABLE 24
Tree-Ring Dated Sites for Stages of the Pecos Classification from Basketmaker III through Pueblo IV

Basketmaker III		
Site	Laboratory of Tree-Ring Research Reference	Descriptive Reference
Cerro Colorado	Bannister, Hannah, and Robinson 1970	Bullard 1962
LA 6988	Bannister, Robinson, and Warren 1970	None
Twin Lakes Site	"	Bullard and Cassidy 1956a; Johnson 1962
Step House	Robinson and Harrill 1974	Hayes 1964
Long House	"	"
Mesa Verde 1990 (NPS)	"	None
Mesa Verde 1940 (NPS)	"	None
Mesa Verde 1824 (NPS)	"	Hayes 1964
Colorado 5 Mt 1	"	Wheat 1955
Mesa Verde Pit Structure No. 2	"	Lancaster 1968
Mesa Verde Pithouse No. 1	"	Smiley 1949
Mesa Verde 145 (GP)	"	O'Bryan 1950
Mesa Verde 1937 (NPS)	"	None
Site 23 (Morris)	"	E. H. Morris 1939
Jeddito Site 264	Bannister, Robinson, and Warren 1967	Daifuku 1961
NA3941A	Bannister, Hannah, and Robinson 1966	None
Ariz K:12:8 (ASM)	"	Wasley 1960
Cave 7 (Red Rock)	Bannister, Dean, and Gell 1966	E. A. Morris 1959
Cave 6 (Red Rock)	"	"
Cave 2 (Red Rock)	"	"
Broken Flute Cave	"	"
Tse-ya-tso Cave	"	A. A. Morris 1933
Mummy Cave	"	E. H. Morris 1938
Twin Caves	"	None
Vandal Cave	"	Haury 1936
Swallow's Nest	Bannister, Dean, and Robinson 1968	Hargrave 1935

Pueblo I		
Site	Laboratory of Tree-Ring Research Reference	Descriptive Reference
Site 17 (Hall)	Robinson, Harrill, and Warren 1974	None
Site 1 (Hall)	"	E. T. Hall 1944
LA 2122	"	"
Bancos Village	"	Eddy 1966
Sambrito Village	"	"
Una Vida	"	Hawley 1934; Hewett 1936
Pueblo Bonito	"	Hawley 1934; Hewett 1936; Judd 1928, 1930, 1954, 1964; Pepper 1920
Peñasco Blanco	"	Hewett 1936
Hungopavi	"	"
LA 4487	Bannister, Robinson, and Warren 1970	None
Kin Bineola	"	Hewett 1936
Bennett's Peak	"	E. A. Morris 1959
NA7512	Bannister, Hannah, and Robinson 1966	None
Houck Group	"	None
Cross Canyon Group	"	Olson 1971
White Mound Village	"	Gladwin 1945
Ariz K:12:10	"	Wasley 1960
Ariz K:12:8	"	"
Allantown	"	Roberts 1939, 1940
Sliding Ruin	Bannister, Dean, and Gell 1966	Mindeleff 1897
Mummy Cave No. 2	"	Gladwin 1948
Church Rock Site	Bannister, Dean, and Robinson 1968	Guernsey 1931; Taylor 1954
NA8800	"	None
NA8300	"	None
Ignacio 7:36	Dean 1975	Carlson 1963
Ignacio 7:31	"	"
Ignacio 7:23	"	"
Falls Creek Rock Shelter	"	Morris and Burgh 1954
Sanchez Site	"	Eddy 1966

TABLE 24 (continued)

Site	Laboratory of Tree-Ring Research Reference	Descriptive Reference
Pueblo I		
Site 1676 (Mesa Verde)	None	Hayes and Lancaster 1975
Slab House	Robinson and Harrill 1974	None
Morfield Canyon Group	"	None
Mesa Verde 107 (GP)	"	Hayes 1964
Mesa Verde 102 (GP)	"	O'Bryan 1950
Mesa Verde 1 (GP)	"	"
Mesa Verde Area	"	None
Far View Group	"	Fewkes 1917, 1922
Mesa Verde 820 (NPS)	"	None
Site 23 (Morris)	"	E. H. Morris 1939
Site 25 (Morris)	"	"
Site 33 (Morris)	"	"
Colorado A:16:190 (GP)	"	None
Ackmen Group	"	Paul Sidney Martin and Rinaldo 1939
Pershing Site	Bannister, Gell, and Hannah 1966	McGregor 1958, 1961
Baker Ranch	Robinson, Harrill, and Warren 1975	Colton 1946; Gladwin 1943
NA5166	"	McGregor 1950, 1951
Pueblo II		
Site	Laboratory of Tree-Ring Research Reference	Descriptive Reference
Cebolleta Mesa LP:2:35-D	Bannister, Hannah, and Robinson 1970	Dittert 1959; Dittert and Ruppe 1951; Ruppe and Dittert 1952
Jewett Gap Site	"	Martin, Rinaldo, and Barter 1957
Cerro Colorado	"	Bullard 1962
Williams Ranch Site	"	Danson 1957
Aztec Ruin	Robinson, Harrill, and Warren 1974	E. H. Morris 1919a, 1921, 1924, 1928; Richert 1964; R. Gordon Vivian 1959
Bc-362	"	None
Una Vida	"	Hawley 1934; Hewett 1936
Tzin Kletzin	"	Hewett 1936
Pueblo del Arroyo	"	Hawley 1934; Hewett 1936; Judd 1959; R. Gordon Vivian 1959

Pueblo Bonito	"	Hawley 1934; Hewett 1936; Judd 1928, 1930, 1954, 1964; Pepper 1920
Peñasco Blanco	"	Hewett 1936
Kin Kletso	"	Hewett 1936; Vivian and Mathews 1965
Hungopavi	"	Hewett 1936
Chetro Ketl	"	Hawley 1934; Hewett 1921, 1936; Vivian and Reiter 1960
Casa Chiquita	"	Hawley 1934; Hewett 1936
Bc-59	"	None
Pueblo Pintado	Bannister, Robinson, and Warren 1970	Hewett 1936
LA6482	"	None
Prairie Dog Pueblo	"	None
LA2701	"	Olson and Wasley 1956
LA2505	"	Bullard and Cassidy 1956b
Kin Ya-a	"	Hewett 1936
Kin Klizhin	"	"
Kin Bineola	"	"
Salmon Ruin	"	Davis 1965; Irwin-Williams 1972
Tocito	"	None
Rattlesnake Point Group	Robinson and Warren 1971	None
LA641	"	None
Houck Group	Bannister, Hannah, and Robinson 1966	None
Cross Canyon Group	"	Olson 1971
Kin Li Chee	"	None
Ariz K:12:6 (ASM)	"	Wasley 1960
Ariz K:12:5 (ASM)	"	"
Allantown	"	Roberts 1939, 1940
Sliding Ruin	Bannister, Dean, and Gell 1966	Mindeleff 1897
Lenaki	Bannister, Dean, and Robinson 1968	Hargrave 1935
Turkey House	"	Guernsey 1931; Hargrave 1935
RB 551	"	Beals, Brainerd, and Smith 1945
Chimney Rock Group	Dean 1975	Jeancon 1922

TABLE 24 (continued)

Pueblo II		
Site	Laboratory of Tree-Ring Research Reference	Descriptive Reference
Two Raven House	Robinson and Harrill 1974	Hayes 1964
Mug House	"	Hayes 1964; Rohn 1971
Mesa Verde 16 (GP)	"	Lancaster and Pinkley 1954
Mesa Verde 1 (GP)	"	O'Bryan 1950
Far View Group	"	Fewkes 1917, 1922
Ewing Site	"	None
Lowry Ruin	"	Paul Sidney Martin, Roys, and von Bonin 1936
Surprise Village	None	M. Berry 1972
Bare Ladder Ruin	Bannister, Dean, and Robinson 1969	Pierson 1957; Steen 1937
Carter Ranch Site	Bannister, Gell, and Hannah 1966	Martin et al. 1964
Wupatki	Robinson, Harrill, and Warren 1975	Colton 1933, 1946; Stanislawski 1963
Winona Village	"	Colton 1946; McGregor 1937, 1941
Ridge Ruin	"	Colton 1946; McGregor 1941
NA1625	"	Colton 1946; Hargrave 1933; C. H. Jennings 1968
NA1238	"	Colton 1946
Medicine Fort	"	Colton 1946; Gladwin 1944
Juniper Terrace Pueblo	"	Colton 1946; Smith 1952
Heiser Springs Pueblo	"	Colton 1946
NA11327	"	None
NA5149	"	McGregor 1951
NA5137	"	"
Pittsberg Village	"	Colton 1946
Red Hill Site	"	McGregor 1951

Pueblo III		
Site	Laboratory of Tree-Ring Research Reference	Descriptive Reference
Cebolleta Mesa LV:4:14-A	Bannister, Hannah, and Robinson 1970	Dittert 1959
Cebolleta Mesa LP:2:25-V	"	Dittert 1959; Dittert and Ruppe 1951; Ruppe and Dittert 1952
Cebolleta Mesa LP:2:24-D	"	Dittert 1959; Ruppe and Dittert 1952

Cebolleta Mesa LP:2:13-A	"	Dittert 1959; Dittert and Ruppe 1951
Site 616, Mariana Mesa	"	McGimsey 1951, 1957
Site 481, Mariana Mesa	"	McGimsey 1951, 1957
Bg-91	Robinson, Harrill, and Warren 1974	Green, Danfelser, and Vivian 1958
Bg-88	"	None
Starve Out Point	"	None
Bg-52	"	None
Bg-51	"	None
Nogales Cliff House	Robinson and Warren 1971	None
Rattlesnake Point Group	"	None
Burriones Cliff House	"	None
Carricito Community	"	None
Kiva House	"	None
Five Kiva House	Bannister, Dean, and Robinson 1969	Stallings 1936
Neskahi Village	"	None
Upper Desha Pueblo	"	Lindsay et al. 1968
Lost Mesa Group	"	"
Kinnickinnick Pueblo	Bannister, Gell, and Hannah 1966	Colton 1946; Conner 1943
Two Kivas Pueblo	Robinson, Harrill, and Warren 1975	Colton 1932
Wupatki	"	Colton 1933, 1946; Stanislawski 1963
Metate House	"	Colton 1946
Deadman's Fort	"	"
Badger House	Robinson and Harrill 1974	Hayes 1964; Hayes and Lancaster 1975
Mesa Verde 16 (Nordenskiold)	"	Hayes 1964
Mug House	"	Hayes 1964; Rohn 1971
Long House	"	Hayes 1964
Colorado 5 Mt 1253	"	None
Swallow's Nest	"	None
Square Tower House	"	Fewkes 1922; Watson 1948
Spruce Tree House	"	Fewkes 1909

TABLE 24 (continued)

Pueblo III		
Site	Laboratory of Tree-Ring Research Reference	Descriptive Reference
Mesa Verde 11 (Nordenskiold)	Robinson and Harrill 1974	Hayes 1964
Painted Kiva House	"	Fewkes 1922
Mesa Verde 115 (GP)	"	None
Mummy House	"	Fewkes 1916, 1922
Hoot Owl House	"	None
Far View Group	"	Fewkes 1917, 1922
Cliff Palace	"	Fewkes 1911
Casa Colorado	"	None
Bone Awl	"	None
Balcony House	"	Nordenskiold 1893
Lion House	"	E. H. Morris 1919b
Two Kiva House	"	"
Jeddito Site 104	Bannister, Robinson, and Warren 1967	Brew 1941
Jeddito Site 4	"	Brew 1937, 1941
Kokopnyama	"	Hough 1903; Haury and Hargrave 1931; Hargrave 1935
Kin Tiel	Bannister, Hannah, and Robinson 1966	Fewkes 1904; Haury and Hargrave 1931
Prayer Rock Cave	Bannister, Dean, and Gell 1966	Bannister, Dean, and Gell 1966
Three Turkey House	"	Colton 1939
RB 315	Bannister, Dean, and Robinson 1968	None
NA9454	"	None
Nagashi Bikin	"	Hargrave 1935
NA2606	"	Fewkes 1911; Hargrave 1935
Twin Caves Pueblo	"	Fewkes 1911; Hargrave 1935
Kiet Siel	"	Fewkes 1911; Guernsey 1931; Hargrave 1935
Scaffold House	"	Fewkes 1911
Betatakin	"	Fewkes 1911; Judd 1930
Long House	"	Fewkes 1911; Kidder and Guernsey 1919
Hawk's Nest Cliff Dwelling	"	None

Pueblo IV		
Site	Laboratory of Tree-Ring Research Reference	Descriptive Reference
Pink Arrow	Bannister, Robinson, and Warren 1967	Brew 1941; Smith 1952
Kokopnyama	"	Hough 1903; Haury and Hargrave 1931; Hargrave 1935
Kawaikuh	"	Hough 1903; Hargrave 1935; Smith 1952
Awatovi	"	Fewkes 1898a; Smith 1952, 1971; Burgh 1959
Pinedale Ruin	Bannister, Gell, and Hannah 1966	Fewkes 1904; Haury and Hargrave 1931
Showlow Ruin	"	Hough 1903; Haury and Hargrave 1931
Red Rock House	"	Hough 1930
Kinnickinnick Pueblo	"	Colton 1946; Conner 1943; Wilson, Winston, and Berger 1961

The first step in the creation of the bar chart was to determine the period or periods of occupation represented at each site. This was accomplished by plotting the presence or absence of cutting dates for each ten-year increment between the earliest and latest cutting dates at each site. Gaps in individual site records of less than 25 years were ignored and treated as periods of continuous occupation. Gaps of 25 years or greater were plotted as occupational hiatuses. Thus, each of the relevant sites was represented by one or more horizontal bars on a common ten-year increment scale. The second step was to sum the number of sites occupied during each increment for the entire Anasazi area. It should be noted that all of the available tree-ring data from A.D. 1 to A.D. 1500 have been summarized in this manner and are included in Figure 12C even though the pre–A.D. 700 sites have already received detailed treatment. In addition, the late Basketmaker II radiocarbon dates are depicted as horizontal lines. This has been done to demonstrate the essential compatibility of the disparate approaches used in the pre– and post–A.D. 700 sections of this chapter.

The meaning of the bar chart is subject to interpretation. Undoubtedly, some errors must have been made in the ascription of continuities or discontinuities to particular sites owing to the arbitrary 25-year threshold employed. However, there is no reason to suspect that errors of this type would produce any systematic misrepresentations or periodicities. Hence, the bar chart is probably a reasonable depiction of the extant chronometric data base. But, to what degree is the chart representative of the actual chronological patterning of prehistoric events? This is a difficult question to assess since the aggregate of dated sites comprises a nonrandom sample of these events. Two considerations argue for the tentative acceptance of Figure 12C as an accurate reflection of prehistoric occupation patterns. First, the sample size is large enough to foster a degree of confidence in the data trends. Second, Figure 12C may be viewed as an empirical generalization subject to modification as more data become available. If it is seriously in error due to some unknown sampling quirk, future work will lead to major modifications. This possibility seems most unlikely in view of the marked periodicity evident in the chart.

Given that Figure 12C is an acceptable depiction of diachronic variation in the relative number of occupied sites, it also bears on the question of variation in human population size through time. However, the relationship is not direct since site size has not been taken into account. This presents no major problem since most of the questions to be addressed deal with the spatiotemporal distribution of sites rather than people.

Methodological problems aside, the substantive results of this exercise are quite interesting and, again, run counter to expectations. Not only is there a yawning gap between classic Basketmaker II and Basketmaker III, but there is a sharp decline in the number of dated sites—approaching zero—between *every recognized stage of the Pecos Classification.* Far from the smooth continua of development diagrammed in Figure 12A (J. D. Jennings 1974) and 12B (Gumerman and Euler 1976), the present analysis strongly suggests that the course of Anasazi cultural evolution is best characterized as a series of temporally discrete typological entities. Each was abruptly terminated in a manner quite similar to the well-known and generally accepted thirteenth-century Pueblo III "abandonment."

CONCLUSIONS

In the most recently published overview of Anasazi prehistory Lipe (1978) reaffirms the long held belief that

> Anasazi chronology is well understood because dendrochronology is applicable over most of the area and has been used to date many pottery types (Breternitz 1966) and sites. The 1927 Pecos Conference periods (Kidder 1927) have generally agreed-upon dates and are still widely used as convenient temporal units, a practice followed here (Lipe 1978:367).

Certainly there is general agreement regarding the bracketing dates of the stages. But does that mean the chronology is "well understood?" No one could discern in the smooth curves drawn by J. D. Jennings (Figure 12A) or Gumerman and Euler (Figure 12B) that Anasazi evolution consisted of a series of remarkable occupational disruptions. And Lipe's article, which will be read by thousands of undergraduate anthropology students, merely reifies the smoothness of the Anasazi curve. Thus, just as in the case of the erroneous belief in ancient maize, the myth of gradual *in situ* Anasazi evolution will most likely be perpetuated for some time to come.

An historical analysis of the intellectual inertia of Southwestern research would, in and of itself, constitute an interesting line of inquiry. However, it will be more useful to turn from what has been said about the data to a consideration of the data patterning developed herein and shown in Figure 12C. These data constitute a problem worthy of explanation, and the remaining chapter may be viewed as a first approximation of that goal.

5. CLIMATE, MIGRATION, AND ANASAZI EVOLUTION

It is no longer fashionable to link major Anasazi cultural events to climatic factors in a causal manner, and constructs that lean too heavily on migration are thought to verge on indecency. Nonetheless, the data presented in this chapter provide strong evidence that climatically induced migrations occurred frequently in Anasazi prehistory. Further, it is argued that these migrations played a vital role in Anasazi evolution.

Prehistoric Climatic Patterns of the Colorado Plateau

Several palynological reconstructions of prehistoric Southwestern climates have been published (e.g., Schoenwetter and Dittert 1968; Mehringer 1967; Haynes 1968), but the temporal controls on which these studies depend are in every case insufficiently precise to shed light on the current problem. Hence, reliance on dendroclimatology is the only reasonable course to follow even though this approach must perforce depend on the sensitivity to the environment of only one or two arboreal species. The most complete work on the subject of dendroclimatology is H. C. Fritts's "Tree-Rings and Climate" (1976). Fritts stresses the multivariate nature of the problem of determining relationships between climate and tree-ring growth and provides many examples of computer aided applications. A lengthy review of these methods is not warranted here. It will suffice to introduce two principal facets of dendroclimatic research: *standardization* and *calibration*. Once a dendrochronological sequence has been determined for a given region, it is necessary to standardize the raw ring widths (this use of the term "standardize" is not to be confused with standardized scores of zero mean and unit variance). This is because the inner rings of a tree tend to be thicker than the outer rings due to growth processes that vary independently from climatic conditions. Use of raw ring widths would therefore introduce an uncontrolled amount of nonclimatic noise into the analysis. Standardization is accomplished by fitting the raw data to a modified exponential growth curve (Stockton and Fritts 1971). The results of standardization are the *tree-ring indices*. Calibration is the next step in the process. This consists of comparing historic indices to the corresponding climatic variables in order to obtain statements of relationship between indices and climatic types. These statements may then be used to make inferences about past climates from the prehistoric tree-ring indices.

The only relevant calibrations published to date are those of Fritts, Smith, and Stokes (1965) for the Mesa Verde area and Stockton and Fritts (1971) for Arizona. In the latter case historic climatic records from four stations were divided into nine climatic classes from hot and dry (Class 1) to cold and wet (Class 9). The corresponding tree-ring indices were standardized to a mean of zero and unit variance and were subjected to certain filtering processes. These were then divided into nine equiprobable classes from Class 1 (greater than a 1.22σ negative departure from the mean) to Class 9 (greater than a 1.22σ positive departure from the mean). Probabilities were then calculated for the co-occurrence of climatic and ring-width classes. The results are shown in Table 25. Probabilities for intermediate climatic categories are fairly indeterminate, but increase abruptly in the cells corresponding to the co-occurrence of extreme values of both variables. There is nearly a 60% chance that negative departures greater than 1.22σ indicate climates hotter and dryer than normal, and a better than 40% chance that positive departures of the same magnitude indicate climates wetter and colder than normal.

Stockton and Fritts's (1971) calibration may be usefully applied to the interpretation of Southwestern tree-ring indices published by Dean and Robinson (1977, 1978). Since the fluctuating demographic patterns discussed in Chapter 4 rely upon data from the entire southern Colorado Plateau, general climatic trends based on the average indices for all tree-ring stations in that area will be employed to insure analytic comparability.

Complete records for the period from A.D. 680 to A.D. 1500 are available from 17 southern Colorado Plateau stations. Dean and Robinson (1977) present these data as decadal standardized departures from the mean for each station. In order to arrive at a Plateau-wide average for each decade of the sequence, the mean departure per ten-year increment for all stations was calculated, and these values were themselves standardized to achieve a mean of zero and unit variance for the recomputed data set. The results are shown in Figure 13A, juxtaposed with the ten-year increment bar chart of tree-ring dated sites developed in Chapter 4. The shaded portion of Figure 13A corresponds to the plus-and-minus 1.22σ range employed by Stockton and Fritts (1971), and it may be assumed that *negative* departures equal to or greater than the shaded boundary represent decadal periods of less than normal rainfall and greater than normal temperature. The four greatest negative departures fall at regular intervals at approximately A.D. 700, 900, 1100, and 1300. In addition, there are a number of lesser—yet still significant—negative departures that occur at irregular intervals. Each departure corresponds to a marked decline in the number of dated Anasazi sites, and as noted in Chapter 4, the most pronounced of the reductions in site density correspond with the temporal limits of

TABLE 25
Conditional Probability for Each Climatic Class Given a Ring-Width Class

	Ring-Width Class								
Climatic Class	1	2	3	4	5	6	7	8	9
1	.583	.292	.179	.200	.100	.050	.036	.125	.000
2	.083	.125	.179	.050	.100	.200	.143	.000	.025
3	.083	.083	.143	.100	.075	.050	.036	.000	.075
4	.042	.250	.179	.100	.075	.000	.107	.000	.025
5	.042	.083	.179	.150	.225	.150	.107	.000	.075
6	.042	.000	.071	.200	.100	.150	.179	.125	.150
7	.042	.083	.036	.050	.100	.000	.036	.250	.025
8	.042	.000	.036	.100	.150	.100	.107	.250	.200
9	.042	.083	.000	.050	.075	.300	.250	.250	.425

Source: Stockton and Fritts 1971

the Pecos Classification stages. The correspondence is admittedly inexact, but the strength of the relationship is too strong to be ignored. It would appear that drought conditions of sufficient magnitude to affect maize production occurred several times during the Anasazi sequence and, further, that these circumstances were linked in some unspecified manner to the recognzied stage-to-stage transitions.

Only nine stations published by Dean and

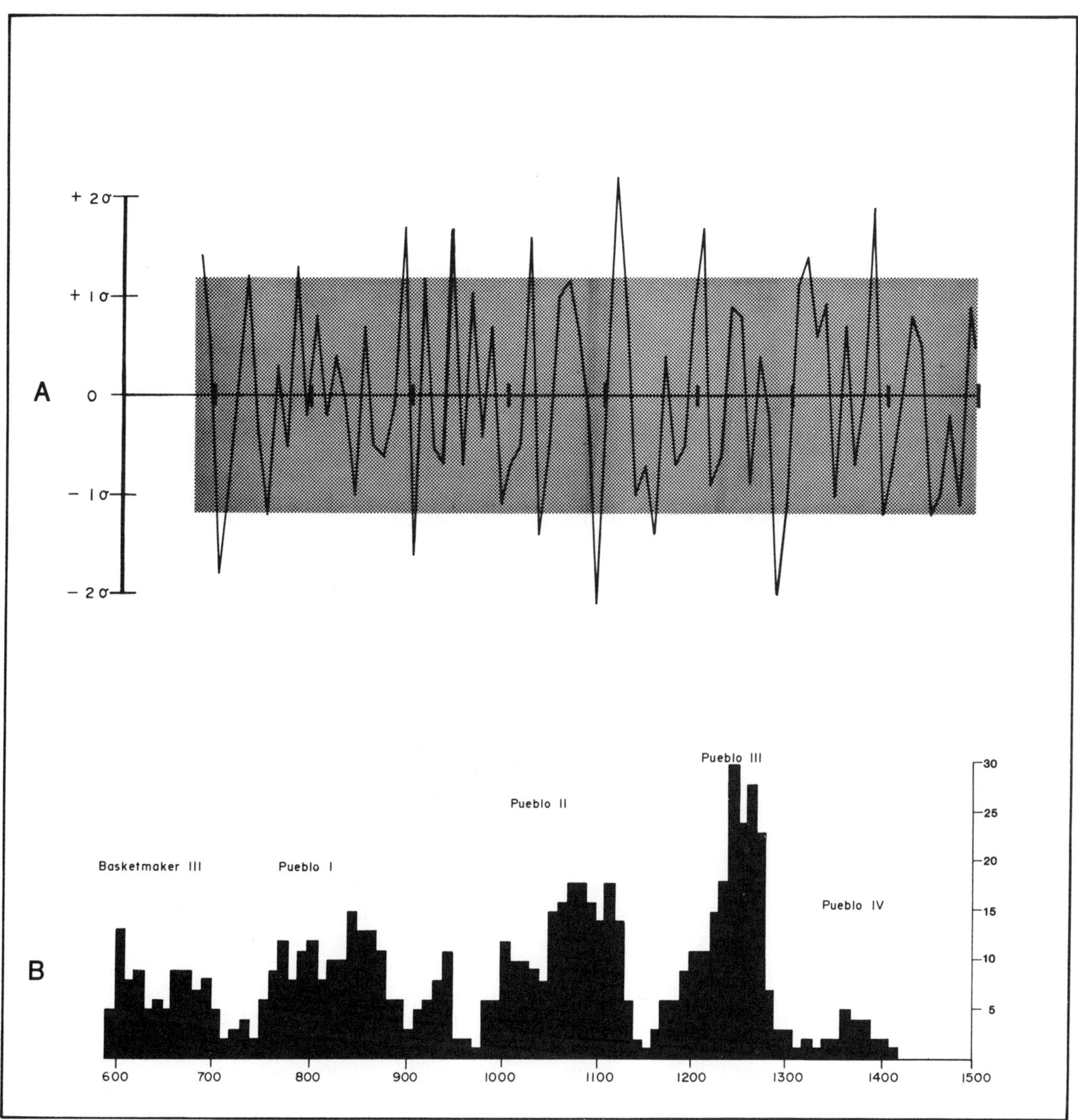

Figure 13. Tree-ring indices (A) and tree-ring dated sites for the period A.D. 680 to A.D. 1500 (B).

Robinson (1978) have records going back in time considerably beyond A.D. 680. Since they are of unequal length, averaging to arrive at a general trend would be misleading. The individual records are plotted in Figure 14 and will be discussed below where relevant. The arbitrary cutoff date of A.D. 750 was chosen to provide some overlap with the more comprehensive portion of the record. The ten-year increment standard errors were calculated from the annual indices by the same method used by Dean and Robinson (1977). That is, the annual indices were standardized to a mean of zero and a variance of one. The ten resultant values for each decade were summed algebraically. These were then multiplied by $\sqrt{n}/n$ where n=10 to obtain the mean decadal departures. The dating ranges of known sites as summarized in Chapter 4 are shown as horizontal bars under the appropriate regional climatic records. Again, there is a close correspondence between strong negative departures and local abandonment. In a few cases, structural cutting dates begin during or even slightly before a major drought. This is most likely attributable to driftwood effect with the actual occupation beginning immediately following the drought interval.

While any attempt to extrapolate the evidence for drought from these few early stations to the Plateau as a whole would be inconclusive, certain points of agreement are evident. The records from Canyon de Chelly, Durango, Natural Bridges, and Navajo Mountain all show a strong negative departure at around A.D. 370, and this equates with the general termination date of classic Basketmaker II. The ensuing tree-ring evidence is chaotic until A.D. 520 when seven of the eight relevant stations show significant departures. These two climatic events are in close agreement with the palynological evidence for reduced effective moisture during the Basketmaker II/Basketmaker III interval (Mehringer 1967).

Although I have taken the simplest and most direct route to the interpretation of the climatic evidence, the concordance of natural and cultural events is convincing. As a point of clarification, it bears mentioning that thin tree-rings do not necessarily correlate with low precipitation during the growing season. Rather, tree-ring growth is more closely associated with winter and spring precipitation during the 15-month period prior to ring growth (Fritts 1976). However, protracted (e.g., decadal) winter-spring drought is normally accompanied by low summer precipitation, and more importantly it has the general effect of inhibiting the growth of ground cover thereby encouraging arroyo cutting. It is interesting in this respect that Stockton and Fritts (1971) were able to successfully retrodict the 1880–90 episode of Colorado Plateau arroyo cutting strictly on the basis of strong negative departures in the tree-ring data.

Discussion

The conclusion seems inescapable that the Anasazi sequence was regularly interrupted by drought-induced "abandonments" similar in scope and magnitude to the well-known thirteenth-century Pueblo III exodus. The latter is the only widespread Anasazi abandonment recognized by Southwesternists, and even in that case most recent workers have tended to deemphasize the importance of drought as a causal factor.

> Climatic change has often been invoked as a cause. Early tree ring workers (Douglass 1929) recognized a series of very narrow rings, thought to represent a "Great Drought" in the late 1200s, coincident with abandonment of the large cliff dwellings of Mesa Verde and the Tsegi canyons. The general explanatory power of this widespread drought faded, however, when it became clear that most Plateau areas had already been abandoned by this time. The tree ring record (Fritts et al. 1965) also reveals several serious earlier droughts that were not accompanied by widespread abandonments (Lipe 1978:378).

Lipe's reference to the notion that "most Plateau areas had already been abandoned" has little empirical support. As the chronometric data represented in Figure 12C indicate, there were more contemporaneously occupied sites during late Pueblo III than at any other time in Anasazi prehistory. Furthermore, Pueblo III sites tended to be much larger than in any earlier period; hence, population must have been on the upswing. Lipe's statement, therefore, appears to be incorrect. As for his reference to the work of Fritts, Smith, and Stokes (1965) on Mesa Verde, it should be made clear that the dendroclimatolo-

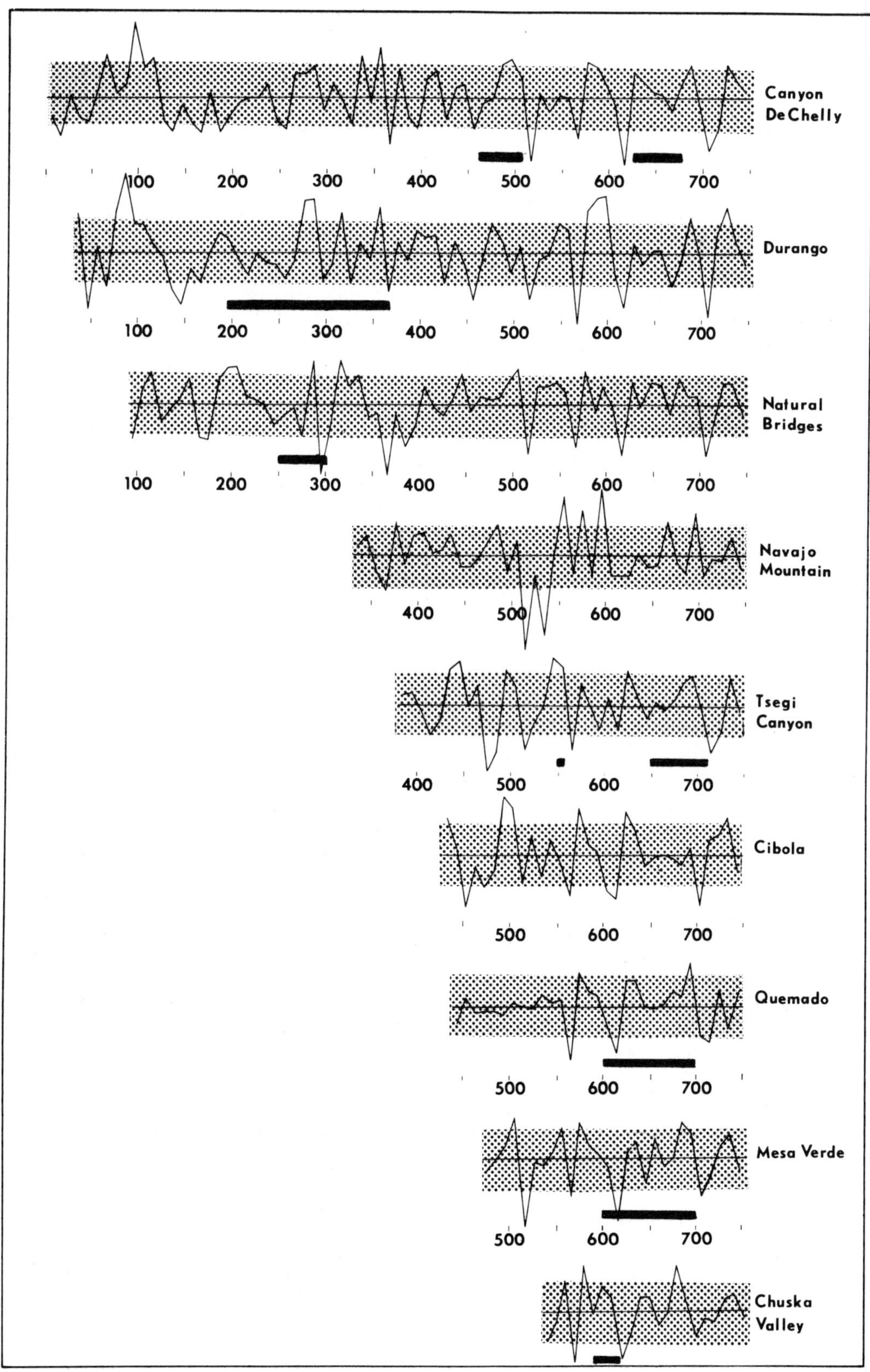

Figure 14. Tree-ring indices for the nine stations with the longest developed records. The horizontal bars represent the documented periods of occupation in the respective areas.

gists were assessing the impact of apparent droughts on the prehistoric settlement of Mesa Verde *as interpreted by archeologists*. The latter were merely asserting the standard *in situ*, cultural continuity story line. Had the archeologists interpreted the many gaps in the Mesa Verde record as abandonments, Fritts, Smith, and Stokes (1965) would have arrived at quite different conclusions, e.g., that numerous abandonments had occurred in response to numerous droughts. It seems clear that the evidence presented in this and earlier chapters is most parsimoniously interpreted in this manner. What remains is to demonstrate the relevance of cyclical abandonment to the processes of Anasazi stage transitions in general.

ANASAZI TRANSITIONS: A PLATEAU PERSPECTIVE

"Abandonment," in the present context, refers to the roughly contemporaneous cessation of occupation of large numbers of Anasazi villages. Use of this term is not intended to suggest that the entire southern Colorado Plateau was ever completely evacuated. As will be seen, the evidence *does* support the fact that significant numbers of people migrated out of the Anasazi region (as traditionally defined) southward and eastward to the southern Basin and Range province during periods of drought. However, population movements *within* the Plateau province in response to drought conditions played an important role in Anasazi evolution, and these are the principal concern of this section.

In overview, the general model of Plateau transition processes is quite simple. During periods of average to relatively abundant precipitation, sites were fairly evenly distributed over the landscape, and it seems probable that most areas of the Plateau were capable of supporting farming populations. However, during major drought intervals, maize farming was not feasible except in a limited number of favorable environmental settings, most of which were high elevation (6600 to 7000 ft.) locales. This is most likely due to the fact that precipitation varies directly with elevation over most of the Plateau (Hunt 1967). Drought-induced abandonment of a large number of small, widely dispersed Anasazi farmsteads and the subsequent migration of these groups to a few refuge areas resulted in population aggregation and the forced coexistence of diverse cultural entities. These circumstances fostered the coalescence of cultural traditions and the syntheses of material culture traits that produced the typological hallmarks diagnostic of the ensuing stage(s) of development. With the amelioration of climate, the drought refugia were abandoned. This is most likely explained by the fact that mean annual temperature and the length of the growing season are *inversely* related to altitude (Hunt 1967). Thus, farming groups that had successfully exploited the high elevation locales due to the extended frost-free period associated with drought conditions were forced to return to lower elevations with the shift to a cooler and moister climatic regime. Hence, the population was once again dispersed over broad areas of the Plateau. Repitition of this process through the several cycles indicated in Figure 13 accounts for the major stage transitions of the Anasazi evolution. In this view, Anasazi prehistory may be characterized as consisting of relatively long periods (ca. 200 years) of cultural stasis, punctuated by relatively brief intervals of cultural transformation.

This sketch provides at least a provisional explanation of why the definitional criteria of the Pecos Classification stages emerge immediately on the heels of major droughts. Furthermore, it does so without inviting accusations of environmental determinism. The cultural transformations that occurred during the contact situations call for culturological explanations; the environmental variation that mediated the contact situation is treated as a catalytic aspect of the process.

In the following more detailed examination of the various transitions, particular syntheses of material culture traits will be noted where relevant and critical transition sites identified where possible. Additional facets of the model will also be introduced in order to account for apparently contradictory data. Since the archeological visibility of transition sites is much greater at the more recent end of the time scale, it will be useful to begin with the Pueblo III/Pueblo IV transformation where the picture is clearest and then proceed in a step-by-step manner toward the earlier, more fragmentary end of the record.

Pueblo III to Pueblo IV

As shown in Figure 13, there was a drastic reduction in the number of Pueblo III sites at around A.D. 1280 shortly following the onset of a severe drought. The geographic distribution of dated Pueblo III sites is shown in Figure 15A. Their abandonment corresponds to the initiation of settlement at high-elevation sites along the Mogollon Rim (the southern boundary of the Colorado Plateau). Reoccupation of low-elevation locales did not occur until approximately A.D. 1360. Refuge sites occupied between A.D. 1280 and 1360 are shown in Figure 15B. These include Kinnickinnick Pueblo (Colton 1946; Conner 1943; Wilson, Winston, and Berger 1961), Pinedale Ruin and Showlow Ruin (Haury and Hargrave 1931). Figure 15C depicts the distribution of Pueblo IV sites dated to A.D. 1360 and later. These include the terminal occupation of Showlow Ruin and the classic Pueblo IV settlements on Antelope Mesa including Awatovi (Smith 1971), Kawaikuh (Hough 1903), Kokopnayama (Hough 1903; Haury and Hargrave 1931), and Pink Arrow (Brew 1941). The Homolovi group near Winslow, Arizona (Fewkes 1898b), and a number of sites in the Black Mesa area (Windham and Dechambre 1978) were most likely occupied in the same period. Hence, the distribution of low-elevation Pueblo IV sites is probably somewhat more widespread than indicated in Figure 15C.

Late Pueblo III sites range from small to moderately large villages and cliff dwellings. Highly distinctive black-on-white pottery types dominate

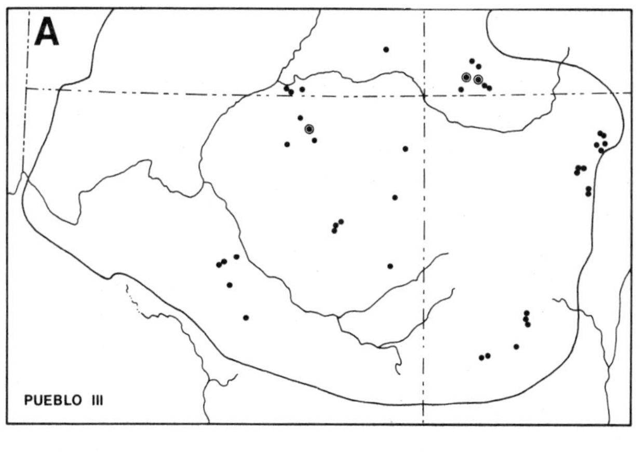

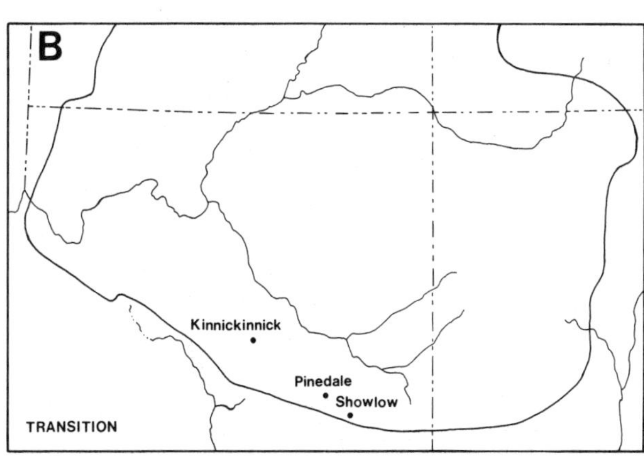

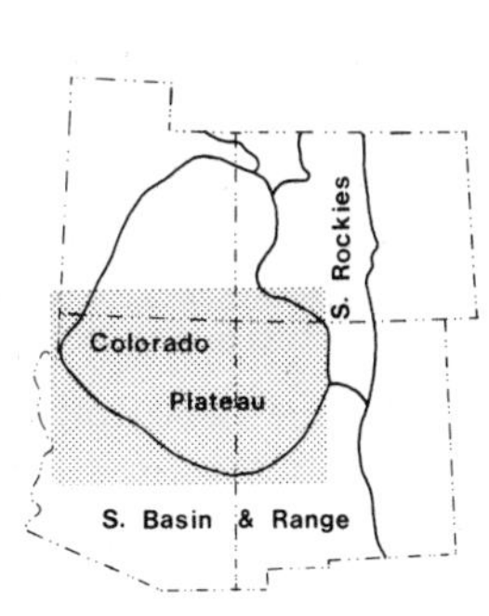

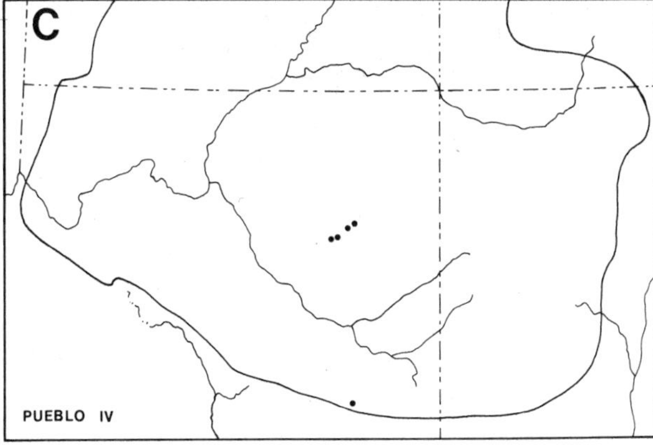

Figure 15. Distribution of dated sites from A.D. 1150 to A.D. 1450. Each dot represents a site; circled dots are site clusters. A, Pueblo III sites; B, sites transitional from Pueblo III to Pueblo IV; C, Pueblo IV sites.

the decorated ceramic assemblages. Polychrome types are present in low frequencies. The situation is reversed in the high-elevation transition sites where the late black-on-white types are in the minority while Jeddito Black-on-orange, Jeddito Black-on-yellow and a wide variety of closely related polychromes predominate. The instantaneity of this reversal strongly suggests that these ceramic types were created *in situ* at these high-elevation refugia. A similar situation may be suggested for Pueblo de los Muertos in the El Morro Valley of New Mexico (Watson, LeBlanc, and Redman 1980). The site is located above 7000 ft. in elevation and was constructed in the early 1280s. Polychromes predominate to the near exclusion of black-on-white types.

All of the refuge sites are large by Southwestern standards, ranging from 200 to over 700 rooms. Many appear to have been built according to preconceived plans over fairly brief periods of time. This is consistent with the notion of rapid population aggregation implied by the general model.

It seems reasonable to assert that the process of aggregation at these large sites as well as the process of population dispersion following their abandonment was closely related to the genesis of the enigmatic Saladoan phenomenon of southern Arizona and New Mexico (cf. Doyel and Haury 1976). This possibility will be briefly explored in a later section. What can be said without equivocation is that these processes were clearly related to the reoccupation of the interior Plateau area by Pueblo IV populations at around A.D. 1360. Jeddito Black-on-orange and Jeddito Black-on-yellow, which made their first appearance at Kinnickinnick shortly after A.D. 1300, are the most abundant decorated types in evidence at the Antelope Mesa sites (Figure 15C).

The proposed model of the Pueblo III/Pueblo IV transition, then, may be summarized as follows: (1) An essentially synchronous, Plateau-wide abandonment of the late Pueblo III sites by A.D. 1280 as a consequence of drought; (2) migration to high elevation sites on the Mogollon Rim in Arizona and the El Morro Valley of eastern New Mexico; (3) coalescence of diverse cultural traditions and the consequent syntheses of new artifact types at these transitional sites; (4) A northward movement of populations archeologically recognizable as Pueblo IV Anasazi at around A.D. 1360 coincident with a return to more mesic climatic conditions.

This account differs markedly from the standard interpretation, which asserts that the "Great Drought" of the thirteenth century did not result in the complete abandonment of the Kayenta area. Rather, the Pueblo III populations are thought to have contracted their range and moved directly to the Hopi Mesas (one of which is Antelope Mesa) where they evolved *in situ* into the Pueblo IV stage and finally emerged as the Pueblo V Hopi of historic times (see, for instance, Smith 1971; Gumerman and Euler 1976). In that view, the sites I have described as transitional are treated as "peripheral" to the main line of continuous development in the "culture center." The assumption of Pueblo III–Pueblo IV *in situ* continuity may be a logical entailment of gradualist evolutionism, but it is *not* a demonstrated fact. The most frequently cited empirical support for continuity is Watson Smith's seriation of the Awatovi ceramics (Smith 1971). Awatovi is one of the largest sites on Antelope Mesa, and it definitely contains both Pueblo III and Pueblo IV components. But the presumed overlap of these two components is not supported by the available data. The sample used for the Awatovi seriation consisted of 50-cm arbitrary levels of room-fill materials; hence, the association of Pueblo III and Pueblo IV ceramics was preordained by the excavation techniques employed. That the seriation "worked" proves nothing about continuity or the lack of it. The method requires typological overlap within the analytic units, and hence cannot stand as independent empirical evidence for *temporal* overlap.

As for other lines of evidence, not one of the very large number of tree-ring cutting dates from Awatovi or any of the other Antelope Mesa sites falls between A.D. 1280 and 1360. It would appear that the Pueblo III inhabitants of Awatovi abandoned the site at about the same time as all the other major Pueblo III sites on the Plateau and for the same reason. Awatovi, Kokopnayama, Kawaikuh, and Pink Arrow then remained unoccupied until the northward migration from the transitional sites at A.D. 1360. This possibility has never been seriously considered even though Smith himself offers physical evidence consistent with a significant hiatus in the occupation of Awatovi.

> An early structure of probably two stories constituted the initial pueblo, but this was later abandoned and filled with debris, either all at once or gradually, and on its remains there later rose another masonry structure also probably of two stories (Smith 1971:6).

Because of the way in which Awatovi was excavated, it is impossible to tell from Smith's report whether the first and second stages of building were associated respectively with Pueblo III and Pueblo IV ceramics. A sequence of Pueblo III—hiatus—Pueblo IV seems most compatible with all the relevant data, and it is likely that this interpretation will be confirmed as soon as stratigraphic excavation techniques are employed at any of the Antelope Mesa sites.

Pueblo II to Pueblo III

As shown in Figure 13, the reduction in the number of sites at the end of Pueblo II was nearly as drastic as at the termination of Pueblo III. The phenomenon appears to have been related to climatic conditions, but the response was not as immediate as in the case of the Pueblo III abandonment. The negative departure in the tree-ring indices at A.D. 1100 is equivalent in magnitude to the one at A.D. 1280, but there was only a slight decline in the number of dated sites coincident with it. The really drastic reduction occurred three to four decades later following a rapid upswing in the indices to plus two sigma, and another negative departure of lesser magnitude but greater duration than the first at around A.D. 1140. It may be that the decade of increased precipitation following the A.D. 1100 drought caused massive downcutting of arroyos, thus destroying *akchin* irrigation fields (Hack 1942) on a major scale. Alternatively, it may simply be the case that the cumulative effects of two severe droughts in a 50-year period were enough to cause abandonment. Whatever interpretation of these data is offered, it can hardly be doubted that climate played an effective role in the dislocation of Pueblo II populations.

Figures 16A and 16C depict the geographic distribution of dated Pueblo II and Pueblo III sites. The temporal partition has been drawn at A.D. 1150 to correspond with the low point in the number of sites during the transition period. The *only* well-dated site that links the two periods together is Wupatki (Figure 16B), with cutting dates that range from A.D. 1130 to 1215 (Robinson, Harrill, and Warren 1975). The Citadel and a number of other Wupatki Basin sites probably fall in the same period but lack adequate tree-ring evidence. Wupatki has long been thought of as a cultural "melting pot" or trade center due to the cultural heterogeneity of the material remains (Colton 1946; Stanislawski 1963; Hartman and Wolf 1977). The site is a large, multistory pueblo with a Chacoan great kiva and a Casa Grande style Hohokam ball court. Associated ceramics represent Sinagua, Cohonina, Kayenta, and Chacoan cultural traditions. The remains of parrots, macaws, shell ornaments, and copper bells also indicate Chacoan or Hohokam relationships (Stanislawski 1963).

It seems clear, in light of the temporal distribution of sites in Figure 13 and the geographic distribution shown in Figure 16, that the cultural mix seen at Wupatki resulted from drought-induced migration rather than diffusion or trade. None of the well-dated Plateau sites were fully contemporaneous with Wupatki, and its initial occupation took place during a major drought that apparently caused the abandonment of the Chaco Canyon pueblos as well as the small but numerous Kayenta Pueblo II villages.

Unlike the drought refugia of other transition periods, Wupatki is not a high-elevation site, therefore orographic rainfall cannot be held to account for the agricultural viability of this locale during the mid-twelfth century drought. Rather, the attractiveness of the Wupatki Basin during the Pueblo II/Pueblo III transition is attributable to the moisture-retaining volcanic ash that blanketed the area after the eruption of Sunset Crater in A.D. 1064–65 (Hartman and Wolf 1977). It was originally proposed (Colton 1946, 1960) that the eruption initiated a prehistoric "land rush" as the diverse cultural groups mentioned above migrated *en masse* to the Wupatki Basin to take advantage of the newly available farm lands. Colton's interpretation has since given way to explanations based on trade or diffusion. However, it now appears that Colton was partially correct. That is, Wupatki was the product of a number of migrating populations, but the major influx of people into the Wupatki Basin did not actually occur until 50 or 60 years after the eruption. The ash fall was never an adequate inducement to attract successful farming populations away from their agriculturally productive homelands. Rather, it provided a refuge for populations forced to abandon a large number of Pueblo II villages during the 1100s due to severe drought.

All of the ceramic types diagnostic of the ensuing Pueblo III stage in the Kayenta area were first developed in the Wupatki Basin and these spread rapidly over the southern Plateau as climatic conditions ameliorated and populations dispersed. In general, the "unit pueblos" typical of the Pueblo II stage were replaced by larger multi-storied villages and cliff dwellings during Pueblo III. This is, of course, quite consistent with the derivation of the Pueblo III tradition from large, complex, multi-cultural transition sites like Wupatki.

Obviously, the Wupatki Basin sites are not numerous enough to have accommodated the entire Pueblo II population. Areas adjacent to the Colorado Plateau that were colonized during this period will be discussed in a later section. Within the Plateau only one additional site bears mention as a possible refuge locality. This is Coombs Village, located in south-central Utah (Lister 1959; Lister, Ambler, and Lister 1960; Lister and Lister

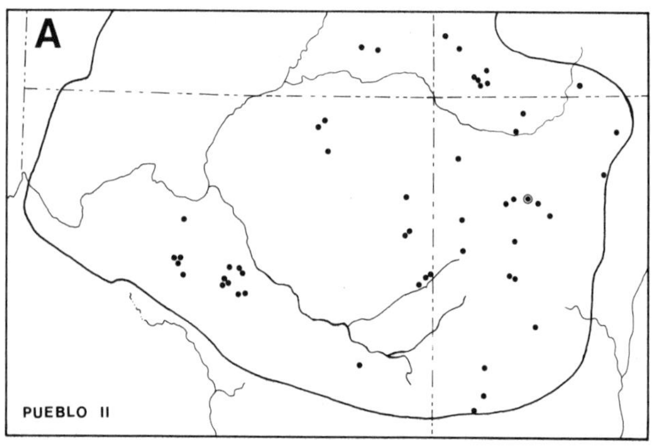

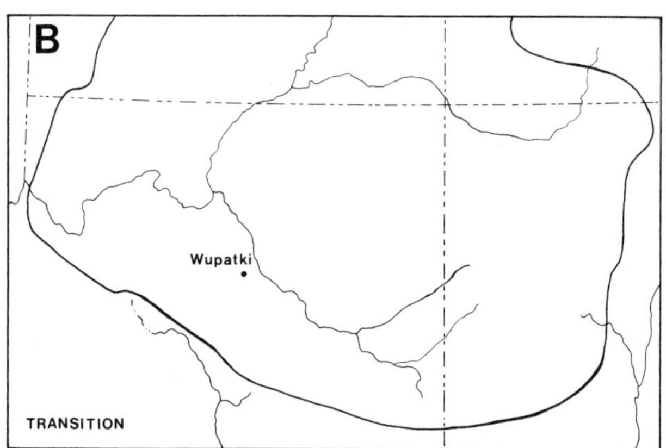

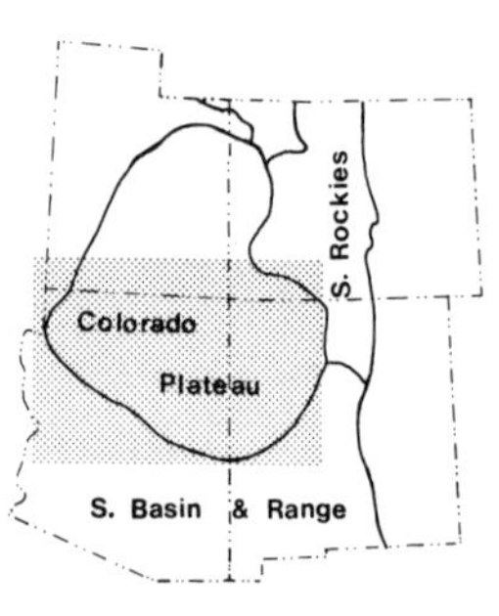

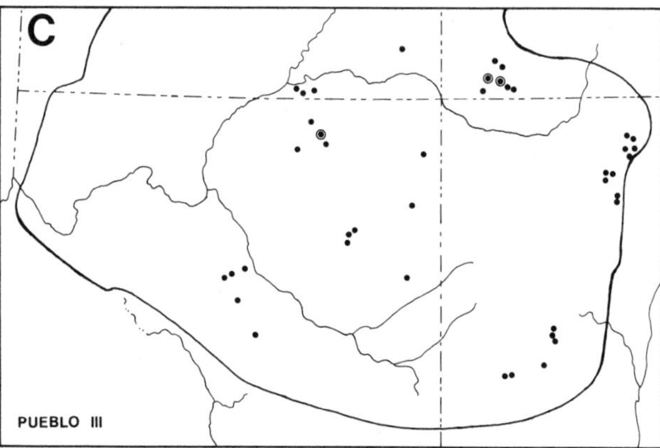

Figure 16. Distribution of dated sites from A.D. 950 to A.D.1300. Each dot represents a site; circled dots are site clusters. A, Pueblo II sites; B, sites transitional from Pueblo II to Pueblo III; C, Pueblo III sites.

1961; Bannister, Dean, and Robinson 1969). It is a large village situated adjacent to Boulder Creek on the Aquarius Plateau at an elevation of 6900 feet and, hence, is more typical of refuge sites than the Wupatki example. The site is not sufficiently well dated to appear in Table 24 or Figure 16 but it seems likely that it was occupied in the mid-twelfth century (Bannister, Dean, and Robinson 1969). Both Anasazi and Fremont ceramics are represented at Coombs Village and the site may record the route for the introduction of Pueblo II design elements to the northern Colorado Plateau and eastern Great Basin.

Pueblo I to Pueblo II

The characterization of the typical Pueblo II village given above does not take into account the large Bonito phase settlements of Chaco Canyon. These are usually classified as Pueblo III sites even though they fall into the Pueblo II time period and were abandoned at about the same time as all the other Pueblo II sites. However, since the Chacoan tradition ceased to exist as a recognizable archeological entity after the cultural synthesis (evidenced at Wupatki) that produced the Kayentan Pueblo III stage, Chacoan sites—both large and small—are readily classifiable as Pueblo II.

The process of transition from Pueblo I to Pueblo II is virtually identical to that already discussed for the more recent transformations, although there is an interesting set of sites that constitute a minor variation on the usual pattern. Figure 17 depicts the distributions of Pueblo I, Pueblo I–II transition, and Pueblo II sites. The partition line has been drawn at A.D. 950 even

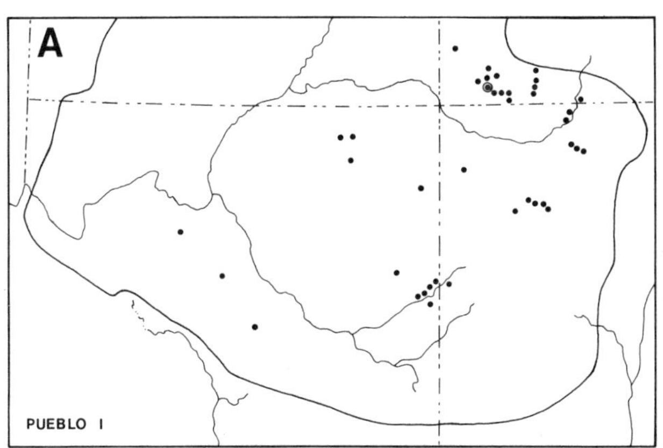

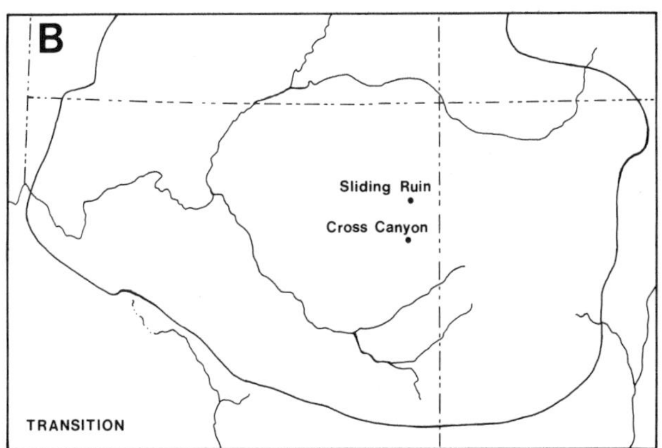

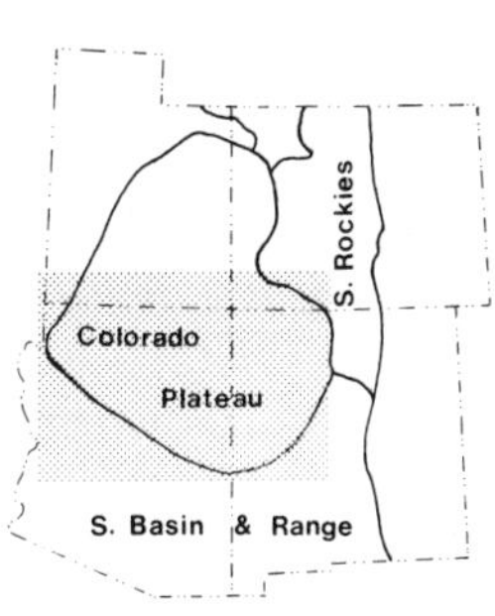

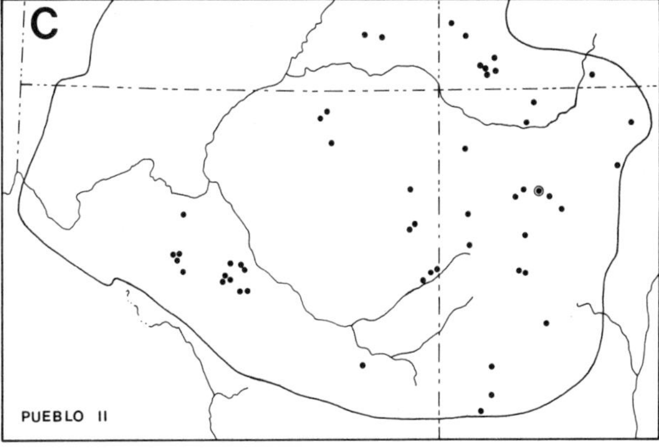

Figure 17. Distribution of dated sites from A.D. 750 to A.D. 1150. Each dot represents a site; circled dots are site clusters. A, Pueblo I sites; B, sites transitional from Pueblo I to Pueblo II; C, Pueblo II sites.

though the relevant drought interval occurred between A.D. 900 and 910 (see Figure 13). This is because the brief pulse of construction activity between A.D. 910 and 950 is, for the most part, readily classified as Pueblo I. All represent movement—following the A.D. 900 drought—into *unoccupied* regions. As a consequence, no coalescence with other groups occurred, and these sites display no discernible change in material remains from the pre–A.D. 900 Pueblo I pattern. It is of considerable interest that four of these sites represent an early construction period at Chaco Canyon. The sites are Pueblo Bonito, Una Vida, Peñasco Blanco, and Hungopavi; and the masonry construction of the early rooms in each of these large settlements is clearly distinguishable from that used in the remainder of the construction sequence (Bannister 1965). The tree-ring evidence indicates that the actual construction of the major portion of these settlements did not begin until A.D. 1025 or later (Robinson, Harrill, and Warren 1974). This suggests that the sequence comprised two discrete components and that the few early structures were intentionally incorporated into the massive room blocks of the later Chacoan "towns." That there exists a 50-year gap in cutting dates for Chaco Canyon as a whole tends to reinforce this interpretation (Robinson, Harrill, and Warren 1974). It might be argued that such a gap could be produced through the stockpiling of construction beams. However, Hawley (1959) reports a similar bimodal distribution of tree-ring dates from firewood recovered from a trash midden at Chetro Ketl, another major Chaco Canyon ruin. This gives added support to the notion of a significant occupational hiatus. I, therefore, find it difficult to accept R. Gwinn Vivian's (1970) assertion that Chaco Canyon was continuously occupied from A.D. 850 to 1150.

As shown in Figure 17B, only two sites were occupied through this transition from Pueblo I to Pueblo II. These are NA8013 of the Cross Canyon Group (Olson 1971) and Sliding Ruin (Bannister, Dean, and Gell 1966). The Cross Canyon Group is located on the Defiance Plateau of northeastern Arizona at an elevation slightly below 7000 feet and is adjacent to a perennial stream (Olson 1971). The advantage of such a location during a drought interval has already been discussed in relation to the Pueblo III–Pueblo IV transition. Site NA8013 consists of a masonry room block, a Chaco style kiva, and an early prototype of a Chacoan great kiva. The site was abandoned just prior to the construction of the Bonito phase pueblos in Chaco Canyon to the east, suggesting a lineal relationship. The site also appears to document the earliest occurrence of Black Mesa Black-on-white pottery, the primary diagnostic of Pueblo II in the Kayenta area to the west. Then too, the village plan of NA8013 is virtually identical to the "unit pueblo" configuration that typifies Pueblo II in that area.

Sliding Ruin is located roughly 20 miles north of the Cross Canyon Group in Canyon de Chelly. It is a masonry cliff dwelling consisting of from 30 to 50 rooms and three circular kivas. Unfortunately, details are lacking regarding the ceramic types present and the nature of the architecture. However, Canyon de Chelly is certainly an excellent candidate for a drought refuge area. The canyon drains a large area of the Defiance Plateau, and the average frost-free period in the canyon bottoms is in excess of 146 days (McDonald 1976). In addition, a site as large as Sliding Ruin occurring at such an early date (A.D. 936 to 983) is a likely precursor (at least in terms of size) of the Chaco Canyon great houses.

Again, I wish to emphasize that these two sites probably were not the only loci of Pueblo I–Pueblo II transition. A program of survey and excavation on the Defiance Plateau and the Chuska Mountains to the north and east would very likely lead to the discovery of a considerable number of high elevation transitional sites. Furthermore, I doubt that a complete understanding of this transition will ever be accomplished so long as only Colorado Plateau data are considered. As shown in Figure 13, the gap between the onset of the A.D. 900 drought and the beginnings of what may properly be considered Pueblo II (ignoring the intervening "blip" of terminal Pueblo I sites) constitutes the greatest discontinuity in the post-Basketmaker Anasazi record. This is also the only period during which significant amounts of Anasazi ceramics are found as intrusives in Hohokam sites in southern Arizona (Gladwin et al. 1937; Wasley and Johnson 1965; Haury 1976). The standard interpretation is that these intrusives represent "trade" wares. I suggest that actual population movement should not be excluded as a possibility. The nature of Hohokam/Anasazi relationships at a Pueblo I–II time depth is an unexplored question, the answer to which might shed light on this period of Anasazi evolution.

Basketmaker III to Pueblo I

Environmental circumstances during this transition were much the same as those described for the Pueblo II–Pueblo III situation. A major negative departure at A.D. 700 is followed immediately by a two-decade increase in effective moisture followed by a second drought interval centered at A.D. 750. I have set the transition boundary at A.D. 750 since that appears to mark the lower limit of sites that may be unequivocally assigned to Pueblo I. Figure 18 shows the distribution of Basketmaker III and Pueblo I sites, as well as the lone candidate for the Basketmaker III–Pueblo I transition. This is Morris's Site 23 in the La Plata District of southwestern Colorado (E. H. Morris 1939). The site is situated at an elevation of approximately 6600 feet and is within walking distance of the La Plata River. It is the earliest dated example of the standard Pueblo I village and consists of crescent-shaped rows of jacal surface rooms with associated pithouses. Site 23 contained at least 17 such units arranged in a roughly linear configuration over 1000 m in length (E. H. Morris 1939; Robinson and Harrill 1974). La Plata Black-on-white and La Plata Black-on-orange were the principal components of the decorated ceramic assemblage. The former is stylistically similar to Kana-a Black-on-white, which is diagnostic of Pueblo I in the Kayenta region. The

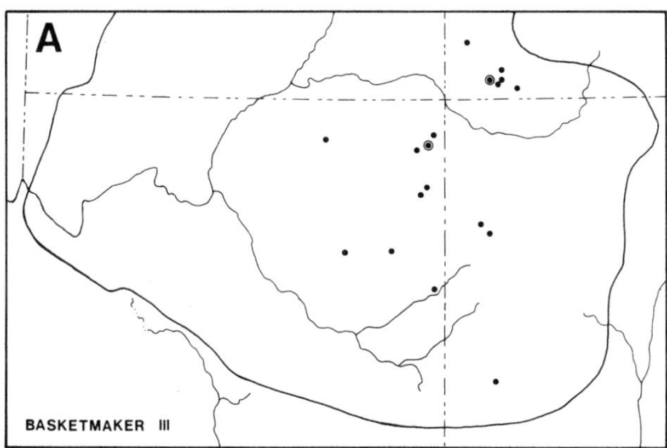

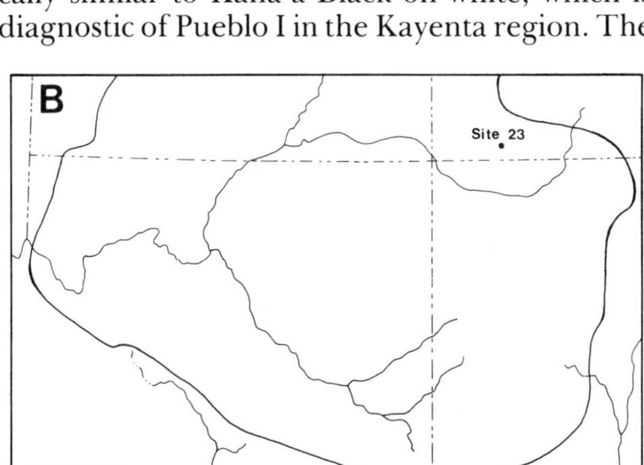

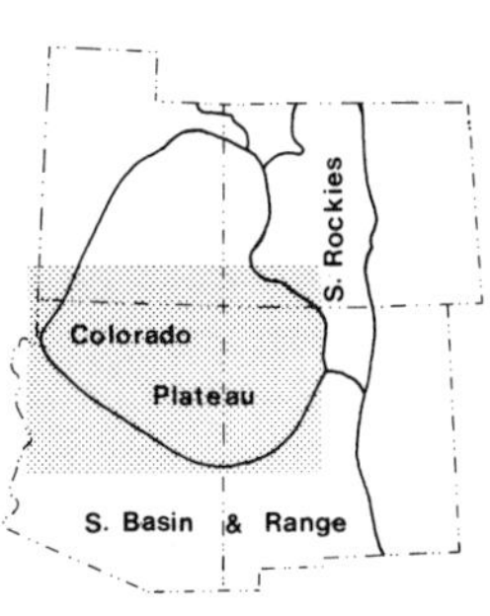

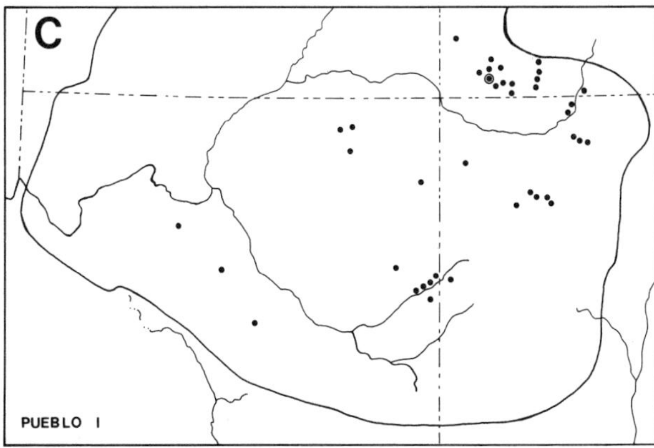

Figure 18. Distribution of dated sites from A.D. 600 to A.D. 950. Each dot represents a site; circled dots are site clusters. A, Basketmaker III sites; B, sites transitional from Basketmaker III to Pueblo I; C, Pueblo I sites.

latter is clearly related to Abajo Red-on-orange, which is diagnostic of Pueblo I in the northern San Juan drainage.

Changes in ceramics and pithouse architecture between Basketmaker III and Pueblo I were hardly drastic. The most significant aspect of the transformation was the change in village pattern from haphazardly arranged clusters of pithouses in Basketmaker III to units consisting of east-west oriented surface rooms with one to three associated pithouses during Pueblo I.

Basketmaker II to Basketmaker III

Figure 19 depicts the distribution of Basketmaker II and Basketmaker III sites as well as the few dated structures that fall in between these periods of occupation. No attempt will be made to analyze the postulated transformation from early to late Basketmaker II in terms of the general transition model owing to the lack of adequate descriptions for most of the early structures. As a consequence, the locations of both early and late Basketmaker II sites are included in Figure 19A.

As demonstrated in Chapter 4, late Basketmaker II and Basketmaker III cluster tightly into discrete periods; hence, it was unnecessary to draw an arbitrary dividing line between these stages. Late Basketmaker II spans the period from A.D. 200 to 375. Basketmaker III begins at A.D. 600 and lasts until A.D. 700–750, depending on the definitional criteria employed. Unlike the series of transitions considered above, there are

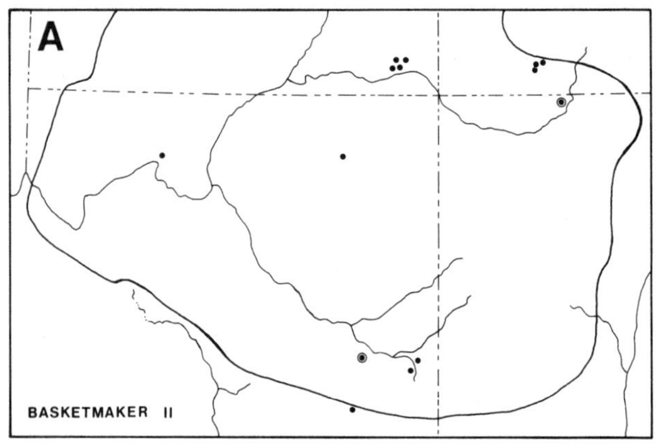

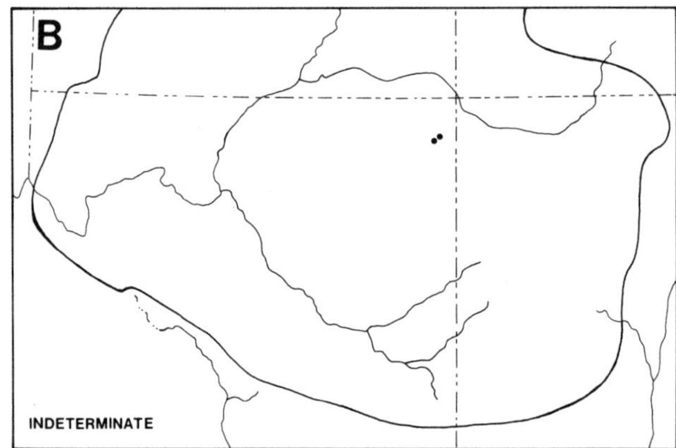

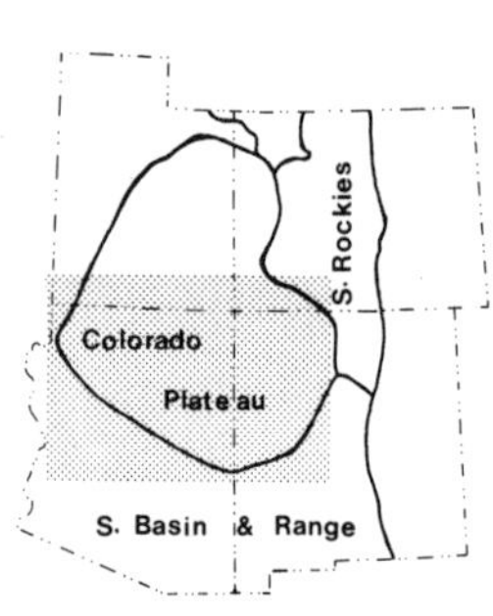

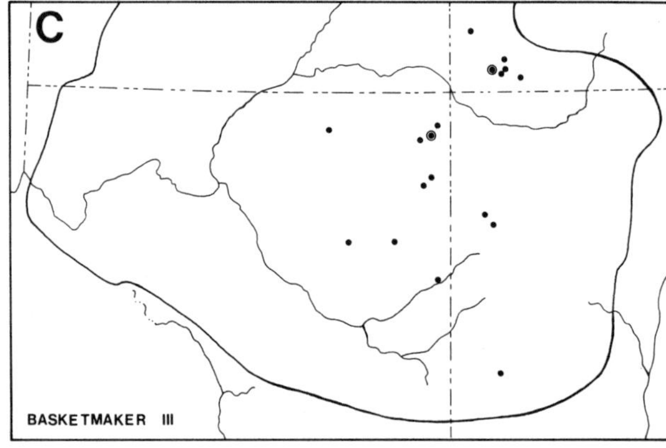

Figure 19. Distribution of dated sites from 185 B.C. to A.D. 750. Each dot represents a site; circled dots are site clusters. A, Early and classic Basketmaker II sites: 185 B.C. to A.D. 375; B, sites of indeterminate status: A.D. 375 to A.D. 600; C, Basketmaker III sites: A.D. 600 to A.D. 750.

no sites that bridge the greater than two-century gap separating these stages. The only evidence of Plateau occupation for the intervening period consists of a few dated pithouses, all of which appear to be short-lived.

The sudden abandonment of late Basketmaker II sites is probably attributable to a drought interval, although the supporting climatic data are scant in comparison to the cases discussed earlier. The nine records of tree-ring indices with the greatest time depth are plotted in Figure 14. The statistical manipulations employed in their construction have already been outlined. In Figure 14 the shaded band is equal to plus-or-minus 1.64σ (90% confidence interval), rather than the 1.22σ used in the previous climatic chart (Figure 13), because in this case we are dealing with single records rather than the average values from several stations; and the probability that ring width may have been influenced by factors other than climate—e.g., disease, soils, slopes, etc.—is somewhat greater. The wider significance band should help to eliminate these potential sources of noise.

Only two of the areas occupied during late Basketmaker II have climatic records of sufficient time depth to be of immediate relevance: Durango and Natural Bridges. In both cases, site abandonment corresponds quite closely to negative departures in the indices. As mentioned earlier, the Canyon de Chelly, Durango, Natural Bridges, and Navajo Mountain records all show a significant negative departure at around A.D. 370. This may be indicative of an early Plateau-wide drought similar in scope and effect to those that occurred later in the sequence. Unfortunately, none of the other records go back in time beyond A.D. 400.

At any rate, the late Basketmaker II stage came to an abrupt halt at A.D. 375, and the dense clustering of sites that may unequivocally be called Basketmaker III does not begin until A.D. 600. Before discussing the few intervening sites, it bears mentioning that Basketmaker III is best defined as a synthesis of elements already in existence in late Basketmaker II. In other words, it appears that Basketmaker III was a consequence of climatically induced coexistence of previously distinct Basketmaker II populations despite the fact that no likely candidates for transition sites have yet been identified. In support of this contention, I point out that the architectural descriptions offered in Chapter 4 reveal major distinctions between eastern and western Basketmaker II houses. The relevant western sites include Veres, Pittman, Lone Tree Dune, Tumbleweed Canyon, and the Bluff Site. The eastern sites include the many examples from the Navajo Reservoir District and the Durango area. Prior to the end of late Basketmaker II, a few structures in the western region had four-post support superstructures, whereas the technique was unknown in the east. On the other hand, many of the eastern structures had large antechambers, while these features were absent in the western sites. The standard Basketmaker III house has both features and is best seen as a combination of the two Basketmaker II architectural traditions. Similarly, the bow and arrow was in use only in the eastern region prior to the Basketmaker II abandonment (Reed and Kainer 1978), but it had completely replaced the atlatl by the onset of Basketmaker III. And finally, some Basketmaker II sites had ceramics while others did not, and the available descriptions (poor as they may be) leave little doubt that there was a considerable degree of variability in surface finish, color, temper, and firing atmosphere. By the beginning of Basketmaker III, every site contained a nearly identical assemblage consisting of Lino Gray and Lino Black-on-gray or the equivalent local types. This, too, suggests a synthesis of features from the earlier period. The problem for research is an elucidation of events during the 225-year interlude. There are a few clues, but the picture is still unclear.

For instance, there is some indication that Canyon de Chelly was used as a refuge area during the latter part of the fourth and portions of the fifth century. Earl Morris (1925, 1938) excavated several houses in the talus slope below Mummy Cave, located ten miles upstream from the confluence of Canyon de Chelly and Canyon del Muerto. This work was done in the 1920s and 1930s and, as might be expected, provenience data for the tree-ring specimens are imprecise.

Cutting dates of timbers thought to have come from talus-slope structures range from A.D. 348 to 485. The structures were

> roughly made circular houses, 12 to 25 feet in diameter. They had walls of sandstone slabs or posts set leaning inwards, plastered with mud and roofed with logs covered with earth. One burned house had several pottery vessels, charred baskets, sandals and planting sticks near a sunken hearth. . . . Each of these houses was surrounded by a number of storage bins. These were of irregular shape and depth, and were two to six feet in diameter. They were lined with large thin slabs set on edge, the cracks and joints being sealed with mud reinforced with shredded bark, reed leaves or corn husks. Two had roofs in place consisting of jug-like necks of adobe reinforced with sticks and covered with circular slabs. Some of the cists held corn, gourds and seeds (Bannister, Dean, and Gell 1966:16).

Donald Morris (personal communication, 1978) has recently obtained tree-ring cores from similar storage structures in Canyon de Chelly that date in the 420s and 430s. This evidence seems to indicate that limited agriculture was being practiced in the canyons during the fifth century.

There is also evidence for a brief episode of building activity in northeastern Arizona during the sixth century. One cluster of dates at around A.D. 500 comes from houses in Obelisk and Broken Flute caves (E. A. Morris 1959) in the Prayer Rock District of northeastern Arizona. The houses have four-post support systems, but lack antechambers; ceramics and the bow and arrow were present. A lone date of A.D. 555 comes from a pithouse in the Klethla Valley of northeastern Arizona (Ambler and Olson 1977). If the date is correct, this would be the earliest known instance of the combination of four-post support and an antechamber in the same structure. The Klethla Valley may eventually prove to be a very important area for understanding the transition from Basketmaker II to Basketmaker III. However, more than one date will be required to establish occupation during this period.

As Figure 14 reveals, climate was fairly erratic from A.D. 370 to 600 in all the areas of record, and southern Colorado Plateau populations were apparently quite small and dispersed. In all likelihood, individual households had to relocate frequently in order to find suitable habitats for crop growth.

During the seventh century, climatic indices are excellent for nearly all of the areas. The cultural syntheses of the previous two centuries—whatever their exact nature and loci—had produced Basketmaker III, the associated populations of which covered the southern Colorado Plateau shortly after A.D. 600. Basketmaker III was apparently a period of cultural stability, exhibiting no signs of significant change until the severe droughts of the early and middle eighth century.

Summary and Discussion

The foregoing treatment of Anasazi prehistory stresses the importance of major population dislocations and the effects of climatically induced aggregation. Smaller-scale adaptive adjustments are also apparent in the record. One possibility is suggested by an apparent anomaly detectable in the general model of Anasazi evolution: Most of the proposed refuge localities were occupied *prior* to the onset of major droughts. A good example is found in the intensively investigated Pueblo de los Muertos and Scribe S sites in the El Morro Valley of New Mexico (Watson, LeBlanc, and Redman 1980). The sites are located immediately adjacent to one another at an elevation of over 7000 feet. Scribe S consists of a number of small, scattered room blocks occupied from approximately A.D. 1250 to 1275, i.e., just prior to the drought of the A.D. 1280s. Pueblo de los Muertos is a massive pueblo of over 700 rooms that was constructed rapidly, shortly after the onset of drought conditions. This suggests that Anasazi populations may have been practicing a bimodal settlement strategy during the late 1200s, planting crops at high-elevation sites like Scribe S as well as at the more numerous low-elevation sites. Simultaneous utilization of both types of environmental setting would have served as a buffer against year-to-year climatic variation. With the shift to protracted drought, the low-elevation component of the buffered agricultural system was eliminated. The high-elevation component witnessed an unprecedented population influx and the consequent construction of large communities such as Pueblo de los Muertos. I suspect that similar patterns will emerge at the other refuge locales as soon as studies comparable in extent to the El Morro Valley project are undertaken. If this proves to be the case, periodic aggregation in drought refugia will be seen as an expectable consequence of "business-as-usual": the rapid shift of an equilibrium equation to one of its extreme values. Population dispersion following the cessation of drought conditions may also be viewed in this way from a strictly adaptive perspective. However, the sociocultural units of dispersion undoubtedly reflected the organizational structure formed in the various refuge sites and were therefore more complex than the units typical of the previous stage. These organizational consequences are, of course, less readily discerned than the changes in art and architecture discussed above. Nonetheless, they are of inestimable value to the development of cultural evolutionary theory and should be a primary focus of future fieldwork.

While the importance of specific adaptive mechanisms pertinent to particular times and places is not to be denied, the general model of Anasazi evolution thus far developed is of greater interest because it stresses the significance of evolutionary tempo. It marks a clear point of departure from the gradualist formulations that have dominated Southwestern thinking for over a half-century. Recent syntheses that might be viewed as competing perspectives are not, in my estimate, sufficiently consistent with the climatic and chronometric evidence. For instance, Lipe's (1978) overview of the Southwest summarizes other investigators' interpretations of the data rather than summarizing and critically evaluating the "raw" data. As a consequence, his paper inadvertently incorporates the tendency of most investigators to interpret local sequences as continuous, and therefore elevates this usually unstated bias to the level of an empirical generalization. The preordained conclusion is that uniform, gradual, endogenous development has occurred in each of the defined Southwestern subareas, e.g., Anasazi, Mogollon, Hohokam, etc. There is very little room for migration as a major Anasazi adaptive strategy, and no room at all for climate as a significant mediating factor.

In another example, Euler et al. (1979) allow that a great number of migrations and other population adjustments have typified the Anasazi sequence. However, the entire model is a hodgepodge of asynchronous migrations that obscure the macropatterning of the data. The main problem with the construct lies in a disparity of critical evaluation between the climatic reconstruction, on the one hand, and the cultural reconstruction, on the other. The climatic aspects of the paper are quite sound and in many ways are much more meticulously worked out than the simple arguments offered here. However, the cultural chronologies are nothing more than "summaries of summaries" that fall considerably short of the level of effort expended on climatic and hydrologic research. As a consequence, the fit between climatic and cultural events is muddled, and no general patterns reveal themselves.

The alternative presented here is based on an exhaustive review of the data, and the chronometric sample size is sufficiently large that it seems very unlikely that the general pattern will be significantly altered by further research.

ANASAZI TRANSITIONS: A SOUTHWESTERN PERSPECTIVE

There are certain implications of the Anasazi model which have not, as yet, been discussed. Of primary importance are the unrealistically high growth rates suggested in Figure 13. As discussed earlier, the relationship between trends in the tree-ring bar chart and actual variations in human population size is a complex matter not readily amenable to quantification. Nonetheless, it is reasonable to argue that some of the trends are quite inconsistent with the growth rates anticipated for a *closed* population at a preindustrial level of technology. For example, the Pueblo II/Pueblo III refuge site of Wupatki is the only well-dated Plateau village known to have been occupied at A.D. 1150. During the ensuing 100 years, the number of Pueblo III sites increased to thirty. Obviously, there were more than thirty Pueblo III sites actually occupied at this time and, as mentioned earlier, Wupatki was probably not the only refuge locality occupied at A.D. 1150. But if we accept Figure 13 as a representative sample of Plateau sites, then a thirtyfold increase in the number of Anasazi villages in three or four generations is indicated. Accurate room counts are not available for all of these Pueblo III villages but it seems clear from the available descriptions that many are as large or larger than Wupatki. Thus the increase cannot be explained as a fragmentation of large villages into a greater number of small ones. Following the more appropriately quantitative arguments of Cowgill (1975), anomalous demographic circumstances of this sort suggest that the increases were augmented to a considerable degree by immigration. By the same token, many of the precipitous declines in site occupation suggest emigration to regions outside the Plateau since it is doubtful that the identified refugia were large enough to accommodate all the refugees set in motion by Plateau-wide droughts.

The situation, then, may have been something like the following: (1) During drought periods, a portion of the Plateau Anasazi population crowded into the few existing microenvironments that could support maize farming; (2) the remainder left the Plateau, most likely moving into the southern Basin and Range province of Arizona and New Mexico and the southern tip of the Rocky Mountain province in the area around Santa Fe; (3) with the amelioration of climatic conditions, significant numbers of people returned to the Plateau. Leaving aside for the moment any consideration of *why* the various return migrations occurred, this model implies that a bar chart of tree-ring dated sites for the Hohokam, Mogollon, and eastern Pueblo areas would reveal a distribution complementary to that of the Plateau. Unfortunately, this interesting possibility cannot be tested for the entire sweep of Southwestern prehistory since the tree-ring data for the southern Basin and Range and Rocky Mountain provinces are scant prior to about A.D. 1200. The only sources of chronometric data suitable for testing the complementarity hypothesis during the pre–A.D. 1200 era are the radiocarbon bar charts presented in Chapter 3, Figure 3. These are repeated in Figure 20 with some additional elaboration. It should be emphasized that the radiocarbon bar charts were constructed differently from the tree-ring bar charts and are not even remotely related to population size. They simply depict changes in the *relative probability* of occupation through time; they are not to be interpreted as population indices. Nonetheless, the major trends in these charts (i.e., peaks and troughs) should provide a reliable indication of the *direction* of change (increase or decrease). The delineation of such trends is sufficient for the present purposes since the implication being tested is occupational complementarity, not the magnitude or rate of actual population change.

The charts do, in fact, display complementary trends at a number of points and therefore tend to support the notion of periodic population adjustment between the Colorado Plateau and the southern Basin and Range provinces. The first instance of this has already been discussed in connection with the introduction of maize to the Plateau. As noted in Chapter 3, the Basketmaker II peak increases sharply as the San Pedro portion of the Basin and Range curve declines, suggesting a northward migration of early farming populations. Similarly, the demise of Basketmaker II correlates with an increase in the Basin and Range curve beginning at some time prior to A.D. 500. This apparently marks the onset of Pioneer Hohokam if the recent reassessments of Hohokam chronology are correct (Plog 1978; Wilcox 1979; Berry and Marmaduke 1980). The SU Site (Paul Sidney Martin 1943; Martin and Rinaldo 1940, 1947), located in the mountainous zone south of the Mogollon Rim, was also occupied during this period, from around A.D. 460 to 500 (Bannister, Hannah, and Robinson 1970). It thus appears that Southwestern ceramic technology first occurred on the Plateau and was later introduced to the Hohokam and Mogollon areas of the Basin and Range via migration during the Basketmaker II–III hiatus.

The Basketmaker III–Pueblo I break revealed in the tree-ring record is not replicated in the Plateau radiocarbon curve. This is not surprising given the relatively short duration of that particular discontinuity and the small number of radiocarbon dates available for Basketmaker III sites. However, the more lengthy Pueblo I–Pueblo II break *is* replicated by the radiocarbon evidence, and this corresponds to the Hohokam peak for the Basin and Range curve. This, of course, is quite consistent with the fact that Pueblo I and Pueblo II ceramics are the prevalent intrusives in Hohokam sites.

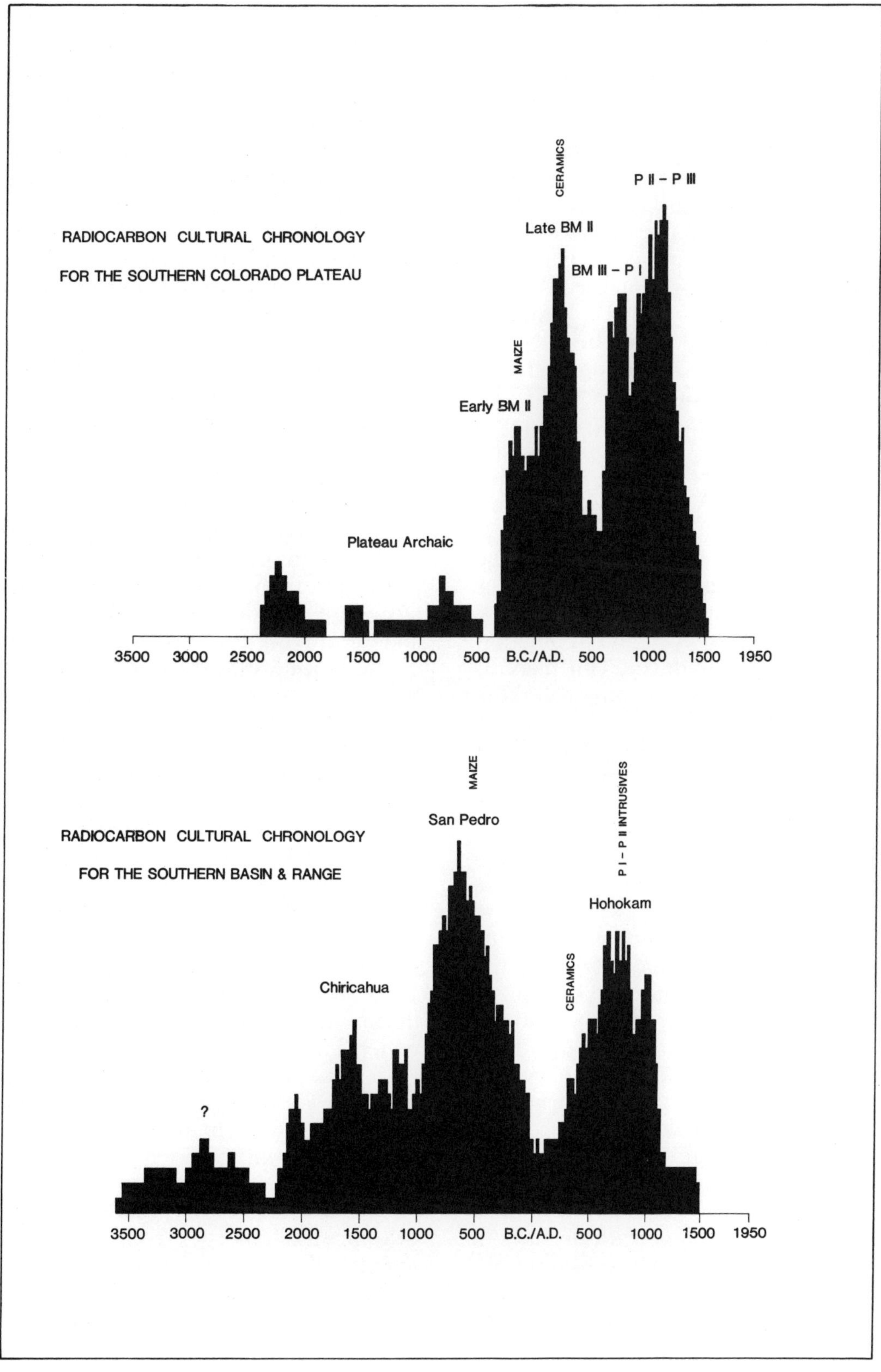

Figure 20. Radiocarbon bar charts for the southern Colorado Plateau and the southern Basin and Range province.

No Pueblo III peak is indicated in the Plateau curve because very few excavators have attempted to date Pueblo III sites by the radiocarbon method. I suspect that the rather drastic Pueblo II–Pueblo III discontinuity would be prominently reflected in the chart if a sufficient sample of dates were available. At any rate, the absence of data for this critical period in both the Plateau and Basin and Range provinces precludes further investigation into what has been termed the Anasazi "takeover" of the Mogollon area (Wheat 1955; Martin and Plog 1973; J. D. Jennings 1974). At some time after A.D. 1000 the pithouse villages, characteristic of the Mogollon tradition for a millenium, were suddenly replaced by masonry pueblos; and black-on-white ceramics made their first appearance in the area. The event is, unfortunately, poorly dated, but future work will quite likely demonstrate a correspondence between the onset of this southern migration and the A.D. 1100 or 1140 drought on the Plateau. The current estimate of A.D. 1000 is based on the *earliest* dated occurrence of analog Anasazi ceramic types. However, the population movement in question may have taken place at any time during the temporal range of these black-on-white types. Given the model presented here, it probably took place near the recent end of that range, coeval with the abandonment of Chaco Canyon and the founding of Wupatki.

The case for complementarity is on much more solid ground after A.D. 1200 since a large sample of tree-ring dated sites is available for most of the relevant areas. Figure 21 shows two bar charts constructed in the same manner described for Figures 12C and 13. Figure 21A represents the latter centuries of the Colorado Plateau sequence. Figure 21B depicts the same period for the southern Basin and Range province and the southern tip of the Rocky Mountain province. The sites included in Figure 21B are primarily located in the mountainous zone south of the Mogollon Rim in Arizona and in the Rio Grande Valley of New Mexico. No tree-ring dates are available for the Hohokam area. The evidence here seems clear-cut since significant declines in Plateau occupation are matched by significant increases in adjacent areas and vice versa. Specifically, the Pueblo III abandonment of the Plateau corresponds to major influxes south of the Mogollon Rim at sites such as Kinishba (Cummings 1938, 1940), Point of Pines (Haury 1958), Canyon Creek Ruin and a series of related sites in the Sierra Ancha region (Haury 1934). This population intrusion brought Anasazi groups into contact situations with indigenous Basin and Range groups as is well demonstrated in the Point of Pines data (Haury 1958). The ceramic types associated with the enigmatic Saladoan phenomenon (Doyel and Haury 1976) apparently were created as a consequence since they seem to date earliest in this region.

In addition, a number of pueblos in the Rio Grande were first settled following the Anasazi Pueblo III abandonment, and it appears that Stubbs and Stallings (1953) were correct in postulating a major migration from the Mesa Verde area to the northern Rio Grande.

The rapid decline in the number of dated sites in the Basin and Range at around A.D. 1340 is primarily attributable to the abandonment of the large pueblos south of the Mogollon Rim. These abandonments correspond to the reoccupation of the Hopi Mesas during Pueblo IV times. Rio Grande settlement apparently remained stable during this period.

Finally, the decline in Pueblo IV Plateau settlement corresponds to an increase in number of Rio Grande Pueblos. The latter were occupied continuously into the European contact period. One interesting implication of the temporal patterning in Figure 21A is that the Hopi Mesas may have been abandoned shortly after A.D. 1400 and not reoccupied until after A.D. 1500. As Figure 13 shows, Plateau-wide droughts occurred at A.D. 1400 and A.D. 1450, hence the Pueblo IV abandonment of the Mesas is consistent with the general model.

In sum, the juxtaposition of chronometric data from the Plateau and adjacent areas supports the complementarity hypothesis and yields patterns inconsistent with models that stress *in situ* development.

The overall picture of Southwestern demographics that emerges from this analysis is one of dynamic fluxion between the Colorado Plateau and Basin and Range province, combined with significant colonization of the southernmost por-

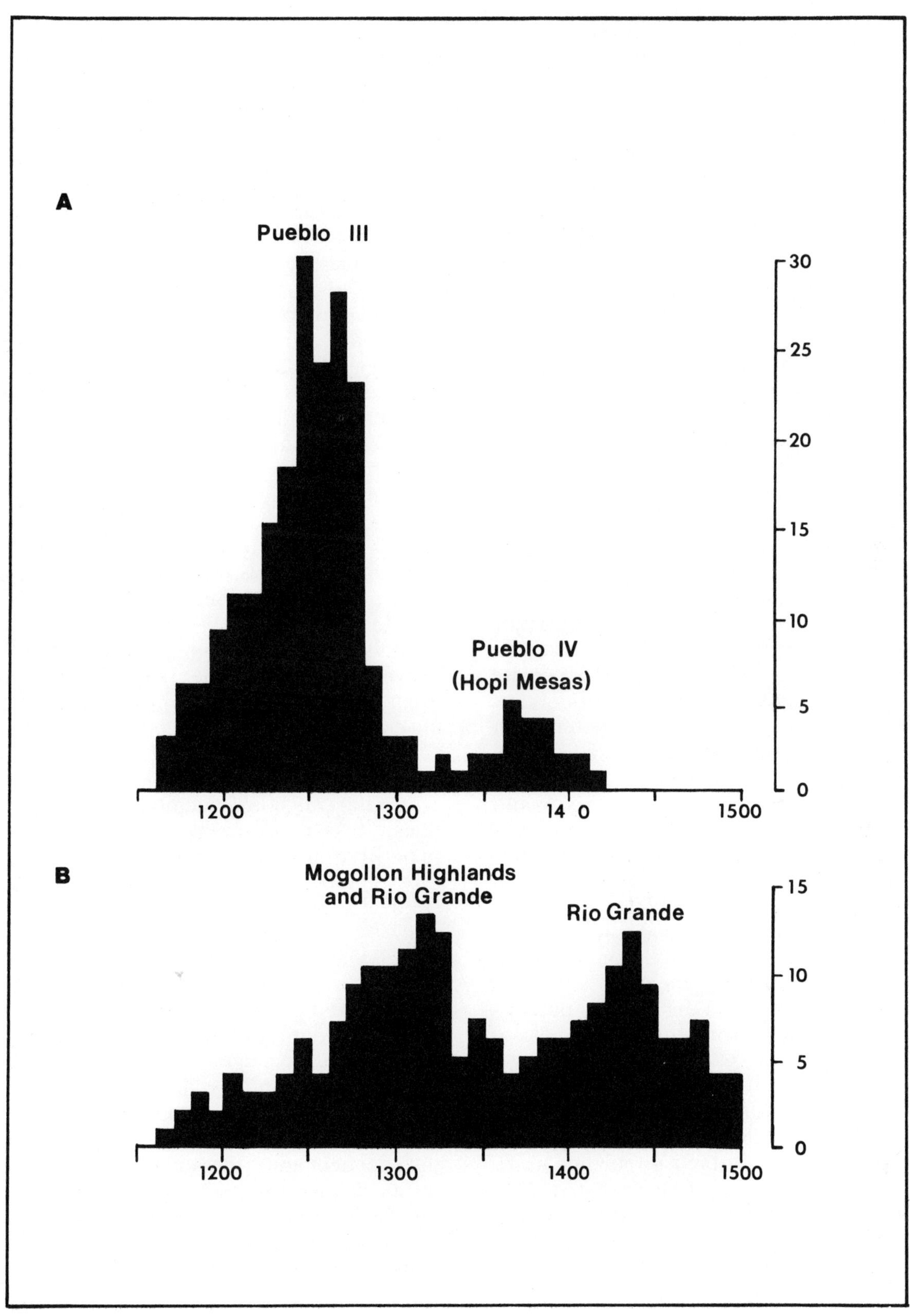

Figure 21. Ten-year increment bar charts of tree-ring dated sites from A.D. 1150 to A.D. 1500. A, Colorado Plateau; B, southern Basin and Range and southern Rocky Mountain provinces.

tion of the Rocky Mountain province late in the prehistoric period. Population exchanges throughout most of the Southwestern agricultural sequence occurred primarily among the Anasazi, Mogollon, and Hohokam regions. The reason for Anasazi abandonment and subsequent emigration to the Basin and Range have already been discussed at length; cyclical drought forced portions of the Plateau population into high-elevation refugia while the rest migrated to adjacent provinces. But why should these groups, who presumably had made a successful adaptive adjustment south of the Mogollon Rim, return to the Plateau with the cessation of drought conditions? One possible answer is found in the agricultural practices of the dry-farming Anasazi, at one end of the spectrum, and the irrigation-farming Hohokam at the other. The same tropical weather systems apply to both areas. A mountainous belt separates the Colorado Plateau from the southern Basin and Range of Arizona and parts of New Mexico. This effectively places the Plateau in a rain shadow insofar as the tropical-based storm pattern is concerned. The major tributaries of the Salt and Gila rivers originate in this same mountainous belt. These factors create an interesting situation in that periods of low rainfall severely limit the agricultural potential of the Plateau while many streams in the Basin and Range remain viable and adequate for purposes of canal irrigation. Such circumstances would prompt a shift in emphasis from Plateau to Basin and Range settlement. However, during periods of increased precipitation much of the Plateau would support dry farming and *akchin* agricultural systems, whereas many Basin and Range river valleys would be subject to disastrous flooding. Southworth (1919) has documented the serious impacts of flood damage on the farming productivity of the Gila Pima during the historic period, and it is likely that the severity of flooding was even greater during the numerous prehistoric periods marked by positive decadal departures in the tree-ring indices (Figure 13). Such circumstances would have prompted population shifts in the reverse direction. The destruction of irrigation systems would not have led to complete abandonment of the southern deserts. Dry-farming was probably feasible in many subareas of the Basin and Range during periods of high precipitation and the old dichotomy between "Riverine" and "Desert" Hohokam (Haury 1950) may still be meaningful if redefined in terms of alternative adaptive strategies.

Thus, in both the Anasazi and Hohokam areas, refugia were available during periods of protracted environmental stress so that, by and large, a gray ware–white ware tradition was maintained on the Plateau and a buff ware tradition was maintained in the southern Basin and Range. However, during these same periods, major population adjustments occurred between the two areas that alternately entailed (1) emigrant Anasazi groups moving into the area dominated by the Hohokam tradition, and (2) emigrant Hohokam groups moving into the area dominated by the Anasazi tradition. In this regard, it is interesting to note that Anasazi design styles (e.g., Kana-a and Black Mesa) are frequently executed on red-on-buff "Hohokam" vessels. And the reverse situation is also true where hachure design elements of the Pioneer period later occur on Pueblo II black-on-white vessels. A similar case could be made for architectural forms in the two provinces. Much of the Mogollon area lies between the Anasazi and Hohokam, and its changing cultural content through time seems to reflect alternating periods of Hohokam and Anasazi cultural domination and various combinations of art and architecture diagnostic of these two entities. This is consistent with the complementarity hypothesis and suggests that the Mogollon concept may be more appropriately analyzed as a cultural amalgum rather than as a unitary tradition.

This is an unusual way to look at the Southwestern prehistoric record, but it is not inconsistent with what is known about ethnographically documented migrations. For example, the Tewa-speaking Hano migrated to the Hopi Mesas in historic times, and by all accounts immediately *became* Hopi insofar as social structure and material culture are concerned (Dozier 1966). The only archeological evidence for this population influx would be a few changes in the ceramic assemblage analogous to those suggested above.

It is therefore reasonable to propose a Hohokam–Mogollon–Anasazi geographic continuum within which there existed a dynamic ebb-and-flow of population. These traditional labels should no longer be thought of as names of "peoples" in the linguistic or ethnic sense. It is quite conceivable that the Anasazi tradition, for instance, was maintained by peoples of diverse linguistic background during any particular stage of the Pecos Classification or by the same or different linguistic stock during sequent stages.

Conclusions

This study has examined space-time systematics for the most accurately dated prehistoric sequence in the world. Without the chronometric precision afforded by the tree-ring method, it would have been impossible to see through the distortions created by gradualist assumptions and discern the punctuated tempo of Anasazi evolution. This example leads to the suspicion that other regional sequences may be similarly distorted. It may be the case that evolutionary sequences, in general, are *characteristically* punctuated, and that smooth transformational continua occur infrequently—if at all. If so, then we should *expect* to find evidence of demographic abruption or some other form of discontinuity between the recognized stages or phases of all regional sequences. I have suggested that this might be true for the Hohokam sequence, and I suspect that this is the case for the Fremont culture of Utah as well. Since chronometric control in both these areas is based primarily on radiocarbon determinations from a relatively small number of sites, it is impossible at present to assess Hohokam or Fremont evolutionary tempos with the same degree of resolution attainable for the Anasazi region. Nonetheless, the gross complementarity evidenced in the radiocarbon bar charts for the Colorado Plateau and southern Basin and Range province is wholly consistent with a punctuational perspective of Hohokam development.

Beyond empirical considerations, there are several compelling reasons for accepting the general model of Southwestern evolution outlined briefly in the preceding section. First, it provides a framework for the explanation of Southwestern phenomena as a whole in terms of endogenous processes, obviating the need to link all major innovations and events to ill-defined Mexican sources. Undoubtedly, Mexican-Southwestern cultural contact occurred—perhaps frequently—but its importance as an external stimulus to Southwestern development has been extremely exaggerated. Internal population movements and the cultural dynamics of coexistence and amalgamation in refugia are sufficient to account for the recognized transformations.

Second, the suggestion that populations moved freely across the "culture area" boundaries of archeologists stresses the significance of migration as a prehistoric adaptive strategy, and perhaps more importantly it draws attention to a fundamental anthropological concept—the independence of language, culture, and genetic heritage. "Hohokam," "Anasazi," and "Mogollon" are labels for distinguishable clusters of material culture traits. They are not the names of mutually exclusive breeding populations nor do they refer to linguistic affiliation. Yet, a one-to-one correspondence between culture and language, culture and genetics, or both, is implicit in much of the archeological literature. Much of this is a function of writing style (e.g., frequent references to "Anasazi groups" or "Hohokam populations" in this work), but there remains a strong undercurrent of *de facto* "ceramics-equals-people" thinking in the Southwest that exerts a powerful, if unstated, influence over the kinds of interpretations that are considered acceptable. For example, I anticipate that the notion of small groups of people abandoning the Colorado Plateau at A.D. 900, moving into viable communities in the southern Basin and Range province, and living amicably under these circumstances while executing Kana-a style ceramic design elements in the local red-on-buff technological medium will *not* readily be accepted as a reasonable or even rational idea. Yet analogous cases are commonplace in the ethnographic literature. The point is that some migrations may be archeologically invisible, some moderately visible, and others highly visible. Typically, only evidence of the latter variety, i.e., the "site unit intrusion," is deemed acceptable; and even these rather clear-cut cases of migration are attributed to diffusion or the nebulous notion of "influence" by many of the Southwestern processualists. In contrast, the general model used here acknowledges the full range of migration/contact situations and anticipates the corresponding levels of empirical visibility.

Finally, acceptance of the model solves a number of traditional anomalies, one of which has been discussed earlier in some detail. I refer to the frequently expressed opinion that the Great Drought could not have caused the thirteenth-century Anasazi abandonment since there had been several earlier droughts of similar magnitude which were *not* accompanied by widespread abandonments. The foregoing analyses have, I believe, adequately refuted this position. Drought-induced population dislocation was a recurrent feature in Anasazi prehistory. Another long-standing anomaly is the fact that new ceramic types tend to occur earlier in "trade" contexts than they do in their supposed areas of "indigenous" manufacture (Plog and Cordell 1979). There is no mystery here either, only a preoccupation with age-area formulations. That is, a great many Southwesternists operate under the implicit assumption that new ideas originate in "culture centers" and radiate outward to the cultural periphery through trade and diffusion. Given the further assumption of cultural lag, the expectation is that innovations should date somewhat earlier in the centers than in the peripheries. The discovery that the actual temporal ordering was the other way around has come as a surprise to most workers, and no plausible explanation has been offered. The difficulty is easily resolved as soon as it is realized that those sites termed "peripheral" in traditional models are the refugia of the model presented here. Those areas traditionally thought of as "culture centers" were depopulated during the refuge (drought) epicycles, but were subsequently reoccupied as climatic conditions ameliorated. Hence, the direction of movement was from refuge area ("periphery") to the interior of the Plateau ("center"). This is, of course, quite consistent with the supposedly anomalous dating of events.

In conclusion, it should be noted that the data upon which this view of Southwestern prehistory is based are less than ideal. This much I acknowledge. However, the Anasazi data seem to form a coherent pattern, and I do not expect this patterning to be altered fundamentally by future work. Anasazi-Hohokam complementarity constitutes a much more conjectural construct, but it is no less plausible than any extant model. Moreover, it provides an intuitively acceptable account of certain demographic oddities and stylistic parallels that are otherwise puzzling. What is required in order to thoroughly test the general model is the strict application of stratigraphic excavation techniques to a wide variety of sites, coupled with the judicious cumulation of well-controlled tree-ring and radiocarbon dates. While I see this as a pan-Southwestern concern, priority should be given to the Hohokam region. This should not be construed as a special condemnation of scholars working in that particular "culture area"; indifferent excavation techniques and capricious extraction of radiocarbon samples are no more prevalent here than in other regions of the Southwest. But the absolute precision and the large sample size of Anasazi tree-ring dates have compensated for the poor quality of fieldwork in that area, whereas no such panacea exists for the Hohokam. What is called for, then, is an emphasis on stratigraphic excavation and the recovery of large numbers of radiocarbon samples from a wide variety of Hohokam sites. A similar research program is called for in the Mogollon "area," and I anticipate that it eventually will be demonstrated that Mogollon (at least its western aspect) is little more than an area-specific rubric for a number of migratory/refugia events—an occupational staccato best thought of as a series of epiphenomena causally related to demographic adjustments within and between the Anasazi and Hohokam areas.

APPENDIX

Southern Colorado Plateau Radiocarbon Dates

Site	Date (B.P.)	Lab No.	Material	Date (A.D./B.C.)	Accept/Reject	Source & Comments
Atlatl Cave	2330±85	DIC588	charcoal	380 B.C.	−	T. Matthews personal communication, 1977. DIC 588 contaminated by amberat. Remainder O.K.
	2700±65	DIC592	charcoal	750 B.C.	+	
	2730±65	DIC590	charcoal	780 B.C.	+	
	4240±70	DIC591	charcoal	2290 B.C.	+	
Broken K Pueblo	790±45	GRN4555	wood	A.D. 1160	+	Vogel and Waterbolk 1967. Tree-ring dated from 1208 to 1259. Only GRN4555 in that range.
	920±65	GRN4347	charcoal	A.D. 1030	−	
	985±50	GRN4351	charcoal	A.D. 965	−	
	990±70	GRN4361	charcoal	A.D. 960	−	
	1140±70	GRN4360	charcoal	A.D. 810	−	
Carter Ranch	830±70	GRN4112	charcoal	A.D. 1120	+	Damon, Haynes, and Long, 1964; Vogel and Waterbolk 1964; Haynes, Damon, and Grey 1966. A425b on humates. Rest come from three different sites/components.
	840±70	GRN4113	charcoal	A.D. 1110	+	
	990±60	GRN4111	wood	A.D. 960	+	
	1020±40	A425a	charcoal	A.D. 930	+	
	1170±180	A425b	humates	A.D. 780	−	
	1370±120	A550	charcoal	A.D. 580	+	
Chilcott Site	780±80	GRN2414	charcoal	A.D. 1170	+	Vogel and Waterbolk 1964
Cly Site	2510±110	A110	charcoal	560 B.C.	+	Haynes, Damon, and Grey 1966
Connie	1695±105	GX1656	wood	A.D. 255	+	F. Plog personal communication, 1978
County Road Locale	545±95	GX1652	wood	A.D. 1405	+	F. Plog personal communication, 1978
County Road Site	2020±95	GX0237	wood charcoal	70 B.C.	+	H. Krueger personal communication, 1978. See text.
	2300±70	GX0272	wood charcoal	350 B.C.	−	
	3095±75	GX0274	wood charcoal	1145 B.C.	−	
Ariz D:7:102	2680±165	GX2747	charcoal	730 B.C.	+	J. Ware personal communication, 1977
Ariz D:7:152	2000±80	I8403	charcoal	50 B.C.	+	J. Ware personal communication, 1977. See text.
	2090±80	I8409	charcoal	140 B.C.	+	
	2100±80	I8410	charcoal	150 B.C.	+	
	2120±80	I8405	charcoal	170 B.C.	+	
	2150±80	I8408	charcoal	200 B.C.	+	
	2170±80	I8407	charcoal	220 B.C.	+	
	2180±80	I8404	charcoal	230 B.C.	+	
	2205±80	I8406	charcoal	255 B.C.	+	
	2210±80	I8402	charcoal	260 B.C.	+	
Dust Devil Cave	1820±80	TX452	charcoal	A.D. 130	+	Valastro and Davis 1970
18 Mile Bend	850±200	M742	wood	A.D. 1100	+	Crane and Griffin 1959

APPENDIX (continued)

Site	Date (B.P.)	Lab No.	Material	Date (A.D./B.C.)	Accept/Reject	Source & Comments
GC-663	1630±90	RL340	charcoal	A.D. 320	+	Thompson and Thompson 1974. See text.
	1690±100	RL336	charcoal	A.D. 260	+	
	1720±100	RL335	charcoal	A.D. 230	+	
	1750±100	RL337	charcoal	A.D. 200	+	
	1810±100	RL338	charcoal	A.D. 140	+	
	1850±90	RL339	charcoal	A.D. 100	+	
GC-671	630±100	RL78	charcoal	A.D. 1320	+	C. Tucek personal communication, 1978
	720±100	RL50	charcoal	A.D. 1230	+	
	780±100	RL79	charcoal	A.D. 1170	+	
	840±110	RL80	charcoal	A.D. 1110	+	
GG-69-1	1655±80	GX2072	charcoal	A.D. 295	+	W. Lipe and R.G. Matson personal communication, 1977. See text.
GG-69-15	1225±110	GX2073	charcoal	A.D. 725	+	W. Lipe and R.G. Matson personal communication, 1977
GG-69-18	1570±80	GX2141	charcoal	A.D. 380	+	W. Lipe and R.G. Matson personal communication, 1977. See text.
	1695±90	GX2142	charcoal	A.D. 255	+	
	1759±176	GX2142 (rerun)	charcoal	A.D. 191	+	
	1870±100	GX2074	charcoal	A.D. 80	+	
GG-69-20	1655±85	GX2143	charcoal	A.D. 295	+	W. Lipe and R.G. Matson personal communication, 1977
GG-70-187	1510±100	GX2076	charcoal	A.D. 440	+	W. Lipe and R.G. Matson personal communication, 1977
	1610±95	GX2075	charcoal	A.D. 340	+	
Glen Canyon	1510±80	A495	charcoal	A.D. 440	+	Haynes, Damon, and Grey 1966
Hay Hollow Canal	895±100	GX1653	wood	A.D. 1055	+	F. Plog personal communication, 1978
Hay Hollow Site	1645±110	GX0804	charcoal	A.D. 305	*	J. Fritz personal communication, 1976. See text. GX0796 was a bone sample. Dates marked with an asterisk are from non-architectural proveniences. Only architectural features from this site are included in the bar charts.
	1685±120	GX0579	charcoal	A.D. 265	+	
	1705±85	GX0806	charcoal	A.D. 245	*	
	1720±90	GX0803	charcoal	A.D. 230	*	
	1755±115	GX0528	charcoal	A.D. 195	*	
	1785±70	GX0539	charcoal	A.D. 165	+	
	1820±80	GX0809	charcoal	A.D. 130	*	
	1845±95	GX0727	charcoal	A.D. 105	+	
	1870±95	GX0796	human bone	A.D. 80	–	
	1895±110	GX0798(?)	charcoal	A.D. 55	+	
	1920±75	GX0798(?)	charcoal	A.D. 30	+	
	1920±85	GX0802	charcoal	A.D. 30	*	
	1945±80	GX0801	charcoal	A.D. 5	*	
	1995±100	GX0580	charcoal	45 B.C.	+	
	2020±110	GX0808	charcoal	70 B.C.	*	
	2030±80	GX0792	charcoal	80 B.C.	+	
	2030±80	GX0799	charcoal	80 B.C.	+	
	2040±120	GX0800	charcoal	90 B.C.	*	
	2095±105	GX0540	charcoal	145 B.C.	+	
	2140±90	GX0805	charcoal	190 B.C.	*	
	2350±95	GX0807	charcoal	400 B.C.	–	
	2420±115	GX0582	charcoal	470 B.C.	–	

APPENDIX (continued)

Site	Date (B.P.)	Lab No.	Material	Date (A.D./B.C.)	Accept/Reject	Source & Comments
Hooper Ranch	570±65 730±60 865±80	GRN4039 GRN3006 GRN4040	charcoal charcoal charcoal	A.D. 1380 A.D. 1220 A.D. 1085	+ + +	Vogel and Waterbolk 1964. At least two components dated.
Hopi Buttes	1040±250 3100±250	W622 W621	charcoal charcoal	A.D. 910 1150 B.C.	+ +	Rubin and Alexander 1960
Ismay Pueblo	1010±100	I4107	charcoal	A.D. 940	−	Buckley and Willis 1970
Kinboko Cave 3	1730±200	W1741	juniper bark	A.D. 220	+	Ives, et al. 1967
Laguna Salada	3520±60	GRN1614	charcoal	1570 B.C.	+	Vogel and Waterbolk 1964
Lone Tree Dune	1700±80	Y1350	charcoal	A.D. 250	+	Stuiver 1969
LA3035	935±130	I1341	charcoal	A.D. 1015	+	Eddy 1966
LA3430	1845±131	TBN?	charcoal	A.D. 105	+	Eddy 1966. See text.
Marble Canyon	4095±100	UCLA741A	split twig figurine	2145 B.C.	+	Berger, Fergusson, and Libby 1965
Site 1291 Mesa Verde	890±150	I1112	charcoal	A.D. 1060	−	Buckley, Trautman, and Willis 1968. Provenience uncertain.
Mineral Creek Pueblo	1000±50 1220±55	GRN4008 GRN2417	charcoal charcoal	A.D. 950 A.D. 730	− −	Vogel and Waterbolk 1964. Too early for Pueblo III context.
No Name Wash	4100±150	RL416	charcoal	2160 B.C.	+	C. Tucek personal communication, 1978
NS #83	1020±85	GX1661	charcoal	A.D. 930	+	F. Plog personal communication, 1978
NS #201	590±90	GX1665	charcoal	A.D. 1360	+	F. Plog personal communication, 1978
NS #195	795±85	GX1660	charcoal	A.D. 1155	+	F. Plog personal communication, 1978
NS #196	1260±90	GX1664	charcoal	A.D. 690	+	F. Plog personal communication, 1978
NS #511	785±90	GX1663	charcoal	A.D. 1165	+	F. Plog personal communication, 1978
NS #1376	1240±95	GX1662	charcoal	A.D. 710	+	F. Plog personal communication, 1978

APPENDIX (continued)

Site	Date (B.P.)	Lab No.	Material	Date (A.D./B.C.)	Accept/Reject	Source & Comments
NA14,277	640±240	UGA2273	charcoal	A.D. 1310	+	W. Marmaduke personal communication, 1978. It seems unlikely that all of these dates are valid, but no additional information is yet available.
	1105±60	UGA2135	charcoal	A.D. 845	+	
	1110±120	UGA2132	charcoal	A.D. 840	+	
	1115±355	UGA2131	charcoal	A.D. 835	+	
	1240±70	UGA2272	charcoal	A.D. 710	+	
	1345±65	UGA2268	charcoal	A.D. 605	+	
	1355±65	UGA2134	charcoal	A.D. 595	+	
	1745±210	UGA2129	charcoal	A.D. 205	+	
NA14,646	1940±75	UGA2100	charcoal	A.D. 10	+	W. Marmaduke personal communication, 1978. See text.
	2040±60	UGA2104	charcoal	90 B.C.	+	
	2145±60	UGA2102	charcoal	195 B.C.	+	
	2180±60	UGA2101	charcoal	230 B.C.	+	
	2185±65	UGA2103	charcoal	235 B.C.	+	
NA14,650	720±85	UGA2250	charcoal	A.D. 1230	+	W. Marmaduke personal communication, 1978. It seems unlikely that all of these dates are valid, but no additional information is yet available.
	855±115	UGA2252	charcoal	A.D. 1095	+	
	905±65	UGA2254	charcoal	A.D. 1045	+	
	955±60	UGA2251	charcoal	A.D. 995	+	
	955±325	UGA2253	charcoal	A.D. 995	+	
	1250±60	UGA2256	charcoal	A.D. 700	+	
NA14,651	575±60	UGA2115	charcoal	A.D. 1375	+	W. Marmaduke personal communications, 1978. It seems unlikely that all of these dates are valid, but no additional information is yet available.
	800±170	UGA2112	charcoal	A.D. 1150	+	
	995±90	UGA2116	charcoal	A.D. 955	+	
	1055±90	UGA2114	charcoal	A.D. 895	+	
NA14,654	975±75	UGA2105	charcoal	A.D. 975	+	W. Marmaduke personal communication, 1978. It seems unlikely that all of these dates are valid, but no additional information is yet available.
	1005±60	UGA2258	charcoal	A.D. 945	+	
	1010±55	UGA2255	charcoal	A.D. 940	+	
	1040±60	UGA2107	charcoal	A.D. 910	+	
	1090±55	UGA2109	charcoal	A.D. 860	+	
	1105±55	UGA2108	charcoal	A.D. 845	+	
	1215±65	UGA2257	charcoal	A.D. 735	+	
	1225±90	UGA2106	charcoal	A.D. 725	+	
	1435±60	UGA2111	charcoal	A.D. 515	+	
	1450±280	UGA2110	charcoal	A.D. 500	+	
NA14,664	690±65	UGA2262	charcoal	A.D. 1260	+	W. Marmaduke personal communication, 1978. It seems unlikely that all of these dates are valid, but no additional information is yet available.
	880±85	UGA2261	charcoal	A.D. 1070	+	
	920±125	UGA2259	charcoal	A.D. 1030	+	
	950±60	UGA2260	charcoal	A.D. 1000	+	
NA14,674	1540±70	UGA2119	charcoal	A.D. 410	+	W. Marmaduke personal communication, 1978
	1785±80	UGA2118	charcoal	A.D. 165	+	
NA14,681	1155±60	UGA2266	charcoal	A.D. 795	+	W. Marmaduke personal communication, 1978. It seems unlikely that all of these dates are valid, but no additional information is yet available.
	1155±60	UGA2265	charcoal	A.D. 795	+	
	1225±70	UGA2263	charcoal	A.D. 725	+	
	1305±60	UGA2267	charcoal	A.D. 645	+	
	1485±60	UGA2264	charcoal	A.D. 465	+	
NA14,682	985±60	UGA2121	charcoal	A.D. 965	+	W. Marmaduke personal communication, 1978.
	1180±55	UGA2122	charcoal	A.D. 770	+	

APPENDIX (continued)

Site	Date (B.P.)	Lab No.	Material	Date (A.D./B.C.)	Accept/Reject	Source & Comments
NA14,683	1120±225	UGA2124	charcoal	A.D. 830	+	W. Marmaduke personal communication, 1978
	1255±60	UGA2125	charcoal	A.D. 695	+	
NA14,868	1235±85	UGA2128	charcoal	A.D. 715	+	W. Marmaduke personal communication, 1978
	1675±115	UGA2127	charcoal	A.D. 275	+	
O'Haco Rock-shelter	650±60	UCLA1876H	yucca fiber sandal	A.D. 1300	+	Briuer 1977
	730±80	UCLA1876C	charcoal	A.D. 1220	+	
	880±60	UCLA1876G	charcoal	A.D. 1070	+	
	2800±60	UCLA1876A	charcoal	850 B.C.	+	
	4170±150	UCR231	charcoal	2220 B.C.	+	
	4200±80	UCLA1876E	charcoal	2250 B.C.	+	
Oven Site	1750±115	I1342	charcoal	A.D. 200	+	Eddy 1966. See text.
Petri Site	1750±100	GX1659	wood charcoal	A.D. 200	+	F. Plog personal communication, 1978
Power Pole Site	1690±150	M1115C	rotton wood	A.D. 260	+	Eddy 1966. See text.
	1740±150	M1115D	rotton wood	A.D. 210	+	
	1830±150	M1115B	rotten wood	A.D. 120	+	
Valentine Village	1420±80	I(MNM)252	charcoal	A.D. 530	–	Eddy 1966. See text.
	1640±90	I(MNM)251	rotten wood	A.D. 310	+	
Sambrito Village	1360±100	TX45	charcoal	A.D. 590	+	Eddy 1966. See text.
	2191±264	TBN306-3	charcoal	241 B.C.	–	
Uells Site	1390±170	I1344	charcoal	A.D. 560	–	Eddy 1966. See text.
Broken Flute Cave	1070±100	C103	wood	A.D. 880	–	Libby 1955. Solid carbon.
Bisti Site	2140±90	A109	charcoal	190 B.C.	–	Haynes, Damon, and Grey 1966. Composite sample.
Pithouse 4	3920±80	A812	charcoal	1970 B.C.	–	Haynes, Grey, and Long 1971
NA5686	3100±110	A47	reed figurine	1150 B.C.	–	Wise and Shutler 1958. Solid carbon.
Rim Valley Pueblo	880±50	GRN4007	charcoal	A.D. 1070	+	Vogel and Waterbolk 1964
Rio Puerco Crossing	680±250	M251	charcoal	A.D. 1270	+	Crane 1956
Table Rock Pueblo	615±55	GRN1997	wood	A.D. 1335	+	Vogel and Waterbolk 1964
Trinidad Pueblo	1000±250	W1910	charcoal	A.D. 950	+	Marsters, Spiker, and Rubin 1969
	1030±250	W1906	charcoal	A.D. 920	+	
Tumbleweed Canyon	1725±50	GRN2801	charcoal	A.D. 225	+	Vogel and Waterbolk 1964

APPENDIX (continued)

Site	Date (B.P.)	Lab No.	Material	Date (A.D./B.C.)	Accept/Reject	Source & Comments
Two Kiva Site	840±100	M1643	wood	A.D. 1110	+	Crane and Griffin 1968
Vernon Site 30	1090±55	GRN1613	charcoal	A.D. 860	+	Vogel and Waterbolk 1964
	1180±50	GRN1690	charcoal	A.D. 770	+	
	1200±55	GRN1689	charcoal	A.D. 750	+	
Walnut Canyon	3500±100	UCLA741B	split twig figurine	1550 B.C.	+	Berger, Fergusson, and Libby 1965; Long 1965
	3880±90	SI86	split twig figurine (Salix)	1930 B.C.	+	
Zero Plaza	2050±120	RL240	charcoal	100 B.C.	+	Dalley 1973
Joint Site	460±105	GX1982	charcoal	A.D. 1490	–	Schiffer 1976. This site has been tree-ring dated between A.D. 1236 and 1247. Only GX1979 falls in that range. The date shown for GX1975 includes a 250-year correction for fractionation.
	515±100	GX1978	wood	A.D. 1435	–	
	795±95	GX1979	wood	A.D. 1155	+	
	905±95	GX1975	maize	A.D. 1045	–	
	960±95	GX1977	charcoal	A.D. 990	–	
	1020±95	GX1976	charcoal	A.D. 930	–	
	1100±120	GX1984	charcoal	A.D. 850	–	
	1145±85	GX1980	charcoal	A.D. 805	–	
	1280±95	GX1983	charcoal	A.D. 670	–	
	1390±100	GX1981	wood	A.D. 560	–	

BIBLIOGRAPHY

Aikens, C. Melvin
1966 Virgin-Kayenta cultural relationships. *University of Utah Anthropological Papers,* No. 79. Salt Lake City.

Ambler, J. Richard, and Alan P. Olson
1977 Salvage archaeology in the Cow Springs area. *Museum of Northern Arizona Technical Series,* No. 15. Flagstaff.

Arnold, J. R., and W. F. Libby
1950 *Radiocarbon dates.* University of Chicago Institute of Nuclear Studies, Chicago.

Bannister, Bryant
1965 Tree-ring dating of the archaeological sites in the Chaco Canyon region, New Mexico. *Southwestern Monuments Association, Technical Series* 6, Part 2. Globe, Arizona.

Bannister, Bryant, Jeffrey S. Dean, Elizabeth A. M. Gell
1966 *Tree-ring dates from Arizona E: Chinle—de Chelly—Red Rock area.* Laboratory of Tree-Ring Research, University of Arizona, Tucson.

Bannister, Bryant, Jeffrey S. Dean, and William J. Robinson
1968 *Tree-ring dates from Arizona C–D: Eastern Grand Canyon—Tsegi Canyon—Kayenta area.* Laboratory of Tree-Ring Research, University of Arizona, Tucson.
1969 *Tree-ring dates from Utah S–W: Southern Utah area.* Laboratory of Tree-Ring Research, University of Arizona, Tucson.

Bannister, Bryant, Elizabeth A. M. Gell, and John W. Hannah
1966 *Tree-ring dates from Arizona N–Q: Verde—Showlow—St. Johns area.* Laboratory of Tree-Ring Research, University of Arizona, Tucson.

Bannister, Bryant, John W. Hannah, and William J. Robinson
1966 *Tree-ring dates from Arizona K: Puerco—Wide Ruin—Ganado area.* Laboratory of Tree-Ring Research, University of Arizona, Tucson.
1970 *Tree-ring dates from New Mexico M–N S, Z: Southwestern New Mexico area.* Laboratory of Tree-Ring Research, University of Arizona, Tucson.

Bannister, Bryant, William J. Robinson, and Richard L. Warren
1967 *Tree-ring dates from Arizona J: Hopi Mesas area.* Laboratory of Tree-Ring Research, University of Arizona, Tucson.
1970 *Tree-ring dates from New Mexico A, G–H: Shiprock—Zuni—Mt. Taylor area.* Laboratory of Tree-Ring Research, University of Arizona, Tucson.

Beals, Ralph L., George W. Brainerd, and Watson Smith
1945 Archaeological studies in northeast Arizona. *University of California Publications in American Archaeology and Ethnology* 44(1). Berkeley.

Bender, Margaret M.
1968 Mass spectrometric studies of carbon 13 variations in corn and other grasses. *Radiocarbon* 10:468–72.

Benedict, James B.
1973 Chronology of cirque glaciation, Colorado Front Range. *Quaternary Research* 3:584–99.

Berger, Rainer, G. F. Fergusson, and W. F. Libby
1965 UCLA radiocarbon dates IV. *Radiocarbon* 7:337–71.

Berry, Claudia F., and William S. Marmaduke
1980 *Cultural resources overview: The middle Gila Basin, Maricopa and Pinal counties, southern Ari-*

zona. 2 volumes. Draft report prepared for U.S.D.I., Water and Power Resources Service, Arizona Project Office, by Northland Anthropological Research, Inc., Flagstaff.

Berry, Michael S.

1972 Surprise Village. In *Highway U-95 archeology: Comb Wash to Grand Flat,* edited by Gardiner F. Dalley, pp. 97–125. Special report of the Department of Anthropology, University of Utah, Salt Lake City.

Bohrer, Vorsila L.

1966 Pollen analysis of the Hay Hollow Site east of Snowflake, Arizona. *Interim Research Report,* No. 12. Geochronology Laboratories, University of Arizona, Tucson.

1972 Paleoecology of the Hay Hollow Site, Arizona. *Fieldiana: Anthropology* 63(1). Chicago.

Brainerd, George W.

1951 The place of chronological ordering in archaeological analysis. *American Antiquity* 16:301–13.

Breternitz, David A.

1966 An appraisal of tree-ring dated pottery in the Southwest. *Anthropological Papers of the University of Arizona,* No. 3. Tucson.

1969 Radicarbon dates: Eastern Colorado. *Plains Anthropologist* 14:113–24.

1970 Archeological Excavations in Dinosaur National Monument, Colorado-Utah, 1964–1965. *University of Colorado Studies, Series in Anthropology,* No. 17. Boulder.

Briuer, Frederick L.

1977 Plant and animal remains from caves and rock shelters of the Chevlon Canyon, Arizona: Methods for isolating cultural depositional processes. Unpublished Ph.D. dissertation, Department of Anthropology, University of California, Los Angeles.

Brew, John O.

1937 The first two seasons at Awatovi. *American Antiquity* 3:122–37.

1941 Preliminary report of the Peabody Museum Awatovi Expedition of 1939. *Plateau* 13:37–48.

Buckley, James D., Milton A. Trautman, and Eric H. Willis

1968 Isotopes' radiocarbon measurements VI. *Radiocarbon* 10:246–94.

Buckley, James D., and Eric H. Willis

1970 Isotopes' radiocarbon measurements VIII. *Radiocarbon* 12:87–129.

Bullard, William R., Jr.

1962 The Cerro Colorado site and pithouse architecture in the Southwestern United States prior to A.D. 900. *Papers of the Peabody Museum of Archaeology and Ethnology, Harvard University* 44(2). Cambridge.

Bullard, William R., Jr., and Francis E. Cassidy

1956a LA 2507. In *Pipeline archaeology,* edited by Fred Wendorf, Nancy Fox, and Orian L. Lewis, pp. 56–60. Laboratory of Anthropology and the Museum of Northern Arizona, Santa Fe and Flagstaff.

1956b LA 2505. In *Pipeline archaeology,* edited by Fred Wendorf, Nancy Fox, and Orian L. Lewis, pp. 43–51. Laboratory of Anthropology and the Museum of Northern Arizona, Santa Fe and Flagstaff.

Burgh, Robert F.

1959 Ceramic profiles in the western mound at Awatovi, northeastern Arizona. *American Antiquity* 25:184–202.

Burleigh, R.

1973 The radiocarbon calendar recalibrated too soon? *Antiquity* 47:309–17.

Carlson, Roy L.

1963 Basket Maker III sites near Durango, Colorado. *University of Colorado Studies, Series in Anthropology,* No. 8. Boulder.

Colton, Harold S.

1932 A survey of prehistoric sites in the region of Flagstaff, Arizona. *Bureau of American Ethnology Bulletin,* No. 104. Washington, D.C.

1933 Wupatki, the Tall House. *Museum Notes* 5:61–64.

1939 Three Turkey House. *Plateau* 12:26–31.

1946 The Sinagua. *Museum of Northern Arizona Bulletin,* No. 22. Flagstaff.

1960 *Black Sand: Prehistory in northern Arizona.* University of New Mexico Press, Albuquerque.

Conner, Sidney

1943 Excavations at Kinnikinnick, Arizona. *American Antiquity* 8:376–79.

Cowgill, George W.

1975 On the causes and consequences of ancient and modern population change. *American Anthropologist* 77:505–25.

Crane, H. R.

1956 University of Michigan radiocarbon dates I. *Science* 124:664–70.

Crane, H. R., and James B. Griffin

1958a University of Michigan radiocarbon dates II. *Science* 127:1098–103.

1958b University of Michigan radiocarbon dates III. *Science* 128:1117–122.

1959 University of Michigan radiocarbon dates IV. In *Radiocarbon Supplement of the American Journal of Science* 1:173–88.

1960 University of Michigan radiocarbon dates V. In *Radiocarbon Supplement of the American Journal of Science* 2:31–48.

1968 University of Michigan radiocarbon dates XII. *Radiocarbon* 10:61–114.

Cummings, Byron

1938 Kinishba—the Brown House. *The Kiva* 4:1–3.

1940 *Kinishba: A prehistoric pueblo of the Great Pueblo Period.* Hohokam Museums Association and the University of Arizona, Tucson.

Daifuku, Hiroshi

1961 Jeddito 264: A report of the excavation of a Basket Maker III–Pueblo I site in northeastern Arizona with a review of some current theories in Southwestern archaeology. *Papers of the Peabody Museum of Archaeology and Ethnology, Harvard University* 33(1). Cambridge.

Dalley, Gardiner F. (ed.)

1973 *Highway U-95 archeology: Comb Wash to Grand Flat.* Special report of the Department of Anthropology, University of Utah, Salt Lake City.

Damon, Paul E., C. W. Ferguson, Austin Long, and E. I. Wallick

1974 Dendrochronologic calibration of the radiocarbon time scale. *American Antiquity* 39:350–66.

Damon, Paul E., C. Vance Haynes, and Austin Long

1964 Arizona radiocarbon dates V. *Radiocarbon* 6:91–107.

Damon, Paul E., and Austin Long

1962 Arizona radiocarbon dates III. *Radiocarbon* 4:239–49.

Danson, Edward B.

1957 An archaeological survey of west central New Mexico and east central Arizona. *Papers of the Peabody Museum of Archaeology and Ethnology, Harvard University* 44(1). Cambridge.

Davis, Emma Lou

1965 Three applications of edge-punched cards for recording and analyzing field data. *In* Contributions of the Wetherill Mesa Archaeological Project, assembled by Douglas Osborne, pp. 216–26. *Memoirs of the Society for American Archaeology,* No. 19. Washington, D.C.

Dean, Jeffrey S.

1969 Chronological analysis of Tsegi phase sites in northeastern Arizona. *Papers of the Laboratory of Tree-Ring Research,* No. 3. Tucson.

1975 *Tree-ring dates from Colorado W, Durango area.* Laboratory of Tree-Ring Research, University of Arizona, Tucson.

Dean, Jeffrey S., and William J. Robinson

1977 *Dendroclimatic variability in the American Southwest.* Laboratory of Tree-Ring Research, University of Arizona, Tucson.

1978 Expanded tree-ring chronologies for the Southwestern United States. *Chronology Series* III. Laboratory of Tree-Ring Research, University of Arizona, Tucson.

De Vries, H.

1958 Variation in concentration of radiocarbon with time and location on earth. *Koninklijke Nederlandse Akademie van Wetenschappen, Proc. Ser. B* 61:94–102.

Dick, Herbert W.

1952 Evidences of early man in Bat Cave and on the Plains of San Augustin, New Mexico. *In* Indian Tribes of Aboriginal America. *Selected Papers of the XXIXth International Congress of Americanists,* Vol. 3, edited by Sol Tax, pp. 158–63. University of Chicago Press, Chicago.

1954 The Bat Cave pod corn complex: A note on its distribution and archaeological significance. *El Palacio* 61:138–44.

1965 Bat Cave. *The School of American Research, Monograph,* No. 27. Santa Fe.

Dittert, Alfred E., Jr.

1959 Culture change in the Cebolleta Mesa region, central western New Mexico. Unpublished Ph.D. dissertation, Department of Anthropology, University of Arizona.

Dittert, Alfred E., Jr., Frank W. Eddy, and Beth L. Dickey

1963 Evidences of early ceramic phases in the Navajo Reservoir District. *El Palacio* 70:5–12.

Dittert, Alfred E., Jr., James J. Hester, and Frank W. Eddy

1961 An archaeological survey of the Navajo Reservoir District, northwestern New Mexico. *Monographs of the School of American Research and the Museum of New Mexico,* No. 23. Santa Fe.

Dittert, Alfred E., Jr., and Reynold J. Ruppe, Jr.

1951 The archaeology of Cebolleta Mesa: A preliminary report. *El Palacio* 58:116–29.

Douglass, Andrew E.

1929 The secret of the Southwest solved by talkative tree-rings. *National Geographic Magazine* 54: 737–70.

1942 Checking the date of Bluff Ruin, Forestdale: A study in technique. *Tree-Ring Bulletin* 9(2):2–4.

1943 Advances in dendrochronology, 1943. *Tree-Ring Bulletin* 9(3):18–24.

1944 Tabulation of dates for Bluff Ruin, Forestdale, Arizona. *Tree-Ring Bulletin* 11(2):10–16.

Doyel, David E., and Emil W. Haury (eds.)
1976 The 1976 Salado Conference. *The Kiva* 42:1–134.

Dozier, Edward P.
1966 *Hano: A Tewa Indian community in Arizona.* Holt, Rinehart and Winston, New York.
1970 *The Pueblo Indians of North America.* Holt, Rinehart and Winston, New York.

Eddy, Frank W.
1958 Sequence of cultural and alluvial deposits in the Cienega Creek Basin, southeastern Arizona. Unpublished Masters thesis, Department of Anthropology, University of Arizona.
1961 Excavations at Los Pinos phase sites in the Navajo Reservoir District. *Museum of New Mexico Papers in Anthropology,* No. 4. Santa Fe.
1966 Prehistory in the Navajo Reservoir District, northwestern New Mexico. *Museum of New Mexico Papers in Anthropology,* No. 15, Parts I and II. Santa Fe.

Eldredge, Niles, and Stephen Jay Gould
1972 Punctuated equilibria: An alternative to gradualism. In *Models in paleobiology,* edited by Thomas J. M. Schopf, pp. 82–115. Freeman, Cooper, San Francisco.

Euler, Robert C., George J. Gumerman, Thor N. V. Karlstrom, Jeffrey S. Dean, and Richard H. Hevly
1979 The Colorado Plateau: Cultural dynamics and paleoenvironment. *Science* 205:1089–101.

Fewkes, Jesse W.
1898a Archaeological expedition to Arizona in 1895. *Seventeenth Annual Report of the Bureau of American Ethnology,* pp. 520–742. Washington, D.C.
1898b Preliminary account of an expedition to the Pueblo ruins near Winslow, Arizona, in 1896. *Smithsonian Institution Annual Report for 1896,* pp. 517–39. Washington, D.C.
1904 Two summers work in Pueblo ruins. *Twenty-second Annual Report of the Bureau of American Ethnology,* pp. 3–195. Washington, D.C.
1909 Antiquities of the Mesa Verde National Park, Spruce Tree House. *Bureau of American Ethnology Bulletin,* No. 41. Washington, D.C.
1911 Antiquities of the Mesa Verde National Park, Cliff Palace. *Bureau of American Ethnology Bulletin,* No. 51. Washington, D.C.
1916 The Cliff Ruins in Fewkes Canyon, Mesa Verde National Park, Colorado. In *Holmes Anniversary Volume,* pp. 96–117. Washington, D.C.
1917 A prehistoric Mesa Verde pueblo and its people (Far View House). *Smithsonian Miscellaneous Collections* 72(1):47–64. Washington, D.C.
1922 Archaeological field work on the Mesa Verde National Park (1921). *Smithsonian Miscellaneous Collections* 72(15):64–83. Washington, D.C.

Fitting, James E.
1973 An early Mogollon community: A preliminary report on the Winn Canyon Site. *The Artifact* 11(1, 2).

Fitting, James E., David G. Anderson, and Timothy C. Klinger
1972 Archaeological survey and excavation in Dark Thunder Canyon. *Southwestern New Mexico Research Reports,* No. 9. Gila, New Mexico.

Flint, Richard F., and Edward S. Deevey
1961 Editorial statement. *Radiocarbon* 3:v.

Ford, Richard I.
1975 Re-excavation of Jemez Cave, New Mexico. *Awanyu* 3:12–27.

Fritts, Harold C.
1976 *Tree rings and climate.* Academic Press, New York.

Fritts, Harold C., David G. Smith, and Marvin A. Stokes
1965 The biological model for paleoclimatic interpretation of Mesa Verde tree-ring series. *In* Contributions of the Wetherill Mesa Archaeological Project, assembled by Douglas Osborne, pp. 101–21. *Memoirs of the Society for American Archaeology,* No. 19. Washington, D.C.

Fritz, John M.
1974 The Hay Hollow Site subsistence system, east central Arizona. Ph.D. dissertation, University of Chicago. University Microfilms, Ann Arbor.

Galinat, Walter C.
1959 Plant remains from the LoDaisKa Site. *In* Excavations at the LoDaisKa Site, by Henry J. Irwin and Cynthia C. Irwin, pp. 104–13. *Proceedings of the Denver Museum of Natural History,* No. 8. Denver.

Gladwin, Harold S.
1943 A review and analysis of the Flagstaff culture. *Medallion Papers,* No. 31. Gila Pueblo, Globe, Arizona.
1944 Tree-ring analysis; problems of dating I: The Medicine Valley sites. *Medallion Papers,* No. 32. Gila Pueblo, Globe, Arizona.
1945 The Chaco branch: Excavations at White Mound and in the Red Mesa Valley. *Medallion Papers,* No. 33. Gila Pueblo, Globe, Arizona.
1948 Excavations at Snaketown IV: Review and conclusions. *Medallion Papers,* No. 38. Gila Pueblo, Globe, Arizona.

1957 *A history of the ancient Southwest.* Bond Wheelwright, Portland.

Gladwin, Harold S., Emil W. Haury, E. B. Sayles, and Nora Gladwin

1937 Excavations at Snaketown: Material culture. *Medallion Papers,* No. 25. Gila Pueblo, Globe, Arizona.

Glassow, Michael A.

1972 Changes in the adaptations of Southwestern Basketmakers: A systems perspective. In *Contemporary archaeology: A guide to theory and contributions,* edited by Mark P. Leone, pp. 289–302. Southern Illinois University Press, Carbondale.

Gould, Stephen Jay, and Niles Eldredge

1977 Punctuated equilibria: The tempo and mode of evolution reconsidered. *Paleobiology* 3:115–51.

Green, Roger C., Maryanne A. Danfelser, and R. Gwinn Vivian

1958 Interpretation of Bg 91: A specialized Largo-Gallina surface structure. *El Palacio* 65:41–60.

Guernsey, Samuel J.

1931 Explorations in northeastern Arizona. *Papers of the Peabody Museum of Archaeology and Ethnology, Harvard University* 12(1). Cambridge.

Gumerman, George J., and Robert C. Euler

1976 *Papers on the Archaeology of Black Mesa, Arizona.* Southern Illinois University Press, Carbondale.

Hack, John T.

1942 The changing physical environment of the Hopi Indians of Arizona. *Papers of the Peabody Museum of Archaeology and Ethnology* 35(1). Cambridge.

Hall, Edward T., Jr.

1944 Early stockaded settlements in the Governador, New Mexico. *Columbia Studies in Archaeology and Ethnology* 2(1). New York.

Hall, Henry J.

1973 The excavation of Zero Plaza. In *Highway U-95 archeology: Comb Wash to Grand Flat,* edited by Gardiner F. Dalley, pp. 63–74. Special report of the Department of Anthropology, University of Utah, Salt Lake City.

Hall, Stephen A.

1977 Late Quaternary sedimentation and paleoecologic history of Chaco Canyon, New Mexico. *Geological Society of America Bulletin* 88:1593–618.

Hanson, N. R.

1969 *Perception and discovery.* Freeman, Cooper, San Francisco.

Hargrave, Lyndon L.

1933 Pueblo II houses of the San Francisco Mountains, Arizona. *Museum of Northern Arizona Bulletin,* No. 4. Flagstaff.

1935 *Report on archaeological reconnaissance in the Rainbow Plateau area of northern Arizona and southern Utah.* University of California Press, Berkeley.

Hartman, Dana, and Arthur H. Wolf

1977 Wupatki: An archaeological assessment. *Museum of Northern Arizona Research Paper,* No. 6, Flagstaff.

Haury, Emil W.

1934 The Canyon Creek Ruin and cliff dwellings of the Sierra Ancha. *Medallion Papers,* No. 19. Gila Pueblo, Globe, Arizona.

1936 Vandal Cave. *The Kiva* 1:1–4.

1938 Southwestern dated ruins: II. *Tree-Ring Bulletin* 4(3):3–4.

1950 *The stratigraphy and archaeology of Ventana Cave, Arizona.* University of Arizona Press, Tucson.

1957 An alluvial site on the San Carlos Indian Reservation. *American Antiquity* 23:2–27.

1958 Evidence at Point of Pines for a prehistoric migration from northern Arizona. *In* Migrations in New World culture history, edited by Raymond H. Thompson, pp. 1–6. *University of Arizona Bulletin* 29(2), *Social Science Bulletin,* No. 27. Tucson.

1962 The greater American Southwest. In *Courses toward urban life,* edited by Robert J. Braidwood and Gordon Willey, pp. 106–31. Aldine, Chicago.

1976 *The Hohokam: Desert farmers and craftsmen.* University of Arizona Press, Tucson.

Haury, Emil W., and Lyndon L. Hargrave

1931 Recently dated pueblo ruins in Arizona. *Smithsonian Miscellaneous Collections* 82(11). Washington, D.C.

Haury, Emil W., and E. B. Sayles

1947 An early pit house village of the Mogollon culture. *University of Arizona Bulletin* 18(4), *Social Science Bulletin,* No. 16. Tucson.

Hawley, Florence M.

1934 The significance of the dated prehistory of Chetro Ketl, Chaco Canyon, New Mexico. *Monographs of the School of American Research and University of New Mexico,* No. 2. Santa Fe and Albuquerque.

1959 Reversal of trash layers at Chetro Ketl, New Mexico. In *The Archaeologist at work,* edited by Robert H. Heizer, pp. 328–42. Harper and Brothers, New York.

Hayes, Alden C.
1964 The archaeological survey of Wetherill Mesa, Mesa Verde Nationl Park, Colorado. *National Park Service Archaeological Research Series,* No. 7-A. Washington, D.C.

Hayes, Alden C., and James A. Lancaster
1962 Site 1060, a Basketmaker III pithouse on Chapin Mesa, Mesa Verde National Park. *Tree-Ring Bulletin* 24(1, 2):14–16.
1968 Site 1060, a Basketmaker III pithouse on Chapin Mesa. *In* Contributions to Mesa Verde archaeology: V. Emergency archaeology in Mesa Verde National Park, Colorado, 1948–1966, edited by Robert H. Lister, pp. 65–68. *University of Colorado Studies, Series in Anthropology,* No. 15. Boulder.
1975 *Badger House community, Mesa Verde National Park.* National Park Service, Washington, D.C.

Haynes, C. Vance
1968 Geochronology of late Quaternary alluvium. *In* Means of correlation of Quaternary successions, edited by R. B. Morrison and H. E. Wright, pp. 591–631. *Proceedings of the VII Congress of the International Association of Quaternary Research,* Vol. 8. University of Utah Press, Salt Lake City.

Haynes, C. Vance, and Austin Long
1976 Radiocarbon dating at Snaketown. In *The Hohokam: Desert farmers and craftsmen,* by Emil W. Haury, pp. 333–36. University of Arizona Press, Tucson.

Haynes, C. Vance, Paul E. Damon, and Donald Grey
1966 Arizona radiocarbon dates VI. *Radiocarbon* 8:1–21.

Haynes, C. Vance, Donald C. Grey, and Austin Long
1971 Arizona radiocarbon dates VIII. *Radiocarbon* 13:1–18.

Hewett, Edgar L.
1921 The excavation of Chetro Ketl, Chaco Canyon, 1920. *Art and Archaeology* 11:45–62.
1936 *The Chaco Canyon and its monuments.* University of New Mexico Press, Albuquerque.

Hough, Walter
1903 Archaeological field work in northeastern Arizona. The Museum Gates Expedition of 1901. *Annual Report of the U.S. National Museum for 1901,* pp. 279–358. Washington, D.C.
1930 Exploration of ruins in the White Mountain Apache Indian Reservation, Arizona. *Proceedings of the U.S. National Museum* 78(13). Washington, D.C.

Human Systems Research, Inc.
1973 *Technical manual, 1973 survey of the Tularosa Basin.* Human Systems Research, Tularosa.

Hunt, Charles B.
1967 *Physiography of the United States.* W. H. Freeman, San Francisco and London.

Irwin, Henry J., and Cynthia C. Irwin
1959 Excavations at the LoDaisKa Site. *Proceedings of the Denver Museum of Natural History,* No. 8. Denver.
1961 Radiocarbon dates from the LoDaisKa Site, Colorado. *American Antiquity* 27:114–15.

Irwin-Williams, Cynthia C.
1967 Picosa: The elementary Southwestern culture. *American Antiquity* 32:441–52.
1973 The Oshara tradition: Origins of Anasazi culture. *Eastern New Mexico University Contributions in Anthropology* 5(1). Portales.

(Ed.)
1972 The structure of Chacoan society in the northern Southwest: Investigations at the Salmon Site, 1972. *Eastern New Mexico University Contributions in Anthropology* 4(3). Portales.

Irwin-Williams, Cynthia C., and S. Tompkins
1968 Excavations at En Medio Rock Shelter, New Mexico. *Eastern New Mexico University Contributions in Anthropology* 1(2). Portales.

Ives, Patricia C., Betsey Levin, Charles L. Oman, and Meyer Rubin
1967 U.S. Geological Survey radiocarbon dates IX. *Radiocarbon* 9:505–29.

Jeancon, Jean A.
1922 *Archaeological research in the northeastern San Juan Basin of Colorado during the summer of 1921.* The State Historical and Natural History Society of Colorado and the University of Denver, Denver.

Jelinek, Arthur J.
1965 Radiocarbon dating in the Southwest United States. Paper presented at the Sixth International Conference, Radiocarbon and Tritium Dating, Pullman.

Jennings, Calvin H.
1968 Highway salvage excavations in Medicine Valley, north-central Arizona. *Plateau* 41:43–60.

Jennings, Jesse D.
1966 Glen Canyon: A summary. *University of Utah Anthropological Papers,* No. 81. Salt Lake City.
1967 Review of "Bat Cave." *American Antiquity* 32:123.
1974 *Prehistory of North America.* 2d edition. McGraw-Hill, New York.

Johnson, Alfred E.

1965 The development of western Pueblo culture. Ph.D. dissertation, University of Arizona. University Microfilms, Ann Arbor.

Johnson, Chester

1962 The Twin Lakes Site, LA 2507. *El Palacio* 69:157–71.

Judd, Neil M.

1928 Pueblo Bonito and its architectural development. *Proceedings of the Twenty-third International Congress of Americanists,* pp. 70–73. New York.

1930 Dating our prehistoric pueblo ruins. *Explorations and Field-Work of the Smithsonian Institution in 1929,* pp. 167–76. Washington, D.C.

1954 The material culture of Pueblo Bonito. *Smithsonian Miscellaneous Collections* 124. Washington, D.C.

1959 Pueblo del Arroyo, Chaco Canyon, New Mexico. *Smithsonian Miscellaneous Collections* 138(1). Washington, D.C.

1964 The architecture of Pueblo Bonito. *Smithsonian Miscellaneous Collections* 147(1). Washington, D.C.

Karlstrom, Thor N. V., George J. Gumerman, and Robert C. Euler

1974 Paleoenvironmental and cultural changes in the Black Mesa region, northeastern Arizona. In *Geology of northern Arizona,* edited by Thor N. V. Karlstrom et al., pp. 495–518. Geological Society of America, Rocky Mountain Section Meeting, Flagstaff.

Kehoe, Thomas F.

1966 The small side-notched point system of the northern Plains. *American Antiquity* 31:827–41.

1973 The Gull Lake Site: A prehistoric bison drive site in southwestern Saskatchewan. *Milwaukee Public Museum Publications in Anthropology and History,* No. 1. Milwaukee.

Kidder, Alfred V.

1927 The Southwestern Archaeological Conference. *El Palacio* 23:554–61.

Kidder, Alfred V., and Samuel J. Guernsey

1919 Archaeological explorations in northeastern Arizona. *Bureau of American Ethnology Bulletin,* No. 65. Washington, D.C.

Lancaster, James A.

1968 The salvage excavation of sites 353 and 354, Chapin Mesa. *In* Contributions to Mesa Verde archaeology: V. Emergency archaeology in Mesa Verde National Park, Colorado, 1948–1966, edited by Robert H. Lister, pp. 57–60. *University of Colorado Studies, Series in Anthropology,* No. 15. Boulder.

Lancaster, James A., and Jean M. Pinkley

1954 Excavation at site 16 of three Pueblo II mesa-top ruins. *In* Archaeological excavations in Mesa Verde National Park, Colorado, 1950, by James A. Lancaster, Jean M. Pinkley, Phillip F. van Cleave, and Don Watson, pp. 23–86. *National Park Service Archaeological Research Series,* No. 2. Washington, D.C.

Lancaster, James A., and Don Watson

1943 Excavation of Mesa Verde pit houses. *American Antiquity* 9:190–98.

1954 Excavation of two late Basketmaker pit-houses. *In* Archaeological excavations in Mesa Verde National Park, Colorado, 1950, by James A. Lancaster, Jean M. Pinkley, Phillip F. van Cleave, and Don Watson, pp. 7–22. *National Park Service Archaeological Research Series,* No. 2. Washington, D.C.

Libby, W. F.

1951 Radiocarbon dates II. *Science* 114:291–96.

1952 *Radiocarbon dating.* University of Chicago Press, Chicago.

1955 *Radiocarbon dating.* 2d edition. University of Chicago Press, Chicago.

Lindsay, Alexander J., Jr., J. Richard Ambler, Mary Anne Stein, and Philip M. Hobler

1968 Survey and excavation north and east of Navajo Mountain, Utah 1959–1962. *Museum of Northern Arizona Bulletin,* No. 45. Flagstaff.

Lipe, William D.

1978 The Southwest. In *Ancient Native Americans,* edited by Jesse D. Jennings, pp. 327–99. W. H. Freeman, San Francisco.

Lipe, William D., and R. G. Matson

1971 Prehistoric cultural adaptation in the Cedar Mesa area, southeast Utah. Unpublished ms. (research proposal submitted to the National Science Foundation).

Lister, Robert H.

1959 The Coombs Site. *University of Utah Anthropological Papers,* No. 41. Salt Lake City.

Lister, Robert H., J. Richard Ambler, and Florence C. Lister

1960 The Coombs Site: Part II. *University of Utah Anthropological Papers,* No. 41. Salt Lake City.

Lister, Robert H., and Florence C. Lister

1961 The Coombs Site: Part III, Summary and conclusions. *University of Utah Anthropological Papers,* No. 41. Salt Lake City.

Long, Austin

1965 Smithsonian Institution radiocarbon measurements II. *Radiocarbon* 7:245–56.

Long, Austin, and Bruce Rippeteau

1974 Testing contemporaneity and averaging

radiocarbon dates. *American Antiquity* 39:205–15.

Lowden, J. A.
1969 Isotopic fractionation in corn. *Radiocarbon* 11:391–92.

Mangelsdorf, Paul C., Herbert W. Dick, and J. Camara-Hernandez
1967 Bat Cave revisited. *Harvard University Botanical Museum Leaflets* 22:1–31. Cambridge.

Mangelsdorf, Paul C., and C. E. Smith
1949 New archaeological evidence on evolution of maize. *Harvard University Botanical Museum Leaflets* 13:213–60. Cambridge.

Marsters, Beverly, Elliot Spiker, and Meyer Rubin
1969 U.S. Geological Survey radiocarbon dates X. *Radiocarbon* 11:210–27.

Martin, Paul Schultz
1963 *The last 10,000 years.* University of Arizona Press, Tucson.

Martin, Paul Schultz, and James Schoenwetter
1960 Arizona's oldest cornfield. *Science* 132:33–34.

Martin, Paul Sidney
1943 The SU Site: Excavations at a Mogollon village, western New Mexico, Second Season, 1941. *Field Museum of Natural History, Anthropological Series* 32(2). Chicago.
1967 Hay Hollow Site (200 B.C.–A.D. 200). *Field Museum of Natural History Bulletin* 38(5):6–10. Chicago.
1972 Foreword to Paleoecology of the Hay Hollow Site, Arizona, by Vorsila L. Bohrer, pp. 1–5. *Fieldiana: Anthropology* 63(1). Chicago.

Martin, Paul Sidney, and Fred Plog
1973 *The archeology of Arizona.* Doubleday, Natural History Press, Garden City.

Martin, Paul Sidney, and John B. Rinaldo
1939 Modified Basketmaker sites, Ackmen-Lowry area, southwestern Colorado, 1938. *Field Museum of Natural History, Anthropological Series* 23(3). Chicago.
1940 The SU Site: Excavations at a Mogollon village, western New Mexico, 1939. *Field Museum of Natural History, Anthropological Series* 32(1). Chicago.
1947 The SU Site: Excavations at a Mogollon village, western New Mexico, Third Season, 1946. *Field Museum of Natural History, Anthropological Series* 32(3). Chicago.

Martin, Paul Sidney, John B. Rinaldo, and Eloise R. Barter
1957 Late Mogollon communities: Four sites of the Tularosa phase, western New Mexico. *Fieldiana: Anthropology* 49(1). Chicago.

Martin, Paul Sidney, John B. Rinaldo, Elaine A. Bluhm, Hugh C. Cutler, and R. Grange, Jr.
1952 Mogollon cultural continuity and change: The stratigraphic analysis of Tularosa and Cordova caves. *Fieldiana: Anthropology* 40. Chicago.

Martin, Paul Sidney, John B. Rinaldo, William A. Longacre, C. Cronin, Leslie G. Freeman, Jr., and James Schoenwetter
1962 Chapters in the prehistory of eastern Arizona, I. *Fieldiana: Anthropology* 53. Chicago.

Martin, Paul Sidney, John B. Rinaldo, William Longacre, Leslie G. Freeman, Jr., James A. Brown, Richard H. Hevly, and M. E. Cooley
1964 Chapters in the prehistory of eastern Arizona, II. *Fieldiana: Anthropology* 55. Chicago.

Martin, Paul Sidney, Lawrence Roys, and Gerhardt von Bonin
1936 Lowry Ruin in southwestern Colorado. *Field Museum of Natural History, Anthropological Series* 23(1). Chicago.

Matson, R. G., and William D. Lipe
1978 Settlement patterns on Cedar Mesa: Boom and bust on the Northern Periphery. In *Investigations of the Southwestern Anthropological Research Group, Proceedings of the 1976 Conference,* edited by Robert C. Euler and George J. Gumerman, pp. 1–12. Museum of Northern Arizona, Flagstaff.

McDonald, James A.
1976 An archaeological assessment of Canyon de Chelly National Monument. *Western Archeological Center Publications in Anthropology,* No. 5. National Park Service, Tucson.

McGimsey, Charles R., II
1951 Peabody Museum Upper Gila Expedition—Pueblo Division preliminary report, 1950 season. *El Palacio* 58:299–312.
1957 Seven prehistoric settlements in west central New Mexico. Unpublished Ph.D. dissertation, Department of Anthropology, Harvard University.

McGregor, John C.
1937 Winona Village, a XIIth century settlement with a ballcourt near Flagstaff, Arizona. *Museum of Northern Arizona Bulletin,* No. 12. Flagstaff.
1941 Winona and Ridge Ruin. Part I: Architecture and material culture. *Museum of Northern Arizona Bulletin,* No. 18. Flagstaff.
1950 Excavation of Cohonina sites, 1949. *Plateau* 22:68–74.

1951 *The Cohonina culture of northwestern Arizona.* University of Illinois Press, Urbana.

1958 The Pershing Site. *Plateau* 31:33–36.

1961 The Pershing Site in northern Arizona. *Plateau* 34:23–27.

Mehringer, Peter J., Jr.

1967 Pollen analysis and the alluvial chronology. *The Kiva* 32:96–101.

Mendenhall, W., and J. E. Reinmuth

1971 *Statistics for management and economics.* Duxbury Press, Belmont, California.

Mindeleff, Cosmos

1897 Cliff ruins of Canyon de Chelly, Arizona. *Sixteenth Annual Report of the Bureau of American Ethnology* 16:79–198. Washington, D.C.

Minnis, Paul E.

n.d. Domesticating plants and people in the greater Southwest. Paper prepared for the School of American Research Advanced Seminar entitled "The Origins of Plant Husbandry in North America," March 2–8, 1980, Santa Fe.

Morris, Ann A.

1933 *Digging in the Southwest.* Doubleday, Doran, New York.

Morris, Earl H.

1919a The Aztec Ruin. *Anthropological Papers of the American Museum of Natural History,* No. 26, Part I. New York.

1919b Preliminary account of the antiquities of the region between the Mancos and the La Plata rivers in southwestern Colorado. *Thirty-third Annual Report of the Bureau of American Ethnology,* pp. 161–205. Washington, D.C.

1921 The house of the Great Kiva at the Aztec Ruins. *Anthropological Papers of the American Museum of Natural History,* No. 26, Part II. New York.

1924 Burials in the Aztec Ruin. *Anthropological Papers of the American Museum of Natural History,* No. 26, Part III. New York.

1925 Exploring the Canyon of Death. *National Geographic Magazine* 48:263–300.

1928 Notes on excavations in the Aztec Ruin. *Anthropological Papers of the American Museum of Natural History,* No. 26, Part V. New York.

1936 Archaeological background of dates in early Arizona chronology. *Tree-Ring Bulletin* 2(4):34–36.

1938 Mummy Cave. *Natural History* 42:127–38.

1939 Archaeological studies in the La Plata District, southwestern Colorado and northwestern New Mexico. *Carnegie Institution Publication,* No. 533. Washington, D.C.

Morris, Earl H., and Robert F. Burgh

1954 Basketmaker II sites near Durango, Colorado. *Carnegie Institution Publication,* No. 604. Washington, D.C.

Morris, Elizabeth A.

1959 Basketmaker caves in the Prayer Rock District, northeastern Arizona. Unpublished Ph.D. dissertation, Department of Anthropology, University of Arizona.

Nelson, Charles E.

1967 The archaeology of Hall-Woodland Cave. *Southwestern Lore* 33(1):1–13.

Nelson, Paula R.

1964 North American man's oldest home? *Chicago Natural History Museum Bulletin* 35(11). Chicago.

Nie, Norman H., C. Hadlai Hull, Jean G. Jenkins, Karin Steinbrenner, and Dale H. Bent

1975 *Statistical package for the social sciences.* McGraw-Hill, New York.

Nordenskiold, Gustav

1893 *The cliff dwellers of the Mesa Verde, southwestern Colorado: Their pottery and implements.* P. A. Norstedt and Soner, Stockholm and Chicago.

O'Bryan, D.

1950 Excavations in Mesa Verde National Park, 1947–48. *Medallion Papers,* No. 39. Gila Pueblo, Globe, Arizona.

Olson, Alan P.

1971 Archaeology of the Arizona Public Service Company 345KV line. *Museum of Northern Arizona Bulletin,* No. 46. Flagstaff.

Olson, Alan P., and William W. Wasley

1956 An archaeological traverse survey in west-central New Mexico. In *Pipeline archaeology,* edited by Fred Wendorf, Nancy Fox, and Orian L. Lewis, pp. 256–390. Laboratory of Anthropology and Museum of Northern Arizona, Santa Fe and Flagstaff.

Olsson, I. U. (ed.)

1970 Radiocarbon variations and absolute chronology. *Proceedings of the 12th Nobel Symposium, Uppsala, 1969.* Wiley Interscience, New York.

Pepper, George H.

1920 Pueblo Bonito. *Anthropological Papers of the American Museum of Natural History,* No. 27. New York.

Pierson, Lloyd

1957 A brief archaeological reconnaissance of

White Canyon, southeastern Utah. *El Palacio* 64:222–30.

Plog, Fred
1974 *The study of prehistoric change.* Academic Press, New York.
1975 Systems theory in archeological research. In *Annual Review of Anthropology* 4:207–24. Palo Alto.
1978 Explaining culture change in the Hohokam preclassic. Paper presented at the 43rd Annual Meeting of the Society for American Archaeology, Tucson.
1980 Explaining culture change in the Hohokam preclassic. *In* Current issues in Hohokam prehistory, edited by David Doyel and Fred Plog, pp. 4–22. *Arizona State University Anthropological Research Papers,* No. 23. Tempe.

Plog, Fred, and Linda S. Cordell
1979 Escaping the confines of normative thought: A reevaluation of Pueblo prehistory. *American Antiquity* 44:405–29.

Ralph, Elizabeth K.
1971 Carbon-14 dating. In *Dating techniques for the archaeologist,* edited by Henry N. Michael and Elizabeth K. Ralph, pp. 1–48. MIT Press, Cambridge.

Reed, Alan D., and Ronald E. Kainer
1978 The Tamarron Site, 5LP326. *Southwestern Lore* 44(1, 2).

Reed, Erik K.
1964 The greater Southwest. In *Prehistoric man in the New World,* edited by Jesse D. Jennings and Edward Norbeck, pp. 175–91. University of Chicago Press, Chicago.

Reeves, Brian
1973 The concept of the Altithermal cultural hiatus in Northern Plains prehistory. *American Anthropologist* 75:1221–253.

Richert, Roland
1964 Excavation of a portion of the East Ruin, Aztec Ruins National Monument, New Mexico. *Southwestern Monuments Association, Technical Series* 4. Globe, Arizona.

Roberts, Frank H. H., Jr.
1929 Shabik'eschee Village, a late Basketmaker site in the Chaco Canyon, New Mexico. *Bureau of American Ethnology Bulletin,* No. 92. Washington, D.C.
1939 Archaeological remains in the Whitewater District, eastern Arizona. Part I: House types. *Bureau of American Ethnology Bulletin,* No. 121. Washington, D.C.
1940 Archaeological remains in the Whitewater District, eastern Arizona. Part II: Artifacts and burials. *Bureau of American Ethnology Bulletin,* No. 126. Washington, D.C.

Robinson, William J., and Bruce G. Harrill
1974 *Tree-ring dates from Colorado V: Mesa Verde area.* Laboratory of Tree-Ring Research, University of Arizona, Tucson.

Robinson, William J., Bruce G. Harrill, and Richard L. Warren
1974 *Tree-ring dates from New Mexico B: Chaco-Gobernador area.* Laboratory of Tree-Ring Research, University of Arizona, Tucson.
1975 *Tree-ring dates from Arizona H–I: Flagstaff area.* Laboratory of Tree-Ring Research, University of Arizona, Tucson.

Robinson, William J., and Richard L. Warren
1971 *Tree-ring dates from New Mexico C–D: Northern Rio Grande area.* Laboratory of Tree-Ring Research, University of Arizona, Tucson.

Robinson, W. S.
1951 A method for chronologically ordering archaeological deposits. *American Antiquity* 16:293–301.

Rodden, R. J.
1959 Mechanical and chemical analysis of the soils of the LoDaisKa Site. *In* Excavations at the LoDaisKa Site, by Henry J. Irwin and Cynthia C. Irwin, pp. 91–99. *Proceedings of the Denver Museum of Natural History,* No. 8. Denver.

Rohn, Arthur H.
1971 Wetherill Mesa excavations, Mug House, Mesa Verde National Park, Colorado. *National Park Service, Archaeological Research Series,* No. 7–D. Washington, D.C.
1977 *Cultural change and continuity on Chapin Mesa.* The Regents Press of Kansas, Lawrence.

Rubin, Meyer, and Corrine Alexander
1960 U.S. Geological Survey radiocarbon dates V. In *Radiocarbon Supplement of the American Journal of Science* 2:129–85.

Ruppe, Reynold J., and Alfred E. Dittert, Jr.
1952 The archaeology of Cebolleta Mesa and Acoma Pueblo: A preliminary report based on further investigation. *El Palacio* 59:191–217.

Sayles, E. B., and Ernst Antevs
1941 The Cochise culture. *Medallion Papers,* No. 29. Gila Pueblo, Globe, Arizona.

Scheffé, H. A.
1959 *The analysis of variance.* Wiley, New York.

Schiffer, Michael B.
1976 *Behavioral archeology.* Academic Press, New York.

Schoenwetter, James, and Alfred E. Dittert, Jr.
1968 An ecological interpretation of Anasazi settlement patterns. In *Anthropological Archeology in*

the *Americas*, edited by Betty J. Meggers, pp. 41–66. The Anthropological Society of Washington, Washington, D.C.

Schoenwetter, James, and Frank W. Eddy
1964 Alluvial and palynological reconstruction of environments, Navajo Reservoir District. *Museum of New Mexico Papers in Anthropology*, No. 13. Santa Fe.

Schulman, Edmund
1949a Early chronologies in the San Juan Basin. *Tree-Ring Bulletin* 15(4):24–32.
1949b An extension of the Durango chronology. *Tree-Ring Bulletin* 16(2):12–16.
1951 Miscellaneous ring records, III. *Tree-Ring Bulletin* 17(4):28–29.
1952 Extension of the San Juan chronology to B.C. times. *Tree-Ring Bulletin* 18(4):30–35.

Sharrock, Floyd W., Kent C. Day, and David S. Dibble
1963 1961 excavations, Glen Canyon area. *University of Utah Anthropological Papers*, No. 63. Salt Lake City.

Shutler, Richard
1961 Lost city: Pueblo Grande de Nevada. *Nevada State Museum Anthropological Papers*, No. 5. Carson City.

Simmons, Alan H.
1981 Paleo-subsistence and technology in the San Juan Basin Archaic: A comparative study from northwestern New Mexico. Paper presented at the 46th Annual Meeting of the Society for American Archaeology, San Diego.

Smiley, T. L.
1949 Pithouse Number 1, Mesa Verde National Park. *American Antiquity* 14:167–71.
1951 A summary of tree-ring dates from some Southwestern archaeological sites. *University of Arizona Bulletin*, No. 22, *Laboratory of Tree-Ring Research Bulletin*, No. 5. Tucson.

Smith, Watson
1952 Excavations in Big Hawk Valley, Wupatki National Monument, Arizona. *Museum of Northern Arizona Bulletin*, No. 24. Flagstaff.
1971 Painted ceramics of the western mound at Awatovi. *Papers of the Peabody Museum of Archaeology and Ethnology, Harvard University* 38(8). Cambridge.

Southworth, C. H.
1919 *The history of irrigation along the Gila River*. Hearings before the Committee on Indian Affairs, House of Representatives, Sixty-sixth Congress, First Session. Vol. 2, Appendix A, pp. 103–223. Government Printing Office, Washington, D.C.

Spaulding, Albert C.
1958 The significance of differences between radiocarbon dates. *American Antiquity* 23:309–11.

Stallings, W. S., Jr.
1936 Dates from Five Kiva House, Utah, *Tree-Ring Bulletin* 3(2):13-14.

Stanislawski, Michael B.
1963 Wupatki Pueblo: A study in cultural fusion and change in Sinagua and Hopi prehistory. Unpublished Ph.D. dissertation, Department of Anthropology, University of Arizona.

Steen, Charlie R.
1937 Archaeological investigations at Natural Bridges National Monument. *Southwest Monuments Monthly Report* 17:327–37. Denver.

Stockton, Charles W., and Harold C. Fritts
1971 Conditional probability of occurrence for variations in climate based on width of annual tree-rings in Arizona. *Tree-Ring Bulletin* 31:3–24.

Struever, Stuart S., and Kent D. Vickery
1973 The beginnings of cultivation in the Midwest-riverine area of the United States. *American Anthropologist* 75:1197–220.

Stubbs, Stanley A., and W. S. Stallings, Jr.
1953 The excavation of Pindi Pueblo, New Mexico. *Monographs of the School of American Research and the Laboratory of Anthropology*, No. 18. Santa Fe.

Stuiver, Minze
1969 Yale natural radiocarbon measurements IX. *Radiocarbon* 11:545–658.

Stuiver, Minze, and Hans E. Suess
1966 On the relationship between radiocarbon dates and true sample ages. *Radiocarbon* 8:534–40.

Symms, E. L.
1977 Cultural ecology and ecological dynamics of the ceramic period in southwestern Manitoba. *Plains Anthropologist Memoir*, No. 12. Lincoln.

Taylor, Walter W.
1954 An early slabhouse near Kayenta, Arizona. *Plateau* 26:109–16.

Thomas, David H.
1976 *Figuring anthropology*. Holt, Rinehart and Winston, New York.

Thompson, Richard A., and Georgia Beth Thompson
1974 *A preliminary report of excavations in the Grand Canyon National Monument, sites: GC-670, GC-671, GC-663*. Report prepared for the National Park Service by Southern Utah State College.

Valastro, S., Jr., and E. Mott Davis
1970 University of Texas at Austin radiocarbon dates VII. *Radiocarbon* 12:249–80.

Vivian, R. Gordon
1959 The Hubbard Site and other tri-wall structures in New Mexico and Colorado. *National Park Service, Archaeological Research Series,* No. 5. Washington, D.C.

Vivian, R. Gordon, and Tom W. Matthews
1965 Kin Kletso: A Pueblo III community in Chaco Canyon, New Mexico. *Southwestern Monuments Association, Technical Series* 6, Part 1. Globe, Arizona.

Vivian, R. Gordon, and Paul Reiter
1960 The great kivas of Chaco Canyon and their relationships. *Monographs of the School of American Research and the Museum of New Mexico,* No. 22. Santa Fe.

Vivian, R. Gwinn
1970 An inquiry into prehistoric social organization in Chaco Canyon, New Mexico. In *Reconstructing prehistoric Pueblo societies,* edited by William A. Longacre, pp. 59–83. A School of American Research Book, University of New Mexico Press, Albuquerque.

Vogel, J. C., and H. T. Waterbolk
1964 Groningen radiocarbon dates V. *Radiocarbon* 6:349–69.
1967 Groningen radiocarbon dates VII. *Radiocarbon* 9:107–55.

Wasley, William W.
1960 Salvage archaeology on Highway 66 in eastern Arizona. *American Antiquity* 26:30–42.

Wasley, William W., and Alfred E. Johnson
1965 Salvage archaeology in the Painted Rocks Reservoir, western Arizona. *Anthropological Papers of the University of Arizona,* No. 9. Tucson.

Watkins, T. (ed.)
1975 *Radiocarbon: Calibration and prehistory.* Edinburgh University Press, Edinburgh.

Watson, Don
1948 Ancient cliff dwellers of Mesa Verde. *National Geographic Magazine* 94:349–76.

Watson, Patty Jo, Steven A. LeBlanc, and Charles L. Redman
1980 Aspects of Zuni prehistory: Preliminary report on excavations and survey in the El Morro Valley of New Mexico. *Journal of Field Archaeology* 7:202–18.

Wendorf, Fred
1953 Archaeological studies in the Petrified Forest National Monument. *Museum of Northern Arizona Bulletin,* No. 27. Flagstaff.

Whalen, Norman M.
1971 Cochise culture sites in the central San Pedro drainage, Arizona. Ph.D. dissertation, University of Arizona. University Microfilms, Ann Arbor.

Wheat, Joe Ben
1955 Mogollon culture prior to A.D. 1000. *American Anthropological Association Memoir,* No. 82. Washington, D.C.

Wilcox, David
1979 The Hohokam regional system. *In* An archaeological test of sites in the Gila Butte–Santan region, south-central Arizona, by Glen Rice, David Wilcox, Kevin Rafferty, and James Schoenwetter, pp. 77–116. *Arizona State University Anthropological Research Papers,* No. 18, *Technical Paper,* No. 3. Tempe.

Willey, Gordon R., and Philip Phillips
1958 *Method and theory in American archaeology.* University of Chicago Press, Chicago.

Wilson, John P., Jon H. Winston, and Alan J. Berger
1961 Burials at Kinnikinnick Pueblo. *Plateau* 34:28–32.

Windham, Michael D., and David J. Dechambre
1978 *Report on the cultural resources in the former Navajo-Hopi Joint Use Area (FY1978).* Report submitted to the Bureau of Indian Affairs, Flagstaff Administrative Office, by the Department of Anthropology, Northern Arizona University, Flagstaff.

Winter, Joseph C., and Henry G. Wylie
1974 Paleoecology and diet at Clyde's Cavern. *American Antiquity* 39:303–15.

Wise, Edward N., and Dick Shutler, Jr.
1958 University of Arizona radiocarbon dates. *Science* 127:72–74.

Wood, John J.
1967 Archaeological investigations in northeastern Colorado. Unpublished Ph.D. dissertation, Department of Anthropology, University of Colorado.

Yamasaki, Fumio, Chikako Hamada, and Tatsuji Hamada
1977 Riken natural measurements IX. *Radiocarbon* 19:62–95.

Yarnell, Richard A.
1976 Early plant husbandry in eastern North America. In *Culture change and continuity: Essays in honor of James B. Griffin,* edited by Charles E. Cleland, pp. 265–73. Academic Press, New York.

INDEX